DISSENT IN AND FOR THE CHURCH

Dissent In and For the Church

Theologians and *Humanae Vitae*

by CHARLES E. CURRAN,
ROBERT E. HUNT
and the "Subject Professors"
with JOHN F. HUNT and TERRENCE R. CONNELLY

A Search Book
Sheed & Ward • New York

The translations of the Documents of Second Vatican Council are those translated by the National Catholic Welfare Conference, Washington, D. C.

Library of Congress Catalog Card Number 70-92530
Standard Book Number 8362-0050-0 (Paperback Edition) and 8362-0064-0 (Library Edition)

Manufactured in the United States of America

Acknowledgments

This volume represents the joint efforts of the twenty Catholic University professors and their legal and academic counsel. The professors collaborated on their theological defense presented to the Board of Inquiry and on all the other aspects involved in the long and tedious process of the Inquiry. Naturally there were some who devoted more of their time to the Inquiry and to the preparation of this volume, but it would be an impossible task to single out particular individuals. Perhaps the most remarkable aspect of the defense of our declaration and action was the communal and collaborative effort on the part of all involved, and this testifies in an eloquent manner to the basic Christian and academic commitments of the professors themselves.

We, the "subject professors," will never be able to express adequately our gratitude to the law firm of Cravath, Swaine & Moore of New York City, and in particular to Mr. John F. Hunt, Jr., and Mr. Terrence R. Connelly, his associate. Without legal counsel of such stature and skill, our case could not have been presented so forcibly. Their contributions and their personal interest in "their clients" remain a happy memory for all.

Robert K. Webb, Professor of History at Columbia University and Editor of *The American Historical Review,* despite an already overcrowded calendar, volunteered to serve as our academic counsel. His competence and help in this role made even more emphatic his commitment to academic life and his willingness to undergo great personal sacrifice for this commitment.

The staff of the National Office of the American Association of University Professors, without making any prejudgments on the case, was always most competent and gracious in furnishing us with authoritative interpretations and directions.

The expert witnesses mentioned by name in the text who willingly testified on our behalf gave to our case the prestige and authority of their own outstanding reputations.

The members of the Inquiry Panel, Dean Donald E. Marlowe, Professor E. Catherine Dunn, Dean Frederick R. McManus, Professor Antanas Suziedelis, Reverend Doctor Eugene I. Van Antwerp and Professor Kenneth L. Schmitz, generously gave many hundreds of hours of their otherwise busy lives in order conscientiously to discharge their responsibilities on behalf of the University in connection with the Inquiry. In their work they exhibited an intellectual honesty and scholarly dedication that enhances the reputation of the University with which they are associated.

Herder & Herder graciously permitted us to use some materials which were originally published in *Contraception: Authority and Dissent,* ed., C. E. Curran (New York, 1969).

Preface

During the present decade, it has become increasingly clear that the Roman Catholic Church is not a monolithic structure, secure from the concerns of its constituencies. The debates surrounding the Second Vatican Council sparked ferment and renewal within the Church. As this has become characterized by protest and dissent, the Church has experienced the same phenomenon which has confronted other institutions in our culture. Priests protest against their bishops; laymen form groups independent of ecclesiastical direction; underground movements virtually separate themselves from the institutional church; men and women leave the religious life for secular occupations in greater number than ever before. In the context of this unrest, conflicting forces polarize within the Church; Pope Paul VI has spoken frequently in a fearful, even reactionary, manner about the contemporary tumult in the Church.

The singular event causing the greatest stir and having the most far-reaching effect on the future of the Church is the dissent from Pope Paul's Encyclical on birth control, *Humanae Vitae*. Never before in history has an authoritative papal teaching met such widespread, immediate and public dissent. Most significantly, those who express disagreement with the Pope's conclusions on artificial contraception do not necessarily consider themselves disloyal Catholics cut off from union with the Church and with the Bishop of Rome.

Dissent from the Encylical was widespread. Theologians and clerics, laymen and laywomen from all over the globe voiced their disagreement. Surprisingly, the most concerted opposition to the absolute condemnation of artificial contraception came from theologians in the United States of America. The Catholic Church in the United States has produced comparatively few theologians who have contributed either to the intellectual life of the Church or of American society. The reaction of American theologians was focused in the statement released in Washington, D.C., on July 30, 1968, in the name of eighty-seven American theologians. That Statement by Catholic Theologians was ultimately endorsed by more than 600 Catholic academicians qualified in the sacred sciences, including moral theologians, canon lawyers, philosophers, biblical scholars and teachers in related specialties.[1]

This response to the Encyclical triggered further reactions. Liberal elements in the Roman Catholic Church applauded; conservative elements labeled the dissent treason; and very many both within and outside the Roman Catholic Church were somewhat confused. The challenges to the loyalty of the "dissenters" posed a central question: Could a Roman Catholic dissent from an authoritative papal teaching and still be loyal to his Church? The Theologians' Statement had postulated that it is a common teaching in the Church that Catholics may dissent from such papal pronouncements. But many loyal Catholics had never heard of such a common teaching despite their fervent participation in the life of the Church. Thus, for example, one priest of apparent goodwill but trained in the pre-Vatican II theology was "irritated" by the Statement of the Theologians.[2] Editorials in the Catholic press repeatedly and caustically condemned the dissent of the theologians and characterized it as destructive of the very institution of the Roman Catholic Church. A more perceptive observer recognized the existence of theological opinions in the Church traditionally upholding the right to dissent from authoritative papal teaching; but he added that "it would be preposterous for the theologians to maintain that the authors of such texts ever envisioned or intended to justify a situation like the present public, collective assertion by numerous theologians or similar acts of other groups."[3]

Such challenges impel subscribers to the Statement to explain not only the fact of their dissent from the absolute ban on contraception contained in *Humanae Vitae* but also the manner in which they made their dissent public. This volume, which attempts to fulfill that responsibility, has its genesis in the context of the most notorious challenge in the United States to the loyalty of the "dissenters."

The Theologians' Statement had been drafted and disseminated by a group of theologians comprised primarily of professors from The Catholic University of America, the only national pontifical university supported by all the bishops of the United States. Catholic University has been the scene of a number of incidents reflecting the tensions existing within the Roman Catholic Church, such as the banning of four "liberal" theologians from a campus speaking engagement in 1963 and the week-long strike by both faculty and students which forced the Trustees of the University to rescind their decision not to renew the contract of Charles E. Curran, then an Assistant Professor in the School of Theology, who had been unanimously recommended for promotion to Associate Professor by his own school and the Academic Senate of the University. After the "Curran affair" in the Spring of 1967, the Board of Trustees of the University changed its composition: in the summer of 1968, instead of a preponderance of bishops, including *ex officio* every archbishop in the United States, the Board consisted of 30 members—15 clerics and 15 laymen. This new Board had just come into power under the chairmanship of Dr. Carroll Hochwalt of St. Louis when the storm broke over the papal Encyclical. The unique position of Catholic University, plus the fact that Catholic University theologians spearheaded the theological dissent from the Encyclical, focused attention squarely on the University. The situation was complicated by the fact that the Chancellor of the University is Patrick Cardinal O'Boyle, the Archbishop of Washington, who reacted more strongly than any other American bishop to the dissent from the Encyclical by suspending the priestly faculties of diocesan clergymen who said they would respect the right of dissent the theologians had affirmed.

At a special meeting on September 5, 1968, the Trustees of Catholic University ordered an inquiry in accord with academic norms into the declarations and actions of the Catholic University professors who had publicly expressed dissent from the papal Encyclical. This inquiry was then carried out by a special Board of Inquiry selected by the Academic Senate of the University. The Board of Inquiry, in its five-month labor, heard thirty-eight witnesses and studied more than 3,000 pages of written exhibits and testimony, including over 600 pages of written materials submitted on behalf of the theologians. The Inquiry Board did not conclude its deliberations until April, 1969. At that time it published a detailed report, finding that "the commentary made by the subject professors in their July 30, 1968 statement is adequately supported by theological scholarship, and that their actions in composing, issuing, and disseminating this statement did not violate the professors' commitments to the University or to the academic or theological communities." At their April, 1969 meeting, the University Trustees deferred action on the Inquiry Report and appointed a subcommittee of their own membership to study it. As might have been expected, the Report of the Inquiry Board has been highly praised by some and vehemently attacked by others in the Catholic press, including a very critical article by a Trustee of the Catholic University.[4] The conclusion of the Report that the public dissent from the Encyclical is theologically acceptable portended great repercussions with respect to both the theoretical understanding of the Roman Catholic Church and the practical life style of the Church in the future. The vehemence of the various reactions emphasize the importance which the dissent it vindicates will have in the history and life of the Church and reinforces the need to explain and justify such dissent.

At their June, 1969 meeting, the University Trustees accepted the Report so far as its conclusions that the theologians had not violated their academic responsibilities are concerned, specifically refused to accept its theological conclusions and authorized a reference of the theologians' position to the Bishops' Commission on Doctrine. Since the Report makes clear that the academic responsibility of Roman Catholic theologians requires that they remain within the boundaries of the Roman Catholic faith commitment, assuming the Trustees understood the Report, the import of their June actions is not immediately obvious. (An explanation is offered in the companion volume to this work.)

This volume is substantially the first part of the prepared testimony submitted to the Inquiry Board by the Catholic University professors and their counsel. The second part of the written testimony presented to the Inquiry Board by counsel on behalf of the professors, which demonstrates the propriety and responsibility of their actions in the light of accepted academic norms, forms the nucleus of a companion volume. The first chapter of this volume gives the proper historical context for evaluating the dissent, and in so doing frequently condenses the facts which were established in the case before the Inquiry Board and the history of the Inquiry itself. Chapter two sets forth preliminary considerations concerning the nature of theology and the role of the theologian, while the third chapter develops preliminary considerations about the nature and function of the magisterium. Chapters four and five discuss dissent in and for the Church, specifically the ecclesiology implied and the methodology used in the declarations and actions of the subject professors (and many other Catholic theologians) in respect of *Humanae Vitae*. Chapter six deals with the specific questions of responsible dissent from one particular ethical teaching of the encyclical; namely, the absolute prohibition of the use of artificial contraception. We have incorporated some of the expert testimony given on behalf of the subject professors, although in substance chapters two through seven remain the written testimony which the professors submitted to the Inquiry Board. This written testimony was the fruit of collaboration among the subject professors and was written with the aim and purpose of presenting their theological case in the most cogent manner possible to their six academicians, of whom the Board of Inquiry was composed. While the same materials can be structured and written differently, there is a documentary value in preserving the argument as it was proposed by the Catholic University professors which outweighs any problems created by the multiple authorship of the material and its specific purpose of presenting theological reasoning to a group which, while highly educated, included people in the fields of engineering, literature and psychology. Chapter eight, after summarizing other examples of dissent, draws conclusions concerning the theological dissent of the professors and situates such dissent in the ongoing life of the Church. The final chapter sets forth the pertinent conclusions of the Inquiry Board. This volume, like the original Statement by Theologians, defends dissent from *Humanae Vitae* with the hope that the Roman Catholic Church will thus be able to carry out more faithfully its God-given mission in history.

Notes

1. Robert G. Hoyt, ed., *The Birth Control Debate* (Kansas City: *National Catholic Reporter,* 1968), p. 175.
2. Robert J. Kritland, "Just One Minute, Father Curran!" in *The Catholic World,* 208 (January, 1969), pp. 152–154.
3. Norbert J. Rigali, "Right, Duty, and Dissent," in *The Catholic World,* 208 (February, 1969), pp. 214–218.
4. Robert J. Dwyer, "Under My Hat," in *Twin Circle* (May 18, 25, 1969).

The subject professors dedicate this volume to those who joined them in upholding the right of Catholic dissent from *Humanae Vitae*—especially those unjustly accused of disloyalty without benefit of due process.

Contents

ACKNOWLEDGMENTS v
PREFACE vii

1 The Historical Context 3
2 Preliminary Consideration Concerning the Nature of Theology and the Role of Theologians 29
3 Preliminary Consideration Concerning the Nature and Function of the Magisterium 55
4 Contemporary Ecclesiological Awareness of Catholic Theologians 91
5 Public Dissent in and for the Church 133
6 The Reasonableness of Responsible Dissent from One Particular Ethical Teaching of the Encyclical 155
7 The Dissent from *Humanae Vitae:* Onset and Aftermath 197
8 *Epilogue:* Conclusions of the Catholic University Faculty Board of Inquiry 221

SUBJECT INDEX 230
PROPER NAME INDEX 234

The Professors subject to Inquiry at Catholic University

William W. Bassett
John Cavanagh
Christian Ceroke
Charles E. Curran
Leo A. Foley, S.M.
George T. Dennis, S.J.
Robert E. Hunt
Thomas Joyce, C.M.F.
George A. Kanoti, C.R.
Peter J. Kearney
Daniel C. Maguire
Berard L. Marthaler
Alfred McBride, O. Praem.
Bernard J. McGinn
Roland E. Murphy, O. Carm.
Russell G. Ruffino
Warren Reich
John F. Smolko
Paul K. K. Tong
David W. Tracy

Academic Counsel to the Subject Professors

Robert K. Webb

Legal Counsel to the Subject Professors

John F. Hunt
Terrence R. Connelly

DISSENT IN AND FOR THE CHURCH

1

The Historical Context

On July 29, 1968, in Rome, Pope Paul VI released his Encyclical letter *Humanae Vitae,* in which he reiterated that ". . . every action which either in anticipation of the conjugal act, or in its accomplishment, or in the development of its natural consequences, proposes, whether as an end or as a means, to render procreation impossible" (*Humanae Vitae,* paragraph 14) is absolutely to be excluded as licit means of regulating birth. Similarly, ". . . it is necessary that each and every marriage act must remain open to the transmission of life" (*Humanae Vitae,* paragraph 11). It seemed to many that this pronouncement would have ended a controversy, but in reality it signaled the beginning of an even more intense controversy within the Roman Catholic Church.

In the 1930 Encyclical Letter *Casti Connubii,* Pope Pius XI had formulated the following teaching: "Any use whatsoever of matrimony exercised in such a way that the act is deliberatively frustrated in its natural power to generate life is an offense against the law of God and of nature, and those who indulge in such are branded with the guilt of grave sin" (paragraph 56). This teaching was repeated by the successors of Pius XI and for a long period by all Roman Catholic theologians writing on the topic. The first cautious attacks by Catholic theologians and philosophers against the absolute condemnation of contraception appeared only late in 1963. In June of 1964, Pope Paul VI announced that a special commission had been established to study the question but that in the meantime the norms proposed by his predecessors were in force.

In the ensuing five years the problem of birth control and the Catholic Church was widely discussed and debated not only in scientific journals but in popular magazines and on television. Interest centered on the commission established by the Pope and its recommendations. In June of 1966, the "birth control commission" (officially called the Commission on Problems of the Family, Population and Natality) made its report to the Pope. The Pope remarked in October of that year that he was still studying the question, but the world learned in April of 1967, through extensive documentation published in the United States by the *National Catholic Reporter,* that the majority of the papal commission had recommended a change in the teaching on contraception. The release of this documentation intensified the debate within the Roman Catholic Church.

Rumors circulated in the Spring of 1968 that the Pope was ready to issue an Encyclical restating the absolute ban on artificial contraception. According to some press sources, liberal European bishops and cardinals dissuaded Paul VI from doing so, but, apparently, the matter was not concluded.

On June 27, 1968, "Guidelines for the Teaching of Religion in the Province of Baltimore and the Archdiocese of Washington" were released by the archbishops of these dioceses. The Guidelines firmly asserted that priests or teachers may not say or imply that the teaching of the Church permits or condones artificial contraception. Some professors at the Catholic University of America were asked by priests in Washington for their evaluation of the Guidelines and, seeking theological interpretation, the Association of Washington Priests sent the Guidelines to all the officers of the Catholic Theological Society of America, including Professor Charles E. Curran of Catholic University, who was then Vice-President of that organization. The negative reaction of the Washington Priests' Association to the Guidelines, as well as comments from a telephone interview with Professor Curran in Olean, New York, appeared in a story on the front page of the Sunday, July 28, edition of the *Washington Star*.

Concurrently, rumors were again circulating that the Pope was about to issue an Encyclical reiterating the absolute ban on artificial contraception. A number of Catholic University theologians, then at various places throughout the country for lectures and studies, conferred by telephone among themselves and with other colleagues about possible courses of action. The mass media insisted that an Encyclical was imminent; finally, on Sunday evening, July 28, it was confirmed that *Time* magazine had obtained a copy of the Encyclical which would be released on Monday, July 29, in Rome.

After consultation, a number of Catholic University professors agreed to meet on the afternoon of July 29 on the campus in Washington, D.C., with other theological colleagues from outside Catholic University. Vatican officials had released and offered interpretations of the Encyclical at a press conference in Rome at 4:30 A.M. Washington time. At approximately 5:00 P.M. the group of theologians, who had obtained copies of the full English text of the Encyclical from the Family Life Bureau of the United States Catholic Conference, met in Caldwell Hall on the campus to read, analyze, discuss and evaluate the papal Letter. The group included the following professors from Catholic University: Charles E. Curran, Robert E. Hunt, Daniel C. Maguire, Alfred McBride, and Russell G. Ruffino. Other participants were: Reverend John E. Corrigan, a priest of the Washington diocese teaching on the summer staff of the Department of Religious Education; Reverend Francis X. Murphy, C.SS.R., Professor of Patristic Moral Theology at the Academia Alfonsiana in Rome; Reverend David L. Jones, a priest of the diocese of Oklahoma City-Tulsa with advanced degrees in sacred scripture and theology, who was also a summer lecturer in the Department of Religious Education; Reverend Henry Schreitmueller, Instructor in Theology at Seton Hall University; Reverend Robert Springer, S.J., Professor of Moral Theology at Woodstock College.

Before and during the discussion, the members of the group had been in contact with other theologians throughout the country. It was finally agreed that a statement would be made and released to the press the next day. (The Association of Washington Priests had already reserved a room at the Mayflower Hotel in Washington for a press conference on Tuesday, July 30, at which they were going to discuss their reaction to the Guidelines.)

The draftsmen agreed on a first draft by 9:00 P.M. and then contacted other theologians throughout the country by telephone to learn whether they would be willing to subscribe to the Statement which would be made public at a press conference the next morning. After a long night of telephoning, reading the statement, and explaining its public release, eighty-seven American theologians agreed to endorse the proposed Statement publicly. On July 30, at a 10:00 A.M. press conference, the Statement by Catholic Theologians was released to the press by Professor Curran in the name of the original eighty-seven subscribers. In addition to the draftsmen, the original signers included the following full-time faculty members from Catholic University: William Bassett, Christian Ceroke, George Kanoti, Peter Kearney, Berard Marthaler, Bernard McGinn and David W. Tracy. The original subscribers to the Statement included theologians from many distinguished Catholic universities, colleges and theologates: e.g., Fordham University; Manhattan College; Notre Dame University; St. John's University, Collegeville, Minnesota; St. John's University, Jamaica, New York; St. Bonaventure University; Seton Hall University; Catholic Theological Union of Chicago; Pope John XXIII National Seminary; St. Meinrad School of Theology; Christ the King Seminary.

About ten of the signers were present to explain and elucidate the Statement and answer questions posed by the press. The individual theologians repeatedly emphasized that the Statement of dissent was not a rebellion or a revolution but a loyal act of theological interpretation by loyal Roman Catholics who accept the Petrine office in the Church. Some of the Catholic University professors (Professors Hunt, Maguire, Ruffino and Tracy) explained their position in greater detail at an open forum sponsored that evening on the campus of Catholic University by the Association of Washington Priests and the Washington Lay Association.

On July 31, letters were mailed to approximately 1,200 members of the Catholic Theological Society of America and the College Theology Society on behalf of the original eighty-seven subscribers to the Statement. The letters were co-signed for the original subscribers by John F. Cronin, Professor of Moral Theology, St. Mary's Seminary, Baltimore; Charles E. Curran of Catholic University; and Edwin F. Falteisek, Head of the Department of Pastoral Theology, School of Divinity, St. Louis University. The letters invited all those who were qualified and who agreed in substance with the public Statement of the Theologians to subscribe to the Statement. The accompanying letter described the required qualifications: "Since the Statement is to represent the thinking of those with special competence in the sacred sciences, it is necessary that the signers be qualified as follows: teachers of theology, philosophy, or canon law (or at least possessing a degree in their fields); or, members of a recognized professional society sponsored by the above-mentioned sciences." Eventually over 600 qualified in the sacred sciences publicly subscribed to the Statement.

There is another important aspect of the context within which the theologians made public their dissent to a practical conclusion of the papal teaching. The Statement of the Theologians was not the first public statement on the issue. On July 29 a number of American bishops made statements about the Encyclical. For example, the Archbishop of Washington said: "I call upon all priests in their capacity as confessors, teachers, and preachers of God's word to follow without equivocation, ambiguity or simulation the teaching of the Church on this matter as enunciated clearly by Paul VI."[1] Such a reaction on the part of American bishops was not wholly unexpected. In January, 1968, the American bishops had released their pastoral letter, *The Church in Our Day,* which did not adequately distinguish between the absolute assent of faith and the conditional religious assent which is due to noninfallible authoritative teachings. This letter failed even to mention the possibility of dissent from authoritative, noninfallible teaching.[2]

Two Catholic University professors (Hunt and Tracy) had pointed out this confusion to one of the bishops on the drafting committee of the pastoral, but no changes were made. Thus on the American scene it was obvious that many Catholics, including bishops, were not totally aware of what the Theologians' Statement referred to as the common teaching about the possibility of dissent from authoritative teaching. People who did not have this knowledge faced the false dilemma of either accepting the teaching of the Encyclical or thinking they had to reject their Roman Catholic faith commitment. Undoubtedly, one could propose many reasons to explain why this was not common knowledge in the Church in the United States, but the important matter remains the fact that a large number of Roman Catholics did not know the existence of the right to dissent from authoritative teachings when there is sufficient reason for such dissent.

On July 31 the American bishops did issue a short statement on *Humanae Vitae* through Archbishop John F. Dearden, President of the National Conference of Catholic Bishops, which in its most pointed reference to the teaching of the Encyclical declared: ". . . we, the Bishops of the Church in the United States, unite with him [Pope Paul] in calling upon our priests and people to receive with sincerity what he has taught, to study it carefully, and to form their consciences in its light."[3] No one can really know what effect the Statement of the Theologians had on the subsequent declaration of the American bishops. Would they have adopted a "harder line" if the theologians had not reacted? Would they have remained silent? In reality, however, the American bishops' statement did leave the door open for many different theological interpretations.

On August 1 another press conference was held at the Mayflower Hotel at which all the lay members of the papal birth control commission from the United States publicly agreed in substance, in accord with their respective competencies, with the Statement of the Theologians. Two members of the commission, Dr. André Hellegers and Professor Thomas K. Burch, both of Georgetown University, as well as the only special consultant on history to the papal commission, Professor John T. Noonan, Jr., of the University of California at Berkeley, spoke at the press conference chaired by Professor Maguire. Both Professor Springer of Woodstock College and Professor Curran stated, in reply to reporters' questions, that their

Statement was not irreconcilable with the statement that had been made on July 31 in the name of the American bishops.[4]

The remarks of Professors Springer and Curran drew an immediate response. On August 2, Bishop Joseph L. Bernardin, General Secretary of the National Conference of Catholic Bishops, issued a brief press release stating: "In asking our people to 'receive (the Encyclical *Humanae Vitae*) with sincerity, to study it carefully, and to form their consciences in its light,' the bishops in no way intend to imply there is any divergence between their statement and the teaching of the Holy Father."[5] Thus the controversy continued.

The activity in the next two weeks of August was primarily behind the scenes. The Acting Rector of Catholic University, Very Reverend John P. Whalen, was obviously under heavy pressure. The Chancellor of the University, Cardinal O'Boyle, the Archbishop of Washington, had taken a very firm and public stand against any possible dissent from the Encyclical in his diocese. Editorial opinion in some Catholic newspapers frequently and fiercely attacked the stand taken by the theologians, especially those at Catholic University.

Acting Rector Whalen, during the week of August 4, organized a meeting among certain members of the hierarchy, including Trustees of the University, and various theologians, including professors from the University and other universities and theologians who supported the dissent from the Encyclical and those who deemed it improper. The purpose of the meeting was to discuss the reaction to the Encyclical, with its theological and pastoral overtones. Initially, Cardinal O'Boyle had agreed to attend such a meeting; but later he changed his mind. Instead, in his capacity as Chancellor of the University he had the Acting Rector send, under date of August 9, a special delivery letter to all the faculty members in the School of Theology and the Department of Religious Education, even though the majority of these people were not in Washington for the summer, to ask them to be at the campus for a special meeting with the Chancellor on August 20.

The meeting between bishops and theologians arranged by Acting Rector Whalen took place at the Statler-Hilton Hotel in New York City on August 18 and 19. There was no doubt that Rector Whalen was trying at this meeting to avert any crises for Catholic University, but his hopes were thwarted. It is questionable whether there were then any realistic possibilities for a solution acceptable to all. The controversy was already too far along and the polarization too deep to expect that a single meeting could solve the problem. If bishops and theologians had been previously involved in an ongoing dialogue, the situation might have been different. But in reality there had been little or no dialogue in the past and much mutual suspicion and even distrust. The meeting did help to establish a modicum of rapport and to dissolve some of the suspicion, but an initial meeting called under crisis conditions could not be expected to cure readily what had long been a festering problem.

By previous agreement between Rector Whalen and Professor Curran, there were fourteen participants at the Statler-Hilton meeting, seven who had dissented from the Encyclical and seven who had objected to the public dissent. The seven dissenters included three Catholic University theologians—Professors Curran, Hunt, and Maguire—as well as Professor Walter Burghardt, S.J., of Woodstock College; Bernard Haering, C.SS.R., a German teaching at the Academia Alfonsiana in Rome; Professor James Megivern, C.M., of St. John's University; and Professor John T. Noonan, Jr. The other seven included four bishops: Bishop Joseph Bernardin, General Secretary of the National Conference of Catholic Bishops; Archbishop Philip Hannan of New Orleans, a Trustee of the University; Bishop John Wright of Pittsburgh, who missed the session on Monday, August 19; and Bishop Alexander Zaleski of Lansing, a Trustee of the University and Chairman of the American Bishops' Committee on Doctrine.

Three theologians who disagreed with the dissent also participated: Reverend Paul McKeever, Editor, *Long Island Catholic;* Professor Carl Peter of Catholic University; and Professor Austin Vaughn of St. Joseph's Seminary, Yonkers, New York.

The meeting began with supper on Sunday evening, August 18, followed by a discussion, with another discussion on Monday morning, closing with lunch. The atmosphere was somewhat strained and reserved, but the tension gradually dissolved as the discussion developed. After the dissenting theologians explained the right to dissent as found in the theological manuals, questions arose about the public character of such dissent. In the light of a developing understanding of the Church, the various roles in the Church, the contemporary situation of mass media and modern communications and the "right to know" in the Church, the dissenting theologians argued that theologians might even be obliged to dissent publicly in certain instances. The bishops present voiced concern over the confusion created among the faithful by such dissent, and some wondered if the theologians were not usurping the pastoral teaching office of the bishops. The dissenting theologians explained their position on these matters. Although no changes of position resulted from the meeting, all agreed that continued dialogue would be profitable.

Acting Rector Whalen issued a press statement describing the meeting in very general terms. According to the official minutes of the Board of Trustees of Catholic University a few weeks later, Acting Rector Whalen as well as Bishops Wright and Zaleski reported on the meeting with the theologians. Father Whalen observed that it was a frustrating experience because nothing tangible was achieved. Bishop Zaleski summarized the attitude of the dissenting theologians and felt there were tendencies which "went beyond Vatican I and II, involving a new concept of the role of the Holy Father, de-emphasizing his authority and stressing the consensus of the faithful." Bishop Wright, who had attended less than half the discussion, "thought the attitude at the New York meeting definitely at variance with Vatican II." However, Bishop Wright thought the meeting was a good idea. Obviously the report on this meeting by these two bishops reflected a definite theological cleavage between them and the dissenting theologians.

On Tuesday, August 20, Chancellor O'Boyle held the meeting to which he had "invited" the faculties of Theology and Religious Education. At the last minute, efforts were made to summon to the meeting faculty members from other schools and departments of the University (Philosophy and Canon Law) who had subscribed to the Statement of July 30. The press referred beforehand to the meeting as a showdown; but, although the Chancellor had his civil and canon lawyers and a court reporter in attendance, the tone of the meeting was courteous. The Chancellor never entered into the theological discussion. After verifying the Theologians' Statement itself and those Catholic University faculty members who had endorsed it, he asked the faculty members if they wished to make any comments "in regard to the problems you think the statement might raise for us as a University."

The professors responded, in general, that the Statement raised no real problems since it was a responsible utterance made by loyal Catholic theologians acting within the bounds of their competency. The subscribers cited the historical context of the paragraph of *Lumen Gentium* (the *Constitution on the Church* of Vatican II), which calls for the religious assent of intellect and will that is due authoritative, noninfallible teaching and they recalled that the official response at the Vatican Council to proposed revisions of paragraph 25 (i.e., *modus* 159) acknowledged that the possibility of dissent from such teaching was already recognized under paragraph 25. They also referred to the theological manuals of Dieckmann, Lercher, Palmieri, Straub, Pesch, Hervé, Van Noort, Karrer, and articles in the *New Catholic Encyclopedia.* Pertinent portions of the manuals of Pesch and Lercher were read into the transcript of the meeting. Some professors who had not subscribed to the statement defended the orthodoxy of the declarations and actions of the dissenters.

After being assured that everyone had had an opportunity to set forth his opinions, however, the Chacellor remarked: "Frankly, I believe I will have to refer the matter to the Board of Trustees and ask for a special meeting of the Board." After the faculty comments, Cardinal O'Boyle also asked each faculty member to give him in writing, within a week or ten days, his professional opinion of paragraphs 8 and 9 of the "Statement by Theologians." These two paragraphs referred to the common teaching on dissent in general and then concluded that in this case Catholic "spouses may responsibly decide according to their conscience that artificial contraception in some circumstances is permissible and indeed necessary to preserve and foster the values and sacredness of marriage."

The remainder of the meeting involved a mental and verbal duel between the Chancellor and the dissenters about the possibility of fulfilling the Chancellor's request. It was already August 20; classes were scheduled to begin within a month. The dissenting professors felt they would stand on much firmer ground once the classes were resumed and the students were back on campus. No one present in that room could forget the University-wide faculty and students' strike a year and a half earlier which forced the Chancellor and the other Trustees to rehire and promote Professor Curran.

The dissenters were careful to have the record of the meeting indicate that it in no way constituted a formal hearing. They all admitted an obligation and responsibility to explain further, to wider audiences, their reasons for theological dissent. But even some of the nondissenters present at the meeting said that a deadline of ten days was much too short, for many had previous commitments for the next few weeks. After much discussion the Chancellor finally agreed that the written comments (prepared either by individuals or a group) should be given him by October 1, although he would prefer to receive the materials earlier.

The meeting with the Chancellor thus indicated that his whole concern was the right to dissent itself, not the mode and manner of that dissent. He only requested a theological explanation of the two paragraphs in the Statement which proposed the right to dissent from authoritative teaching, in this instance, *Humanae Vitae.* During the course of the Inquiry that was to follow, the Acting Rector supplied the Inquiry Board with an English translation of the Latin texts cited by the subscribers to the Statement in the August 20 meeting, which had been prepared for Chancellor

O'Boyle by Germain Grisez, a philosopher who took a leave of absence from his post at Georgetown to serve as a special consultant to Cardinal O'Boyle after the birth control controversy erupted.

The translations prepared for the Chancellor were selective, and thus somewhat distorted, and failed to indicate all the points favoring the possibility of dissent. The distortion in this document prepared for the Chancellor is evident from a comparison of the translations with the originals and was acknowledged by the one theologian on the Inquiry Board. The impact of the selective translation of the works cited by the dissenting professors is not clear.

The Chancellor had come to the meeting with a prepared press release. Near the end of the meeting he distributed his release and asked for comments. The dissenting professors pointed out that the press release was his and not theirs, although they were willing to make their comments. In "off the record remarks" the Chancellor indicated his intention of releasing his press statement and of making no further comments to the press. In the Inquiry that was to follow, witnesses testified that the Chancellor said he had no objection if anyone else wanted to talk to the press. Some of the dissenting professors, including Professors Curran and Hunt, did talk informally with the press after the meeting. Although dissenting theologians had not alerted the press, reporters were waiting outside Caldwell Hall where the meeting took place. Articles on the meeting with the Chancellor, including comments from Professors Ceroke, Curran, Hunt and Ruffino, were carried in the papers the next day.

The professors were initially generally satisfied with the Chancellor's meeting, and most of them left Washington to return to what they had been doing during the summer months. Apparently Chancellor O'Boyle was not satisfied. Early in the morning of August 21 he called Acting Rector Whalen and Dean Schmitz of the School of Theology to his chancery office. He was quite irate both about the meeting and the subsequent publicity. Later that day, the Chancellor issued a lengthy press release in which he charged that "two of the dissenting theologians, Professor Charles Curran and Professor Robert Hunt, immediately presented to the news media an account of the meeting that seriously misrepresented my position." The Chancellor continued: "The false and misleading reports of the meeting suggested that my effort to be fair implied a vindication of the claimed 'right of dissent. . . .' Listening with patience does not imply agreement."[6] The Chancellor then returned his focus to paragraphs 8 and 9 of the Statement.

> Those who say that this is "common teaching" about dissent offer no evidence that the Catholic Church ever tolerated dissent of the sort they are carrying on and even instigating. . . . In my judgment, those who give Catholics advice like this are misleading them because, by implication, what they are saying is either that human judgment stands above the law of God or that the Catholic Church is lying when it claims divine authority for its moral teaching. It seems odd to me that those who signed the dissenting statement in which these two paragraphs were included did not find themselves able to render a professional opinion upon them as I requested.[7]

The Encyclical, in the Chancellor's mind, was "the law of God," and professional opinions, coupled with scholarly citations, did not constitute "professional opinion."

The tone and style of Chancellor O'Boyle's comments differed greatly from the Statement by Theologians. Had the dissenting theologians, particularly Professors Curran and Hunt, distorted the position of the Chancellor? The O'Boyle statement of August 21 does not mention any specific charges of distortion. However, the minutes of the special subsequent meeting of the Board of Trustees, held on September 5, make the Chancellor's charges more explicit and specific. According to the official minutes of the meeting, he said: "Yet the *Baltimore Sun,* the *Washington Post* and *Star* quoted Father Curran and Hunt as saying that they 'felt vindicated' and that their 'right of dissent had been approved.'" The minutes also report that "This reaction, the Cardinal thought, was erroneous, based on confusing patient listening with agreement."

The Inquiry Board subsequently did not find any such distortion in the declarations made by Professors Curran and Hunt to the press. The specific accusations made in the minutes cited above are false. The article in the *Baltimore Sun* never quoted either Professor Curran or Hunt. The quotations attributed to the two professors did not appear in any of the newspaper accounts "quoted" in the minutes. It is true that the word "vindicated" did appear in a story written for the National Catholic News Service. But this particular story was "killed" before publication by someone other than the reporter. The reporter in question was called by the Inquiry Panel and testified that Professor Curran had not used the term "vindicated." The reporter, who pointed out that his story was similar in tenor to the stories carried in the daily press, later testified that he used that term to describe the situation because the dissenting theologians did explain to the press that they presented the Chancellor with a number of accepted theological authorities who uphold the right to dissent from authoritative, noninfallible papal teaching. After the long statement by Chancellor O'Boyle, a professor who had not subscribed to the statement publicly came to the defense of his colleagues. Professor Leo Farley issued a statement taking "exception to the Chancellor's account and interpretation of the Tuesday (August 20) meeting."[8]

The reaction following the August 20 meeting with the Chancellor indicated that the whole matter was not going to be dropped. The Chairman of the Board of Trustees of Catholic University, apparently at the instigation of Chancellor O'Boyle, called a special meeting of the Board in Washington on September 5 to consider "the urgent situation the University faces because of the reaction of some faculty members to Paul VI's Encyclical *Humanae Vitae*." Newsmen were already gathered at the Madison Hotel as the members arrived for the 9:30 A.M. meeting. During the course of the day, occasional announcements were made to the press that a statement would be forthcoming shortly, but the meeting dragged on. Obviously there was division within the Board. Finally the press was informed that the Chairman of the Board, Dr. Carroll Hochwalt, would read a statement to the press at 9:00 P.M. When Hochwalt finally did appear to read his statement, he refused to answer any questions or give any added interpretation of the statement.

The official minutes of the Trustees' meeting, which were subsequently supplied to the subject professors, indicate the general trend of the meeting. First the Statement by Theologians was read, and then some of the participants discussed the Statler-Hilton meeting in New York and the August 20 meeting with the Chancellor. Cardinal McIntyre then introduced a long resolution that the Board of Trustees, having "seriously and penetratingly considered the utterances of Father Curran, his followers and associates with regard to the Encyclical *Humanae Vitae*, . . . has come to the conclusion that these statements and other expressed opinions are in obvious conflict with known and practiced teachings of the Church as held for centuries and recently reiterated and confirmed by the Holy Father. . . ." The resolution calls the attitude of the theologians a violation of their Profession of Faith and their contract with the University, and thus a breach of contract which admits of no other consideration than a termination.

Debate followed. Although no vote on the McIntyre resolution was taken according to official minutes, the Chairman appointed a committee to draft a statement in accord with the tenor of the debate. At 3:00 P.M. the meeting reconvened with a reading of the tentative points prepared by the drafting committee. After discussion of these points, a committee was appointed to prepare a final draft. Cardinal McIntyre then withdrew his motion. At 6:00 P.M. the revised draft was presented, discussed and adopted in final form. In substance, the Board called for the Acting Rector to institute an inquiry, in accord with academic norms and process, to determine if the theologians had violated their manifold responsibilities.

The only statement which came from this meeting of the Trustees was the statement read to the press. This news release questioned both the dissent itself and "the style and method of organizing and publicizing their dissent." It is important to underline the fact that, in their statement, the Trustees do question the dissent itself and not merely the "manner and mode." The Board first affirmed that the dissenting members of the faculty were not speaking for the University. It also affirmed *its* loyalty to the Holy Father. The sentence questioning style and manner is introduced by a "moreover." While the Board asserted that final judgments in theological matters belong to the bishops of the Church, it directed the Acting Rector to institute an inquiry to determine whether the professors, by "their *declarations* and actions with regard to the Encyclical," had violated their responsibilities under general norms of responsible academic procedure and under the "Statutes" of the University, which require, among other things, that faculty members "submit unreservedly" to the Pope's Apostolic Authority as the "only safe norm of Truth." Moreover, the condition laid down by the Trustees for the continued teaching of the professors during the course of the Inquiry was their agreement to abstain from "any activities which would involve the name of the Catholic University and which are inconsistent with the pronouncements of the ordinary teaching authority established in the Church—above all, that of the Holy Father." Although there may have been changes of position later, there can be no doubt that on September 5, despite the long explanation given in the Statler-Hilton meeting and the Chancellor's meeting, the Board of Trustees definitely was challenging the right to dissent itself.

Acting Rector Whalen began immediately to carry out his mandate from the Board. On September 9, he proposed four questions to the professors involved, who were then on campus, and explained that if a professor would withdraw his endorsement of the Statement by Theologians, he would not be subject to the Inquiry. One of the questions asked if the theologians were willing to observe during the Inquiry the conditions set down by the Board of Trustees in their September 5 press release. The professors refused. (It should be noted that the professors never did agree with the alien condition of silence imposed by the Board of Trustees, even though Whalen and others gave the impression that the professors had agreed. A special committee of the Academic Senate of the University as well as an official University press release confirm this lack of agreement. The only "agreement" made by the professors was to observe the ban on Inquiry publicity required by governing American Association of University Professors' procedures.)

The action by the Acting Rector on September 9 marked the beginning of what was to be a tedious and tiring Inquiry lasting until April. The subject professors realized the need for counsel and consultation if they were going to be subject to such an Inquiry. On September 10, five of the professors met for three hours with the executive secretary, general counsel and other staff members of the AAUP, who strongly advised the need for legal counsel. The Washington, D.C., chapter of the American Civil Liberties Union offered its services, and Professor Hunt consulted his brother, John F. Hunt, Jr., a New York attorney and member of the law firm of Cravath, Swaine & Moore. At Mr. Hunt's request, the Cravath firm itself agreed to represent the professors during the course of the Inquiry. Mr. Hunt and Terrence R. Connelly as his associate handled the case. At the request of AAUP, Robert K. Webb, Professor of History at Columbia University and Editor of the *American Historical Review,* volunteered his services to act as academic counsel for the subject professors.

Acting Rector Whalen asked the help and cooperation of the Academic Senate in carrying out his mandate from the Board of Trustees. The Senate first appointed a Committee on Committees which was commissioned to nominate two committees to begin the work of the Inquiry. As a result of the Senate action, two committees came into existence: "Committee A," under the chairmanship of Professor J. Kerby Neill, had the task of investigating the agreement reached between the Acting Rector and the theologians concerning the conditions laid down by the Board of Trustees if the professors were to continue to teach pending the findings of the Inquiry. "Committee B," chaired by Dean Donald E. Marlowe, was charged with drawing up the procedures for the inquiry itself, and these procedures were approved by the Academic Senate on October 16. The procedures also outlined the process for the election of the Board of Inquiry itself—one member from each of the three main divisions of the University (the Graduate Schools, the Professional Schools, and the Ecclesiastical Schools); two members at large, one of whom should be from outside the University and competent in the sacred sciences; one alternate from the faculty at large.

Meanwhile, in November, the American bishops released their Pastoral Letter *Human Life in Our Day*. By this time, not only had many other hierarchies throughout the world commented on the Encyclical, but also bishops, theologians, and many in the Church had become better acquainted with the "common teaching in the Church that Catholics may dissent from authoritative, noninfallible teachings of the magisterium when sufficient reasons for so doing exist."

The 1968 Pastoral Letter of the American bishops recognizes the possibility of *theological* dissent from authoritative, noninfallible papal teaching. However, there remain the questions of (1) whether, as the dissenters had claimed, spouses may dissent in practice and (2) how theological dissent may be expressed. The American bishops comment: "The expression of theological dissent from the magisterium is in order only if the reasons are serious and well-founded, if the manner of the dissent does not question or impugn the teaching authority of the Church and is such as not to give scandal. Since our age is characterized by popular interest in theological debate and given the reality of modern mass media, the ways in which theological dissent may be effectively expressed, in a manner consistent with pastoral solicitude, should become the object of fruitful dialogue between bishops and theologians. They have their diverse ministries in the Church, their distinct responsibilities to the faith and their respective charisms."[9]

The subject professors were still expecting that specific charges would be leveled against them. The only communication from the Board of Trustees was the statement which was released to the press on September 5. The Trustees had that day publicly labelled the dissenters' conduct as seriously questionable under norms of responsible academic procedure and had threatened to suspend anyone who repeated such questioned conduct pending the Inquiry. The procedures of the American Association of University Professors, which the Trustees cited as authorizing suspension in this case, permit no suspension unless charges are pending; thus the professors believed that their refusal to recant would bring on charges. Moreover, if one is accused of wrongdoing, it is an elemental principle of justice that the accuser has an obligation to detail the nature of the charges. However, no charges were forthcoming.

On December 23, the acting Rector of the University submitted a letter of comments from a committee of Trustees in response to the Inquiry Board's request, in the absence of charges, for a "clarification or particularization" of the Trustees' September 5 action:

> In giving this directive to the faculty of the University, the Board did not attempt to pre-judge the result of the inquiry. The Board made no charges—leveled no accusations. . . .
>
> Hence, the focus of the present inquiry is on the style and method whereby some faculty members expressed personal dissent from Papal teaching, and apparently helped organize additional public dissent to such teaching. At no time in this inquiry is there any attempt by the Board to question the right of a scholar to have or to hold private dissent on Papal teaching not defined as infallible.
>
> There is a considerable body of commentary on the method and spirit of due dissent in the Catholic Theological community. However, the literature now available in the general academic community on how believing Christians reconcile the tenets of their religious faith with the demands of authentic speculative investigation is almost nonexistent. . . .
>
> It is possible that the current inquiry could result in an historic statement for the entire field of speculative theology. . . .

This letter of comment marked a definite shift of position: according to the letter, the Inquiry was now supposed to concern only the "style and method" of dissent and not the right to dissent itself. This position is contradicted by a number of factors: the specific request in the December 23 letter itself that the Inquiry determine whether the professors had violated their profession of faith; the statement released at the September 5 meeting of the Board of Trustees questioning the responsibility of the professors' *Declarations* as well as their actions and the tenor of the meeting itself; the threat of suspension imposed by the Board of Trustees unless the professors agreed "to abstain for the period of the Inquiry from any activities . . . which are inconsistent with the pronouncements of the ordinary teaching authority established in the Church —above all, that of the Holy Father"; and the questions posed by the Acting Rector to the professors on September 9 and 10. Despite the December 23 letter, the Board of Inquiry understood that the Trustees' September 5 mandate required it to determine whether the asserted right to dissent represented "permissible scholarly views" within the pale of responsible Roman Catholic theological positions. Moreover, Bishop James Shannon, testifying as the Trustees' representative to the Inquiry three weeks after the December 23 letter was written, agreed that the Inquiry Board's concept of its task was "reasonable."

The Board of Inquiry held its first organizational meeting on October 31, 1968, and then devoted the next month to developing its rules of procedure. Pre-Inquiry conferences took place on December 13 and December 27, 1968, and January 10, 1969. In January the professors proposed a detailed statement of the facts which was then discussed and mutually agreed upon. The subject professors in late January transmitted to the Board the first part of their written materials—over 200 pages defending on theological grounds their public dissent from the Encyclical. On February 18, civil and academic counsel submitted on behalf of the subject professors the second part of their written materials defending the responsibility of the declarations and actions of the professors in the light of academic principles and norms.

After the Board questioned the professors about the written materials, expert testimony was advanced on significant aspects of the question of dissent. These expert witnesses were people of outstanding merit who testified from the viewpoint of their respective competences. Those who gave either written or oral testimony in defense of the professors included Dr. Robert Cross, then President, Hunter College, now President, Swarthmore College; Reverend Walter Burghardt, Editor, *Theological Studies;* Dr. John C. Bennett, President, Union Theological Seminary; Reverend John H. Thirlkel, Dean of Theology, St. Mary's Seminary and University, Baltimore; John Noonan, Professor of Law, University of California, Berkeley; Reverend Victor Yanitelli, President, St. Peter's College; Reverend John Hotchkin, Bishop's Committee for Ecumenism and Interreligious Affairs; Reverend Clarence Friedman, Associate Secretary, College and University Department, NCEA; Kenneth Woodward, Religion Editor, *Newsweek;* Reverend Gerard Sloyan, Professor of Religion, Temple University; Reverend Bernard Lonergan, Research Professor of Theology, Regis College, Toronto; and Reverend Theodore Hesburgh, President, Notre Dame University, Indiana.

The hearings ended on March 12, 1969. The professors, through their counsel, sent their proposed findings to the Board. Neither the Trustees nor their counsel proposed any findings. The Board had already begun to draft their findings before consulting the findings proposed by the professors. (The charge was later heard that the Inquiry Board merely adopted the findings proposed by the professors; anyone familiar with the proposed findings and the report would find this assertion ridiculous.) When the Inquiry Board made its report to the Academic Senate at a special meeting on April 1, the Senate unanimously adopted the report. The report exonerated the professors and chided the Trustees for some of their declarations and actions, especially those concerning the threat of suspension employed in their September 5 statement. The report also urged that Catholic University adopt the norms of academic freedom and academic due process recommended in the report.

As noted, the report of the Board of Inquiry did not close the matter. At their meeting in Houston in April, 1969, the Board of Trustees of Catholic University voted only to receive the report and appointed a subcommittee of their members to study it and bring their recommendations to the next regular meeting or to a special meeting. The publication of the report of the Inquiry board again touched off comments pro and con concerning the theological dissent from the Encyclical and illustrated anew the need for a cogent explanation justifying such dissent. Finally, at their June meeting, the Trustees terminated the University proceedings against the professors but authorized reference of the theological issues to the bishops.

The remaining chapters of this volume develop the theological justification for the dissent of the professors at Catholic University and their public promulgation of that dissent. Since the professors were subjected to the Inquiry because they ascribed to the Statement by Catholic Theologians of July 30, 1968, these chapters will focus on that statement and the reasons its preparation and publication were responsible courses of action of Roman Catholic theologians at the Catholic University of America. (The Statement is set forth in its entirety at the conclusion of this chapter.) The argumentation developed in the following chapters supports the conclusion that the substance of the Statement by Theologians, promulgation of the Statement through the mass media, the timing of such promulgation and subsequent subsidiary promulgation were all within the pale of responsible Roman Catholic theological activity. However, this volume does not attempt to prove that other views regarding the Encyclical, or regarding the promulgation of views concerning the Encyclical, are not within the pale of responsible Roman Catholic theological activity.

Full Text of the July 30, 1968, Statement by Catholic Theologians

1. As Roman Catholic theologians we respectfully acknowledge a distinct role of hierarchical *magisterium* (teaching authority) in the Church of Christ. At the same time, Christian tradition assigns theologians the special responsibility of evaluating and interpreting pronouncements of the magisterium in the light of the total theological data operative in each question or statement. We offer these initial comments on Pope Paul VI's Encyclical on the Regulation of Birth.

2. The Encyclical is not an infallible teaching. History shows that a number of statements of similar or even greater authoritative weight have subsequently been proved inadequate or even erroneous. Past authoritative statements on religious liberty, interest-taking, the right to silence, and the ends of marriage have all been corrected at a later date.

3. Many positive values concerning marriage are expressed in Paul VI's Encyclical. However, we take exception to the ecclesiology implied and the methodology used by Paul VI in the writing and promulgation of the document: they are incompatible with the Church's authentic self-awareness as expressed in and suggested by the acts of the Second Vatican Council itself. The Encyclical consistently assumes that the Church is identical with the hierarchical office. No real importance is afforded the witness of the life of the Church in its totality; the special witness of many Catholic couples is neglected; it fails to acknowledge the witness of the separated Christian churches and ecclesial communities; it is insensitive to the witness of many men of good will; it pays insufficient attention to the ethical import of modern science.

4. Furthermore, the Encyclical betrays a narrow and positivistic notion of papal authority, as illustrated by the rejection of the majority view presented by the Commission established to consider the question, as well as by the rejection of the conclusion of a large part of the international Catholic theological community.

5. Likewise, we take exception to some of the specific ethical conclusions contained in the Encyclical. They are based on an inadequate concept of natural law: the multiple forms of natural law theory are ignored and the fact that competent philosophers come to different conclusions on this very question is disregarded. Even the minority report of the papal commission noted grave difficulty in attempting to present conclusive proof of the immorality of artificial contraception based on natural law.

6. Other defects include: overemphasis on the biological aspects of conjugal relations as ethically normative; undue stress on sexual acts and on the faculty of sex viewed in itself, apart from the person and the couple; a static worldview which down-

plays the historical and evolutionary character of humanity in its finite existence, as described in Vatican II's *Pastoral Constitution on the Church in the Modern World;* unfounded assumptions about 'the evil consequences of methods of artificial birth control'; indifference to Vatican II's assertion that prolonged sexual abstinence may cause 'faithfulness to be imperiled and its quality of fruitfulness to be ruined'; an almost total disregard for the dignity of millions of human beings brought into the world without the slightest possibility of being fed and educated decently.

7. In actual fact, the Encyclical demonstrates no development over the teaching of Pius XI's *Casti Connubii* whose conclusions have been called into question for grave and serious reasons. These reasons, given a muffled voice at Vatican II, have not been adequately handled by the mere repetition of past teaching.

8. It is common teaching in the Church that Catholics may dissent from authoritative, noninfallible teachings of the magisterium when sufficient reasons for so doing exist.

9. Therefore, as Roman Catholic theologians, conscious of our duty and our limitations, we conclude that spouses may responsibly decide according to their conscience that artificial contraception in some circumstances is permissible and indeed necessary to preserve and foster the values and sacredness of marriage.

10. It is our conviction also that true commitment to the mystery of Christ and the Church requires a candid statement of mind at this time by all Catholic theologians.

Notes

1. *Washington Evening Star,* July 30, 1968, p. A–4. The article referred to the fact that O'Boyle "released his statement to newsmen by telephone from Pennsylvania."
2. *The Church in Our Day* (Washington, D.C.: U.S.C.C., 1968), pp. 69–73.
3. N.C. News Service (Domestic), July 31, 1968.
4. *Washington Post,* August 2, 1968, p. A–2; *New York Times,* August 2, 1968, p. 1.
5. N.C. News Service (Domestic), August 2, 1968.

6. N.C. News Service (Documentary Service), August 22, 1968; also *Washington Post,* August 22, 1968, p. B–1.
7. *Ibid.*
8. *Washington Post,* August 24, 1968, p. D–4.
9. N.C. News Service (Documentary Service), November 15, 1968, pp. 18, 19.

2

Preliminary Consideration concerning the Nature of Theology and the Role of Theologians

Theology is a scholarly discipline—in the strictest and contemporary sense of the term—whose complexities can be understood only in the light of its history and present methods. An understanding of theology's truly scientific character is prerequisite to proper appreciation of its function in and for the Church. But although the function of the theologian is clearly a scholarly one, it is not merely speculative endeavor. By the very nature of his discipline, the theologian must function in constant reference to the daily and actual living of the Christian life. In fact, all true theology is by its very nature *pastoral;* i.e., it has a direct relationship to the day-to-day life of the Church community.

Theology and the theologian are, by their very nature, directly relevant to countless persons not professionally engaged in the scholarly work itself. Theology is in constant dialogue with the living tradition of the Church. The theologian considers and evaluates the living experience of Christians today in the light of the total experience of the past and the previous theological reflections and formulations which expressed that experience. Furthermore, Vatican II emphasized the role of all the faithful in the Church and, at the same time, the coresponsibility of theologians in communicating to all Christians what they need to know in carrying out their particular responsibilites in and for the Church and the world. It would be a mistake to consider theology as anything other than a truly scientific, scholarly discipline; it would be equally wrong to consider it as purely "abstract" and without necessary relationship to the practice of the Christian life itself. Theology is at one and the same time speculative and practical, scientific and pastoral; the proper function of the theologian is measured by the very nature of his field.

Theology as a Science

Historical Development. Authoritative historians of theology show a development of theology as a science which has ebbed and flowed, not always advancing in a straight line.[2] It is generally held that theology became a science in the strict sense with the medieval rediscovery of the Aristotelian scientific ideal, certain knowledge of things through their causes. It then became possible to structure an ordered and systematic understanding of the Christian faith. The search for systematic, scientific understanding became the complex and enriching challenge of the medieval theologians.

After the medieval achievement, the science of theology in the Catholic tradition underwent a number of changes, some of which were detrimental to theology's truly scientific character. Among the historical factors influencing the changed understanding of theology as a science were the late scholastic decline, Reformation—Counter-Reformation exigencies, seventeenth-century empirical scientific revolution, "enlightenment" attack upon tradition, rise of the subjectivist problem in post-Cartesian philosophy, development of the historico-critical method and the human sciences, and rise of the post-subjectivist problematic.[3]

The Council, however, reasserted the strictly scientific nature of the discipline called theology. "Nevertheless, if reason enlightened by faith studies the mysteries in a serious, dedicated, and humble way, it does achieve . . . some understanding of them and a most profitable one."[4] It is this understanding that theology strives to attain—a knowledge that is not faith but an understanding of faith, a knowledge that is not infused but acquired with human effort, a knowledge that differs radically from philosophical knowledge about God because its object is revealed mystery and because it engages not reason alone but reason enlightened by faith. It is an understanding that although imperfect will continue to grow until faith is dissolved in the vision of God Himself. "Let there be growth . . . and all possible progress in understanding, knowledge, and wisdom whether in single individuals or in the whole body, in each man as well as in the entire Church, according to the stage of their development."[5]

The Council decree further suggested the scientific framework for a systematic theology as the systematic understanding of God and human existence built upon three main methodological factors: analogies from nature, the interconnection of the mysteries (analogy of faith) and the relationship of the mysteries to the final end of man. Further developed, these same factors remain the foundation of the science of theology today. The "analogies from nature" may be drawn from various human sciences and from a pluralism of philosophical positions, and the "analogy of faith" has become far more complex as the return to Christian sources via the historico-critical method has enriched the entire enterprise.

Complexities of Contemporary Scientific Theology. A science develops only after there has been opportunity for reflection and systematization. Since the very nature of "scientific" work has changed and continues to change, theology has also experienced continuing development and growth. Its task, therefore, must be considered in light of the complexities of its developing insights.

Theologians know that man has become more conscious of the historical and cultural limitations which affect all human knowledge and science as well as theology. Historical growth and development have alerted modern theologians to the *development* of doctrine and the consequent need to study it in the light of its historical unfolding. They recognize the need to study the sources of theology by use of historico-critical methodology. This approach, which was also influenced by the advances of the empirical scientific method, has fostered development of a variety of disciplines embraced in the concept of "positive theology": for example, biblical theology, patristic theology, liturgical theology.

The developing meaning and understanding of *science* itself has profoundly affected contemporary theology. The object of science has changed from the Aristotelian-Scholastic ideal ("certain knowledge of things through their causes")—and the resultant concern for universality, necessity and certainty—to the contemporary scientific ideal (complete explanation of all data in terms of their intelligible relationships)—and the resultant concern for development, probability and matter-of-factness. This shift has resulted in a different attitude toward certitude and method in science, which, in turn, has brought about a restructuring in all contemporary, systematic sciences, including theology.

The recognition of the historical and cultural limitations of all human knowing and the changed understanding of the notion of science create basic problems for theology. As a result many contemporary theologians see a need to reevaluate the method employed by the science of theology. In the more contemporary notion of science, greater stress is placed upon a more inductive approach; the contemporary theologian is also faced with a "knowledge explosion." The theologian must be familiar with many diverse specializations: biblical theology, sociology, patristic theology and psychology. More importantly, the theologian must develop a method for evaluating, coordinating and synthesizing all the relevant data. In the light of an appreciation of historical growth and development, the theologian realizes he will never attain the older ideal of absolute certitude. Clear, simple and absolutely complete answers are not considered achievable in contemporary theological investigation. These characteristics of all science today, moreover, are felt even more acutely by the theologian, because theology ultimately deals with the mystery of God. Theology takes its beginning from the faith-commitment of the believer; theological meaning thus can never be fully understandable to any human interpreter.

Although the recognition of complexity and inherent limitations in theology is fairly common among theologians today, it is not peculiar to contemporary theology. Scholasticism at its best (e.g., in the works of St. Thomas Aquinas) always recognized the originating and determining mystery of the faith-data it attempted to understand systematically, and spoke of the role of theology as relating systematically (via the scholastic technique of "negative coherence"; i.e., no *demonstrable* intrinsic contradiction, but no positive demonstration) to a deeper recognition of the mystery of God's revelation to man in Christ Jesus and in his Church. The doctrinal statement of the First Vatican Council leads to the same recognition of the real but partial and analogous understanding proper to the theologian's task. The object of interpretive scientific theology is not only the manifestation of that faith-commitment in the Christian tradition, but also the complex development of that faith-commitment in history and in mystery.

The Problem of Interpretation: Theology and Tradition

The theologian as a scientist is primarily involved in the work of systematic reflection and interpretation. He operates within the context of the Christian theological tradition which must be constantly reinterpreted in the light of the thought patterns and expressions of the present time.

Two Opposite Dangers. Throughout the history of theological interpretation in the Church, there have been two persistent temptations:

a) either simply to accept an unappropriated tradition by a word-for-word repetition of previous formulae without any realization of the historical and cultural limitations inherent in any such human thought and speech. One example is the problem of extrinsicism, or what has come to be called "Denzinger theology," the mere verbal repetition of previously defined or taught formulae found in Henry Denzinger's standard anthology of conciliar, papal and episcopal utterances;

b) or to ignore the tradition and deny it any value, so that theology is reconstructed solely in the light of present experience (e.g., the extremes of the so-called "Modernist" movement at the beginning of this century).

Nevertheless, all the major figures of the Catholic theological tradition (Origen, Augustine, Aquinas and Newman; and, among contemporaries, Congar, Rahner, Lonergan and Schillebeeckx) effectively avoid both false polarities because they have realized the interpretive (hermeneutic) difficulties involved in genuine theological work. These theologians realize the inadequacy of extrinsicist notions of authority and tradition in relation to the theologian's interpretive task—whether such extrinsicism be understood as a simple, uninterpreted and noncontextualized imposition from without (the alternative of the "right") or as a simple, uninterpreted and noncontextualized rejection of tradition (the alternative of the "Enlightenment" and the "Modernist left").

Unfortunately, some contemporary commentators have been unable to properly interpret the theological position of the major figures in the history of theology. Aquinas, for example, is often interpreted either as a "rationalist" or a "fideist," with no recognition of how he transcends either category. Newman has been quoted for "authority" alone in one series of proof-texts or for "conscience" alone in another,[6] with little or no recognition that his or any authentic theologian's thought involves the constant dialectic between faith and reason, authority and conscience, and tradition and scientific theology.

The contemporary insights with respect to the related matters of hermenuetics, of theological method and especially of the development of doctrine have freed the theologian to recognize the dual exigencies inherent in accepting as his data the true meaning of the tradition: the need to recognize the validity of the tradition and, at the same time, the need to recognize its inherent cultural and historical limitations.

Greater Complexities Today of Doctrinal Development. The matter of doctrinal development has become the central question for many Catholic thinkers, particularly during the present century. The contemporary theologian would be aware of the positive advances in understanding this development achieved by the use of the historico-critical method and by the proposed explanations of such figures as Newman, Blondel or Moehler in an earlier generation or Rahner, Congar, Murray or Lonergan in the present generation. Vatican II, with its declarations on collegiality and religious liberty, has made every contemporary theologian particularly familiar with doctrinal development and with the implications of that process for his interpretive endeavors. Moreover, every theologian would further recall that the alternatives of "Modernism" (which attempted to eliminate the reality of the doctrinal principle or tradition by negating its truth-value) or of "manualism" (whose proof-text method denigrated the reality of development) are both inadequate to handle the dual reality of doctrines as truly expressing the faith yet remaining ever open to further refinement and development. Indeed, as the problems associated with eucharistic theology or Christology in recent years make clear, the contemporary theological enterprise has been engaged in a multidimensional and multileveled attempt to understand and to find the categories adequate for expressing the reality of doctrinal development.

In this context the interpretive difficulties of the theologian are manifold. He must consider every theological reality in the light of the best scientific methods developed in the various theological specializations. In doctrinal theology, for example, the theologian must be fully familiar with the doctrinal weight accorded each doctrinal definition, e.g., the actual truth defined in the conciliar decrees on the reality of purgatory and hell (which may be considerably less than or different from what is assumed by the popular Catholic mind). He must be prepared to understand the definition within its historical context, while neither ignoring the truth-value of the definition (the temptation of pure relativism) nor simply repeating extraneous formulations in a later and differently developed context. He must find categories to "bring that reality to speech anew," to develop it, to reexpress it and to rethematize it. The theologian realizes that not every expression will be adequate; hence, he presents his expression to and within the Church community for its theological and sometimes doctrinal critique.

Need to Communicate Interpretations. The contemporary theologian is likewise aware that part of the data of theology is the living experience of man. The Second Vatican Council's *Declaration on Religious Liberty* recognizes that the need for religious liberty was appreciated by many men of goodwill through their human experience before it was formulated and expressed by the Council. Likewise, the call for dialogue with all men of goodwill issued by Popes John XXIII and Paul VI and by the Second Vatican Council confirms that the theologian can learn from the contemporary experience not only of Christians but of all men. Thus the theologian must always be in dialogue with contemporary Christian and human experience.

In the renewal of theology and in the contemporary perspective of Vatican II there has been a demand that theology be more explicitly relevant. The contemporary theologian must be in dialogue with modern science as a key factor in contemporary human experience. He must interpret the tradition for contemporary man and express this interpretation in an idiom which people living today can understand and accept. In approaching his task, the contemporary theologian is sustained by the model of St. Thomas Aquinas, who did not merely repeat the past Christian tradition but, rather, reinterpreted it in the light of the Greek philosophy then current in European universities. The theologian has the responsibility and obligation to make his theological interpretation available to all; he understands that all men are called to hear the good news of Christianity and to have some reflective and systematic understanding of Christian truth to the extent that they are in need of such understanding and capable of assimilating it.

The contemporary scene is marked by a growing popular interest in theological and philosophical questions, due in part to the educational attainments of so many people today. The "popularity" of theology today is evidenced by the number of books published every year on theological topics, some of which have even made "best-seller" lists. The contemporary theologian is continually asked to lecture to widely diverse audiences. The daily press gives extensive coverage not only to religious events but to theology itself. All these factors indicate that many people are looking for the interpretations which the professional theologian can give. But this does not mean that the professional theologian is merely to be a popularizer in the pejorative sense of that term.

The Manualist Tradition and Communication. The same need to communicate theological interpretations in terms of practical evaluation of concrete life situations is clearly evidenced in the handbooks of moral theology which have existed in various forms for many centuries. This genre of theological writing continues to provide practical moral guidance in our time and exemplifies the peculiarly pastoral function of theology. The manuals were and occasionally are still used in the education of Catholic seminarians and priests. Until very recently, most catechetic materials for all levels of instructions were nothing more than popularized and vernacularized versions of the standard manuals of moral theology. Even a cursory glance at the manuals reveals page after page of the most minute directions for the practical living of the Christian life by clergy and faithful. Hardly any possible situation is omitted from consideration by the manualists, and precise, concrete "do's" and "don'ts" are prescribed without equivocation.

Professional theologians have long been called upon to use other types of popular theological literature to communicate their interpretations and give concrete guidance in the living of the Christian life. In contemporary times, for example, most American Catholics are familiar with the "Question Box" format of theological literature employed in Catholic newspapers and periodicals, and with the practice of many parishes to provide regularly sponsored lectures by professional theologians on issues of concrete Christian living. The identifiable pastoral role exercised by professional Catholic theologians during the past four centuries is a fact of Church life.

The Theologian in the Contemporary Ecclesiological Context. Since the theologian functions in and for the Church, the contemporary ecclesiological context is an intrinsic modifying factor of the exercise of his function. The ecclesiological context of the manualist era has been notably modified in recent decades. The pertinent elements of the post-Vatican II ecclesial self-awareness will be detailed in chapter four, but it is well to note here that the Council articulated certain fresh ecclesiological self-conceptions already apparent in the 1950's and early 1960's. Since the Council, Roman Catholic teaching and preaching have stressed that all men are called to perfection and that all Christians are expected to live a full participation in the life of the Church, each according to his proper office or role. The Council and postconciliar theology emphasize the specifically Christian task of building a better human society and the correlative right to the necessary knowledge and guidance for accomplishing this task.

The professional theological community is intensely aware of the coresponsibility among its members and of their collective responsibility with persons holding different offices or exercising different functions in the Church. The theologian recognizes the duty to make his specific contribution, a duty deeply rooted in doctrinal and ecclesiological convictions. To be sure, he is also "conscious of his duties and limitations." He thus acknowledges a distinct hierarchical function and mission in the Church, as well as other functions, ministries and gifts in the Church.

Quantity and Quality of Theological Interpretation. Human prudence attaches weight to the quantity and quality of persons holding a particular conviction. This never constitutes an absolute norm but only a prudential presupposition to be taken into consideration by one about to act. There is also an important principle in theology somewhat related to this aspect of human prudence. Long before the contemporary ecclesiological context the theologian was aware that he does not function in isolation from and independent of other theologians in the Church. The number and stature of theologians holding a particular position has great theological and pastoral significance in Roman Catholicism. Catholic theology has traditionally given interpretive weight to the extent, both quantitative and qualitative, to which a particular teaching is held by theologians. This factor is clearly pertinent to the history of systematic theology.

In the history of systematic moral theology, the problem of acting when one does not have certitude is functionally solved by a principle or system known as "probabilism." Probabilism, first proposed by Bartholomew Medina, O.P., in the sixteenth century, maintains that a person is not obliged to follow a more strict position (even if it is more probable) if there exists a more lenient opinion which is itself truly probable. "Probable opinion" is a word of art meaning a responsible theological view which is or can be supported by truly weighty considerations and arguments, but does not deny that other, even contrary, views may be equally or more supportable. ("Probable" here is to be understood in the Latin sense of "prove-able" or "support-able.")

Generally, the hierarchical magisterium and theologians have agreed that a probable opinion furnishes any individual in the Church a safe and secure norm to follow. The important questions are who determines and what constitutes a probable opinion. In this regard theologians speak of intrinsic and extrinsic probabilism. Intrinsic probabilism is established by the merits of the reasons supporting the opinion, which need not rise to the level of moral certitude. Extrinsic probabilism, by contrast, rests on reason and on the number and quality of theologians who hold the particular view. Standard textbooks of moral theology generally agree that both the theological competency of the individual involved and the number of theologians holding an opinion enter into the determination of extrinsic probability. For example, the theology manuals speak of five or six authors of great repute as constituting a probable opinion; on particular issues, views of one outstanding theologian, e.g., Thomas Aquinas, could constitute a truly probable opinion. The methodology often employed in moral theology textbooks is merely to list the number of theologians maintaining a particular opinion in order to prove its probability.[7]

Theologians, therefore, are frequently asked whether or not a particular opinion is probable. Contemporary theologians must, of course, be engaged in ongoing reinterpretation of past articulations of the principle of probabilism itself. Some theologians today would rightly condemn the excesses that were sometimes associated with extrinsic probabilism. But all contemporary theologians would admit that there is theological and pastoral importance in the number and quality of theologians who maintain a particular position.

The Interpretive Possibility of Dissent

Particular interpretations of theologians may, of course, be truly probable but still run counter to the established opinion or to the teaching proposed by the papal and hierarchical teaching offices. The task of reinterpretation of the total theological tradition in the light of the present self-awareness of the Church may at times involve theologians in the type of particular interpretation which the older manuals labeled a "dissent." That "dissent" is an interpretive or reinterpretive possibility has been clearly acknowledged and taught in the "manualistic" tradition of theology even since the sixteenth century. Even leaving aside the contemporary ecclesiological context, practicing theologians could spontaneously recite a list of subjects in which the possibility of "dissent" was brought to actuality in their own or their colleagues' published works and classroom lectures. This is common knowledge in such areas as theological anthropology (e.g., the doctrine of original sin, monogenistic origin of the human race), sacramentology (e.g., validity of Anglican Orders, specific confessional enumeration of sins, nature of eucharistic presence), ecclesiology (e.g., genuine ecclesiality of separated Christian communities, diverse function of some ecclesial structures), ecclesiastical discipline arising from a doctrinal basis (e.g., obligatory clerical celibacy, many practical liturgical stipulations) and biblical exegesis and theology (e.g., decrees of the Pontifical Biblical Commission). "Dissenting" interpretations and reinterpretations of fallibly-taught doctrines are part and parcel of active theological life. This "right to dissent" from authoritative, fallible teachings of the magisterium must, however, be thoroughly examined and then reinterpreted in the light of contemporary theological advances and the present ecclesiological context.

Dissent as Interpretation in the Earlier Vocabulary of the "Manual" Tradition

The standard, classically recognized "right to dissent" described by the theological authors in the "manual" tradition is to some degree pertinent testimony that a theologian's function of interpretation may, at times, take the form of dissent. "Manual" denotes certain textbook presentations of theology, usually intended for use in seminary theology courses. Such works are a distinct literary genre, whose limitations are well known.[8] The following manuals, to be cited herein, date from 1891 to 1963, and are representative of the textbooks used in seminaries and schools of theology throughout the Catholic world:

1. D. Palmieri, *De Romano Pontifice cum prolegomeno De Ecclesia* (2nd edition, Prato: Giacchetti, 1891) (hereinafter called Palmieri);
2. C. Pesch, *Praelectiones Dogmaticae,* t. I: *Institutiones Propaedeuticae ad Sacram Theologiam* (Freiburg: Herder, 1915) (hereinafter called Pesch);
3. H. Dieckmann, *De Ecclesia,* t. II (Freiburg: Herder, 1925) (hereinafter called Dieckmann);
4. J. M. Hervé, *Manuale Theologiae Dogmaticae,* t. I (Paris: Berche & Pagis, 1934) (hereinafter called Hervé);
5. L. Lercher, *Institutiones Theologiae Dogmaticae* (5th edition by F. Schlagenhaufen), t. I (Barcelona: Herder, 1951) (hereinafter called Lercher);
6. J. Salaverri, *De Ecclesia Christi* in *Sacrae Theologiae Summa,* t. I (Madrid: B.A.C., 1955) (hereinafter called Salaverri);
7. F. A. Sullivan, *De Ecclesia, I*: *Quaestiones Theologiae Fundamentalis* (Rome: Gregorian University Press, 1963) (hereinafter called Sullivan).

Ordinary Papal Teaching: Authoritative but Noninfallible.[9] The manuals describe the "ordinary papal magisterium," or teaching office of the pope, as the day-to-day proposal of Catholic teaching that the pope articulates in his sermons, addresses and encyclicals: "that exercise of his teaching office by which the pope intends to teach, but does not make clear his intention of imposing his judgment as absolutely definitive and irreformable."[10]

The ordinary teaching office of the pope is commonly regarded by theologians as fallible.[11] But the manualists say that the pope's ordinary teaching office is "authoritative" even when fallible. The manuals distinguish between a magisterium *mere docens seu scientificum* (merely teaching or scientific), to which assent is given because of the reasons the teacher offers, and a magisterium *auctoritativum* (authoritative), to which assent is given because of the *authority* of the teacher.[12] The pope, unlike the teacher whose teaching stands or falls by the merit and strength of the arguments he presents, has been given an authority to teach which can require assent even when his reasons are not in themselves convincing.[13] His is a *magisterium authenticum,* where *authenticum* mean not "authentic," but "authoritative" or "official."

Corresponding Obligation of Assent. In the case of such ordinary magisterium, the manuals hold that one is obliged to give "internal, religious assent." Assent is an act "by which what is contained in the decree is affirmed to be true."[14] The assent must be internal and sincere; external conformity or respectful silence is not sufficient.[15] The requisite assent is termed "religious" because its motive is that the pope has been given authority to teach by Christ.[16]

Such "internal, religious assent," however, is to be distinguished from the assent of "divine faith." (There has long been a dispute concerning the existence of a third category of assent called "ecclesiastical faith," which would apply to those infallible statements of the Church that do not concern matters formally revealed.[17]) The motive for an act of divine faith is the unfailing authority of God; the motive for "internal religious assent" is the authority of the teaching office in question.[18] Divine faith is absolutely certain and *super omnia firma,* supremely firm; internal religious assent is not absolutely certain and not supremely firm; internal religious assent is not absolutely or metaphysically certain[19]—most of the authors speak of religious assent as "morally certain."[20]

Divine faith is to be given without qualification or condition; this is not true of internal religious assent. Lercher speaks of religious assent as not objectively certain because it rests upon a motive that does not exclude the possibility of error and is known to be such. It is presumed, however, that in any concrete case the magisterium is not in error. Such presumption does not exclude the possibility of error but only its present likelihood. Most of the manualist authors assert explicitly that religious assent is *conditional.*[21] Palmieri and Pesch do not use that term respecting religious assent, but they imply that such assent is conditional because they acknowledge the possibility of dissent.[22]

The Possibility of Dissent. Although these manualists agree that internal religious assent is subject to conditions, they are rather general in describing those conditions. Salaverri expresses the permissible qualification of assent in the following manner: "unless by an equal or superior authority the Church should decree otherwise."[23] For Sullivan, the condition is "unless the Church should at some time decide otherwise or unless the contrary should become evident."[24] For Lercher, dissent is not permissible "unless a grave suspicion should arise that the presumption is not verified."[25] Pesch speaks of the binding force of pronouncements "so long as it does not become positively clear that they are wrong," and adds that "assent is prudently suspended when there first appear sufficient motives for doubting."[26] Straub is quoted by Salaverri as holding that it is licit to dissent, to doubt or to continue to regard the opposite opinion as probable "if the decree should appear to someone to be certainly false or to be opposed to so solid a reason that the force of this reason cannot be shattered even by the weight of the sacred authority."[27] Palmieri holds that "religious assent is owed when there is nothing which could prudently persuade one to suspend his assent. The assent is morally certain; therefore, should motives appear, whether they be true or false (but from inculpable error), which persuade one to a different view, then in those circumstances the will would not act imprudently in suspending assent."[28]

With the possible exception of Salaverri, then, these manualists admit that a Catholic could have sufficient reason to justify withholding assent to a teaching of the ordinary magisterium of the pope. (Dieckmann and Salaverri alone suggest that only a theologian could find himself in such a position;[29] the others apply the qualification quite generally.) Nor do these authors suggest that the reasons for dissent must be *new* ones, not previously considered by the magisterium.

On the other hand, the manualists insist that the presumption initially favors the teaching of the ordinary magisterium, and that assent may not be suspended rashly or casually from a motive of pride, "excessive love of one's own opinions" or "over-confidence in one's own genius."[30] Palmieri, however, at least suggests that certain cases, such as Celestine III's permission of divorce and remarriage in the case of the heresy of a spouse, or the Galileo matter, may prove "both the exception that we have allowed for and that metaphysically certain assent is not required."[31] Similarly, Sullivan implies error in the ordinary magisterium on the part of Popes Liberius, Vigilius and Honorius.[32]

Error: Detection and Correction. Three of the manualists explore more fully the possibility of error and of its correction, although their consideration of the possibility represents only initial analysis.

Sullivan admits that a pope could make a mistake, but he insists that it would never become the "constant and traditional teaching of the Holy See."[33] In rejecting the claim that the ordinary magisterium of the pope is infallible, Sullivan takes the following position:

> It seems to be possible that a pope, teaching *modo ordinario,* might propose a judgment that would have to be corrected afterward, without the whole Church being drawn into error thereby. In such a case, the divine assistance would be enough to assure that the error would be

corrected before it was generally accepted by the Church and to prevent the erroneous teaching from becoming the traditional teaching of the Holy See.[34]

He asserts that "an error in the ordinary magisterium could be corrected before the whole Church were led into error."[35] But at no point does he indicate how that end might be accomplished in fact.

Dieckmann makes the following statement in a discussion of the assistance of the Holy Spirit that accompanies the daily exercise of the ordinary magisterium:

It must be conceded that the influence of this assistance cannot be determined accurately, so that each doctrinal act could be said to have been made under this special assistance which preserves one from error. If that were true, all the acts would be infallible. The assertion is rather a universal one: generally the Holy Spirit will preserve the organs of the authoritative magisterium from error especially in those decisions which are prepared and issued with the necessary diligence, caution and scholarship.[36]

This concession by a leading manualist contrasts with the fear sometimes voiced that to acknowledge the possibility or fact of error is to deny the assistance of the Holy Spirit.

Pesch approaches the problem obliquely, in a discussion of the process of determining the reasons for a pronouncement:

Since the pope's congregations do not *per se* supply an absolutely certain argument for their teaching, one can and, it may be, one must inquire into the reasons for the teaching. In this way it may come about either that the teaching in question will slowly be received by the whole Church and thus be raised to the level of infallibility, or that the error will be detected.[37]

Lercher approaches the question of dissent more directly than the foregoing three authors:

If the supreme pontiff, exercising his authority, but not at its highest level, obliges all to assent to a thing as true (because revealed or coherent with revelation), he does not seem to be infallible *de jure* nor is it necessary to say that the Holy Spirit would never permit such a decree to be issued, if it should be erroneous.

It is true that the Holy Spirit will never allow the Church to be led into error by such a decree. The way in which error would be excluded would more probably consist in the assistance of the Holy Spirit given to the head of the Church, by which such an erroneous decree would be prevented. But it is not entirely out of the question that the error might be excluded by the Holy Spirit in his way, namely, by the subjects of the decree detecting its error and ceasing to give it their internal assent.[38]

Lercher also makes a similar comment about the decrees of the papal congregations: "If by such a decree the affirmation of the truth of some matter should be objectively false, the Holy Spirit would not permit error: probably by his assistance he would not move the bishops and faithful to give a firm internal assent.[39] It is not out of the question that the Holy Spirit might assist individual bishops or even individual members of the faithful, so that they would not err, when the magisterium teaches authoritatively but not infallibly."[40] The cogency of these statements is not affected by the fact that Lercher is extremely skeptical about whether such a situation justifying dissent will ever arise. Lercher is the only manualist who suggests how the Church could correct an error taught by the ordinary magisterium. Lercher views such correction as the work of the Holy Spirit, but he does not exclude the faithful from participation in this corrective work, that is, from participation in such dissent.

Lercher's position parallels such views as Newman's "on consulting the faithful in matters of doctrine" and Bishop Gasser's (the official relator at the First Vatican Council) insistence that the pope has a moral obligation to consult the Church before approaching an infallible declaration.[41] Lercher's position, moreover, calls to mind a set of traditional discussions from the eleventh century, recently rediscovered by modern scholarship, concerning the possibility of a pope becoming a heretic or a schismatic.[42] Popes, canonists and theologians have acknowledged the possibility of papal heresy or schism, and some nine centuries of theological and canonical discussion have included consideration of what the Church at large could do in such a case.[43]

At least this much is clear: there remain within the Church-at-large norms of doctrine and practice which are not dependent on the pope; that there are circumstances, however unlikely one may judge them to be, in which it could be necessary for the Church to judge and correct the pope; and that the destiny of the Church is not totally committed into the hands of the pope alone.

Dissent as a Legitimate Interpretive Option. The tradition reflected by the manuals, therefore, teaches both the duty of internal religious assent to ordinary papal teaching *and* the possible legitimacy of dissent. In the earlier "manual" vocabulary, dissent clearly is a legitimate interpretive possibility for the competent Roman Catholic, for sufficient reasons, in response to an authoritative, noninfallible teaching of the hierarchical/papal magisterium.

American Bishops on Assent and Dissent. The "right to dissent" articulated in the manuals is acknowledged in many recent pastoral statements of national hierarchies.[44] The American Bishops' Pastoral Letter of 1967, *The Church in Our Day,* sharply departed from the usual theological vocabulary with respect to the forms of assent and failed to indicate even the possibility of dissent. As a result, it not only did not deal with norms for dissent from ordinary magisterial teaching[45] but left the faithful unprepared for the problems generated by the publication of *Humanae Vitae.* Following the theologians' dissent from the Encyclical, this inadequacy in the 1967 Pastoral was only partially corrected in the American Bishops' 1968 Pastoral, *Human Life in Our Day.*[46]

Preliminary Reflections on the Traditional Right of Dissent: Need for Reinterpretation

The perspective of the manuals concerning assent and dissent suffers from serious philosophical and theological limitations. The manuals' analyses of the nature of assent is inadequate, and quite oblivious to the crucial questions raised by Newman in his *Grammar of Assent*. How would the manualists have reacted to Newman's view that assent is by nature unconditional? "No one can hold conditionally what by the same act he holds to be true."[47] The discussion of what Newman terms "opinion" is also of interest to the discussion of a type of "assent" that is merely a "presumption" of truth.[48]

The manuals also tend to pass over rather quickly the problem created by using such words as "authority" and "obedience" when speaking of "teaching." The association of the words "teaching" and "authority" is not without ambiguity. Surely the use of the word "authority" with respect to teaching is at best only analogous to its use with respect to law. Does "authority" to teach derive from a source other than the possession of truth? The manualists seem to think so; Palmieri[49] and Pesch[50] add to the obligation of assent to a word from God that derives from natural law (not to mention common sense) *another* obligation of assent that derives from the "authority" of the Church.

The manuals do not adequately consider the relationship of the roles of the mind and of the will with respect to assent, with the result that the movement from "assent" to "obedience," and vice-versa, seems too facile. Perhaps these difficulties derive from too close association (not to say identification) of the magisterial and juridical functions of authority.[51] Such associations would cause misgivings even if the notion of law involved were properly intellectualist; when it is voluntaristic, the danger of accepting a notion of truth as whatever authority happens to teach is greatly increased.

The shift in theological ideal from the medieval quest for understanding to the post-Tridentine passion for certainty is also not without its importance for the development of the kind of perspective present in the manuals. The foregoing deficiences are suggested merely to indicate the necessity of reinterpreting the manualist tradition in the light of the contemporary theological and ecclesiological context. Such reinterpretation will merely *begin* with the affirmation of the manualists that the possibility of dissent from authoritative teaching is an integral part of the accepted dynamics of theology.

Another aspect of the need for reinterpreting the manualists' presentation of the right to dissent was suggested by Professor John Noonan, of the School of Law, University of California (Berkeley), in the expert testimony he delivered before the Inquiry Panel at Catholic University. Professor Noonan pointed out the importance of taking careful account of the special problems faced by the Roman Catholic Church arising from the nineteenth century political and religious milieu within which many of the manuals were first published. He testified that to restrict the right to dissent to private or semiprivate presentations addressed directly to the Holy See (the curious distinction between "internal" and "external" dissent) could have resulted from the defensive attitude of the Church at that time with respect to the non-Catholic religious community in Europe and all the other complex forces, intellectual and political, which seemed to threaten the Church's survival. The fear that dissenting voices within the Church would be unfairly used against the Church, especially by the Protestant community, may very well have influenced the severe restrictions of the manualists on external or public dissent even from clearly acknowledged fallible teachings of the papal magisterium.

Furthermore, an understanding of the nature and function of the magisterium, or teaching office in the Church, is a prerequisite to any attempt to reinterpret the right to dissent in its present practical context. The manualist articulation of the possibility of dissent evidences a static conception of the relationship between the bishops' teaching office, the theologians' scientific role and the living witness of faithful Christians. Indeed, characterizing a particular theological response to a hierarchical pronouncement as "dissent" from "the magisterium" or from "the teaching of the Church" ignores the history of doctrinal development. A more dynamic view of the workings of the Spirit in the Church would see room and reason for dialogue in the quest for truth, dialogue which would be frustrated in a structure in which the teaching function was firmly and exclusively fixed at one level of communication within the Church. Thus the process of arriving at the teaching of the Church must be re-examined within the framework of co-responsibility in the Church to determine the proper relationship between the theologians' teaching office and the hierarchical magisterium and the relationship of both to the whole Church as "magistral."

This preliminary consideration of the nature of theology and the role of theologians has recalled several points which are essential both to the question of reinterpretation in general and the problem of responsible dissent from the Encyclical *Humanae Vitae* in particular. To summarize, theology is a science in the strict sense, and as a science is limited only by truth and the implications of its data. It would cease to be a science if it were not free to arrive at conclusions which are suggested by its research and supported by its data. A theologian operates in the context of particular traditions and is to be presumed loyal to those traditions. A Roman Catholic theologian theologizes within the context of a Roman Catholic faith-commitment. This theological enterprise is delicate and complex.

As theology sharpens its interpretive skills, it becomes increasingly aware of its multiple possibilities and the inevitability and normalcy of theological pluralism. Catholic theologians welcome the contributions of the hierarchical magisterium, while recognizing (with the traditional manuals) the possibility of "licit dissent." Because of the frequent obscurity of the matters that it treats, theology can never be an individualistic pursuit. It is always a communal endeavor. Theologians must check the thinking of others in their field in order to test their own positions.

Communication among theologians alone would not satisfy the "need to know" of the whole Church, which has always sought the practical guidance of the theological community. Thus, theology is not merely a matter of intellectual exercise but has a distinct pastoral dimension. The theologian has an obligation to bear witness to the achievements of his science by means that are suited to the current state of culture and communications. The specification of that obligation with respect to interpretive possibilities that in the vocabulary of the manualists were labeled "dissents" is itself an object of theological endeavor, particularly through a reinterpretation of the relationship of theologians with the hierarchical magisterium in the context of the ecclesiological theme of co-responsibility.

Notes

1. The self-understanding of the Roman Catholic theologian expressed in this chapter is not unique to the Catholic University Theologians. It is shared by such noted contemporary theologians as M. Chenu, Y. Congar, H. Küng, B. Lonergan, K. Rahner and E. Schillebeeckx. See H. Küng, "The Freedom of Theology," in *Freedom Today* (New York: Sheed & Ward, 1966), pp. 66–108; B. Lonergan, "Theology in Its New Context," in L. K. Shook, ed., *Theology of Renewal,* vol. I (New York: Herder, 1968), pp. 34–46; Y. Congar, "Theology's Tasks After Vatican II," in Shook, *op. cit.,* pp. 47–65; K. Rahner, "Theology and the Magisterium After the Council," *Theology Digest* (Special Sesquicentennial Issue, 1968), pp. 4–16; E. Schillebeeckx, "Toward a Catholic Use of Hermeneutic," in *God the Future of Man* (New York: Sheed & Ward, 1968), pp. 1–49.
2. Y. Congar, *A History of Theology* (New York: Doubleday, 1968).
3. This period in Catholic theology is well summarized in Congar, *op. cit.,* pp. 187–89.
4. Denzinger-Schoenmetzer, *Enchiridion Symbolorum,* 32d edition (Barcelona: Herder, 1963), n. 3016 (hereinafter cited merely as Denz.).
5. Denz., 3020.
6. See the American Bishops' Pastoral Statement, *Human Life in Our Day* (November, 1968), Washington: United States Catholic Conference (U.S.C.C.), *passim,* and the comments of J. Haughey, "The Bishops and Cardinal Newman," *America* 119 (Nov. 30, 1968), pp. 554–55.
7. All standard authors of moral theology manuals treat the moral system of "probabilism" at some length: cf. e.g., the works of Noldin-Schmitt, Regatillo-Zalba, Iorio, Vermeersch, Pruemmer.
8. Y. Congar, *op. cit.,* pp. 177–95.
9. The editors acknowledge their debt of gratitude to Professor Joseph A. Komonchak of St. Joseph's Seminary (Dunwoodie), Yonkers,

N.Y., and Professor Harry McSorley of St. Paul's College, Washington, D.C., for the valuable contribution their research on the problem of dissent in the manualists has made to this section of our presentation. Cf. J. A. Komonchak, "Ordinary Papal Magisterium and Religious Assent," in C. E. Curran, ed., *Contraception: Authority and Dissent* (New York: Herder, 1969), pp. 101–26. In August, 1968 Professor Komonchak prepared, on behalf of the Catholic University theologians, a brief analysis of the manualists' teaching on dissent for use in the Statler-Hilton meeting. He *subsequently* expanded his work to include the background and correct understanding of paragraph 25 of *Lumen Gentium* and offered it to the subject professors for use in their presentation to the Inquiry Board. It is essentially this study which was incorporated into the work herein cited. Professor McSorley also made his study available to the professors.

10. F. A. Sullivan, *De Ecclesia, I: Quaestiones Theologiae Fundamentalis* (Rome: Gregorian University Press, 1963), p. 349. See also L. Lercher, *Institutiones Theologiae Dogmaticae* (5th edition by F. Schlagenhaufen), t. I (Barcelona: Herder, 1951), p. 296, and H. Dieckmann, *De Ecclesia,* t. II (Freiburg: Herder, 1925), p. 91.
11. Sullivan, *op. cit.,* pp. 348–52; J. Salaverri, *De Ecclesia Christi* in *Sacrae Theologiae Summa,* t. I (Madrid: B.A.C., 1955), pp. 709–10.
12. Sullivan, *op. cit.,* pp. 258–59; Salaverri, *op. cit.,* pp. 662–63; Lercher, *op. cit.,* pp. 158, 257; D. Palmieri, *De Romano Pontifice cum prolegomeno De Ecclesia,* 2nd edition (Prato: Giacchetti, 1891), p. 167.
13. Palmieri, *op. cit.,* 719; C. Pesch, *Praelectiones Dogmaticae,* t. I: *Institutiones Propaedeuticae ad Sacram Theologiam* (Freiburg: Herder: 1915), p. 370; Dieckmann, *op. cit.,* p. 116; Lercher, *op. cit.,* pp. 297–98; Salaverri, *op. cit.,* pp. 716–18; Sullivan, *op. cit.,* pp. 345–48.
14. Lercher, *op. cit.,* p. 297; Dieckmann, *op. cit.,* p. 116; Salaverri, *op. cit.,* p. 716; Sullivan, *op. cit.,* p. 347.
15. Palmieri, *op. cit.,* p. 719; Pesch, *op. cit.,* p. 370; Dieckmann, *op. cit.,* p. 116; Lercher, *op. cit.,* p. 297; Salaverri, *op. cit.,* p. 716; Sullivan, *op. cit.,* p. 347.
16. Pesch, *op. cit.,* p. 370; Dieckmann, *op. cit.,* p. 116; Lercher, *op. cit.,* p. 297; Salaverri, *op. cit.,* p. 716; Sullivan, *op. cit.,* p. 347.
17. Y. Congar, "Foi dogmatique et 'foi ecclésiastique,'" in *Catholicisme,* t. IV, col. 1059–67, reprinted in *Sainte Église* (Paris: du Cerf, 1963), pp. 357–73.
18. Palmieri, *op. cit.,* p. 719; Pesch, *op. cit.,* p. 393.
19. Palmieri, *op. cit.,* p. 719; Pesch, *op. cit.,* p. 370; Dieckmann, *op. cit.,* p. 116; Salaverri, *op. cit.,* p. 716.

20. Palmieri, *op. cit.*, pp. 719–20: *"maxime probabile causas erroris deesse"*; Pesch, *op. cit.*, p. 370: *"certitudine morali quadam latiore"*; Dieckmann, *op. cit.*, p. 116; Sullivan, *op. cit.*, p. 348; Salaverri's *certitudo relativa* is identical with what others mean by *certitudo moralis.*
21. Dieckmann, *op. cit.*, p. 116 (quoting Maroto); Lercher, *op. cit.*, p. 297; Sullivan, *op. cit.*, pp. 348, 354; Salaverri, *op. cit.*, pp. 716, 719, where he cites other authors.
22. Palmieri, *op. cit.*, p. 719; Pesch, *op. cit.*, p. 370.
23. Salaverri, *op. cit.*, pp. 716, 720.
24. Sullivan, *op. cit.*, pp. 348, 354.
25. Lercher, *op. cit.*, p. 297.
26. Pesch, *op. cit.*, p. 370.
27. Salaverri, *op. cit.*, p. 719.
28. Palmieri, *op. cit.*, p. 719.
29. Dieckmann, *op. cit.*, p. 116 (again quoting Maroto); Salaverri, *op. cit.*, p. 720; J. M. Hervé, *Manuale Theologiae Dogmaticae,* t. I (Paris: Berche & Pagis, 1934), p. 523.
30. Lercher, *op. cit.*, pp. 298, 307; Salaverri, *op. cit.*, p. 720.
31. Palmieri, *op. cit.*, p. 721; cf., pp. 731–37.
32. Sullivan, *op. cit.*, pp. 349–50; cf., pp. 331–40.
33. Sullivan, *op. cit.*, p. 345.
34. *Ibid.*, p. 350.
35. *Ibid.*, p. 351.
36. Dieckmann, *op. cit.*, pp. 117–18.
37. Pesch, *op. cit.*, p. 370.
38. Lercher, *op. cit.*, p. 297.
39. *Ibid.*, p. 297.
40. *Ibid.*, p. 307.
41. *Collectio Lacensis,* v. VIII (Freiburg: Herder, 1890), p. 401.
42. B. Tierney, *Foundations of the Conciliar Theory* (Cambridge: University Press, 1955); H. Küng, *Structures of the Church* (New York: Nelson, 1964), pp. 249–319. Cf., also the controversy about the force and significance of the "*Sacrosancta*" decree of the Council of Constance, e.g., in P. de Vooght, *Les pouvoirs du Concile et l'autorité du Pape au Concile de Constance* (Paris: du Cerf, 1965), or the reviews of this book in 84 *Downside Review* (1966), pp. 432–35, and in 40 *Revue des Sciences Religieuses* (1966), pp. 195–96.
43. The problem does not concern the Pope only as a *persona privata;* cf. A. Duval, *De Suprema R. Pontificis in Ecclesiam Potestate,* I, 1614, 19th edition (Paris: Lethielleux, 1877), 255–57.
44. See *infra,* chapter seven.
45. American Bishops' Pastoral Statement, *The Church in Our Day* (January, 1968), Washington: U.S.C.C., pp. 69–73.

46. American Bishops' Pastoral Statement, *Human Life in Our Day* (November, 1968) Washington: U.S.C.C., p. 18.
47. J. H. Cardinal Newman, *Grammar of Assent* (London: Longmans, 1906), p. 172.
48. *Ibid.*, pp. 58–60.
49. Palmieri, *op. cit.*, pp. 240–41.
50. Pesch, *op. cit.*, pp. 193–94.
51. On the dangers of "juridicism" in the interpretation of Church documents, see Y. Congar, *The Meaning of Tradition* (New York: Hawthorne, 1964), pp. 120–24; W. Kaspar, *Dogme et Evangile* (Tournai: Casterman, 1967).

3

Preliminary Consideration Concerning the Nature and Function of the Magisterium

The Term "Magisterium." The term "magisterium" does not have a univocal meaning of long standing. In fact, it has only recently become common in the theological vocabulary. In general, the term describes the Church's competence to teach and bear witness to the nature and consequences of God's revelation in Christ. The subject and object of this competence, however, have not yet been theologically treated to an adequate degree. Even in the theoretical order many questions and problems have not been solved.

The magisterium is identified in varying ways throughout the history of the Church, depending on the prevailing ecclesiology, the notion of communications and the culturally conditioned views of authority and truth. Furthermore, the very notion of "teaching" is quite ambiguous. A teacher might be an authority figure who imposes information on passive students or, in accordance with another educational philosophy, he could be someone who leads students to understanding and does not content himself with merely reporting on past discoveries. In the face of such difficulties in specifying the scope of these preliminary considerations on the nature and function of magisterium in the Church, the most workable starting point for the present purposes seems to be a brief recall of the terminology and categories of the "manual" tradition.

Ordinary and Extraordinary Magisterium. A rather consistent terminology developed in the manuals with respect to the magisterium. Until Vatican II, the term "magisterium" was usually used to designate the *hierarchical* magisterium exclusively. The manifestations of the hierarchical magisterium were generally distinguished conceptually as *"ordinary"* or *"extraordinary."* The extraordinary magisterium comprises the teachings of ecumenical councils or *ex cathedra* papal statements. It is taught that infallibility could attach to such teachings under certain rigidly defined conditions; infallibility could also reside in the ordinary magisterium, which includes anything in the realm of Christian faith and morals that is taught "unanimously" and as a matter of faith and morals by all the bishops in union with the pope.

Magisterium as Authoritative. Aside from the question of infallibility, which is being afforded extensive treatment in modern theology, the magisterium has been considered as having an important role in teaching doctrine that is "authentic" or "authoritative" but admittedly noninfallible. The term "authentic" itself has no well developed history as a "word of art" in theological interpretation. However, concerning *authoritative* teaching, Vatican II, in its *Dogmatic Constitution on the Church,* stated that an exercise of "authentic teaching authority" must be "acknowledged with reverence" and sincerely adhered to with "a religious assent of soul." This assent is also described as "submission of will and of mind."[1]

Role of the "Sense" of the Faithful. A broadly based "sense" in the Church, the *sensus fidelium,* however, has always been considered an important criterion of Christian truth along with the hierarchical magisterium. The very early tendency in the Church was to refer to the consensus of all believers as a safe test of orthodoxy. However, this was never understood to be a question of mere "majority rule." The notion of the *sensus fidelium* shows a variety of historical forms depending on the theological and polemical context in which it is found.

Subject Exercising Magisterium

Entire Church as Magistral. The notion of magisterium is rooted in the promise of the Spirit of truth to the company of believers.

The basic proposition of the theology of the magisterium is, in Rahner's words, that "the Church as a whole cannot fall from eschatological grace—hence from truth as grace either—because she is the concrete presence of the definitive self-assertion of God which has occurred in the God-Man."[2] The promise of truth, then, primarily concerns "the church as a whole." The Spirit was not promised only to the hierarchical ministry of the Church. "The body of the faithful as a whole, anointed as they are by the holy One, cannot err in matters of belief."[3] Neither the magisterium nor the Church is simply hierarchical. Neither theologians nor Church officers may claim with any historical accuracy to be, in an exclusive sense, *the* magisterium.

Variety of Ministries. There can be no doubt as to the presence of ministries in the very early Church. The early Church was liberal in creating, shaping and even discarding ministries. There is, however, no indication of an original fixed set of clearly defined "offices" destined for all time. The lists of ministries (I Cor. 12:28-31; Rom. 12:6-8; Eph. 4:11) varied without apology. One person might claim to exercise several of these ministries. These ministries were not the primary reality around which the Church was structured but rather involved functions within the Christian life of service.

Development of the Role of Officers. As the Church took on a more definite form, the role of *officers* achieved more importance and precision. The tripartite division of officers, which we now simply assume, is first mentioned by Ignatius of Antioch in the early second century.[4] By the middle of the second century, the special role of the episcopate was clearly established. Communities such as the Roman Church, which were founded by an apostle, were considered important witnesses to genuine apostolic doctrine.

The theology of the discernment of the Spirit and the theology of office intertwine historically and present a polarity and tension that have still not been thematically resolved. The Church has persistently believed that it is not only its officers who are anointed by the Spirit. At times, however, the teaching prerogatives of the officers have been so stressed that the faithful seem graced only to accept and to obey. At other times the magisterial role of the Church at large has been emphasized.

Stress on Officers as Sole Subject Excercising Magisterium: Historical Stages. Congar states that a revolution in the notion of authority occurred at the time of the Gregorian reforms, when a highly juridical paradigm altered the conception of teaching authority.[5] Church officers, especially the pope (whose office in this period was much affected by what Weiler calls "totalitarian thinking"), came to be seen as *possessing* God's authority rather than imperfectly reflecting it through delegation.[6] As a result, authority, at times, came to be seen as embodied in the officeholder, and the distinction between ecclesiastical and divine authority was blurred.

The reaction at the Council of Trent against the reformers brought about a more systematic stress on the power of officeholders. For centuries, the terms "revelation" and "inspiration" had not been used rather indiscriminately as descriptive of the ultimate source of the authority of teachings of popes and councils. After Trent, the term "assistance" was thought more descriptive of the guiding influence of the Spirit on Church officers. The notion of "assistance," however, has never been precisely explained. (For Suarez, for example, it was "equivalent to revelation.")[7] Despite the absence of theological explanation of this notion of assistance, the "assisted" magisterium of the hierarchy came to be seen more and more as the proximate rule of faith. In the eighteenth century, Billuart stressed that traditions do not constitute a rule of faith unless they have been proposed by a magisterium.[8] In the nineteenth century, the influential Franzelin distinguished between the preservation of truth in the whole Church and the binding promulgation of truth by the hierarchy.[9] Billot, reacting to the Modernist threat, assigned a critical role in preserving truth to the assisted hierarchical magisterium.[10]

The notion of assistance was basic to the definition of infallibility of Vatican I. D'Avanzo and Gasser, speaking for the Deputation of the Faith (the Commission charged with the drafting and presentation of proposed Conciliar texts), asserted that assistance is not a new revelation but a manifestation of the truth which is already contained in the deposit of revelation. Since a strict obligation in conscience binds the pope to seek out the truth in the faith of the living Church,[11] when the pope defines, he does so "in relation to the universal church,"[12] and "representing the universal church."[13] Gasser states that a negligent pope would be impeded by God from a destructive and erroneous use of his powers.[14] The foregoing theories evidence a shift in the notion of teaching authority, from an aspect of the inherent power of the genetic Christian and apostolic experience to an attribute of the power of a proclaiming hierarchy. The term "vicar of Christ" had been first used to denote the Spirit (Tertullian),[15] and the phrase "Charism of truth" was used by Irenaeus not to describe the teaching power of Church officers (as it is in Vatican I *and* Vatican II) but to express the power of the truth itself.[16] The meaning of the phrase "rule of faith" has also changed: "In the Fathers, *regula fidei* (rule of faith) refers to an object, the doctrine we must profess in order to receive baptism in the Church. For modern authors, *regula fidei* means the magisterium."[17] "Teaching authority" in its early usage had reference to the totality of the original Christian experience and not merely to the notion of "the charism of office" as it is used in our modern sense.[18]

Other Factors Influencing the Definition of the Subject Exercising "Magisterium." Despite the stress on office, other factors have influenced Church history in regard to the subject exercising magisterium. There were the ancient axioms: *orbis major urbe* (the whole church is greater than Rome alone), and "what affects all should be treated by all." Moderate conciliar theories also emerged in the twelfth and thirteenth centuries stressing the magisterial role of the universal Church. These notions found blessing at the Council of Constance. From the early centuries, much importance was attached to the aforementioned *sensus fidelium* as a sign of truth.[19] This stress on what the universal

Church believed did not amount to a kind of poll-taking or a statistical approach to truth. It was rather another way of stressing the presence of the Spirit in the whole company of believers.

The Christian realization that the Spirit of God is operative in the entire Church is also very clearly contained in the Russian theology of *sobernost*. This interesting theology relies heavily upon the thought of the early Church fathers in stressing unanimity in love.[20]

During the primacy of the universities in the thirteenth, fourteenth and fifteenth centuries, the magisterium of the theologians was in high repute. The development of universities was the distinguished achievement of medieval Christian culture and was based on the premise that truth would emerge from the free exchange of ideas. Theologians whose ideas were thought too adventuresome (e.g., St. Thomas Aquinas) had the advantage of judgment by their university peers.

Teaching Role of Bishops in the Church. Acknowledgment of the special teaching office of bishops, however, is certainly part of authentic Christian tradition. In a true sense the bishops are in the Church as teachers. As Vatican II's *Decree on the Bishops' Pastoral Office in the Church* says, "Christ gave the apostles and their successors the command and the power to teach all nations, to hallow men in the truth and to feed them. Bishops, therefore, have been made true and authentic teachers of the faith, pontiffs, and pastors through the Holy Spirit, who has been given to them."[21] This same document specifies this teaching role in the following words: "In exercising their duty of teaching—which is conspicuous among the principal duties of bishops—they should announce the Gospel of Christ to men."[22]

It is, of course, clear that the bishops are called upon not merely to proclaim the gospel as it is found in Scripture but also to apply it as best they can to the problems of "civil society with its laws and professions, labor and leisure, the arts and technical inventions, poverty and affluence. . . . Finally, they should set forth the ways by which are to be answered the most serious questions concerning the ownership, increase, and just distribution of material goods, peace and war, and brotherly relations among all countries."[23]

It is not, of course, presumed that the bishops will be able to apply the gospel vision to each and every complex problem of private and social morality in the modern world. It will always be necessary for the bishops, as for all other teachers in the Church, to enlist the assistance of experts in the various fields.

The Second Vatican Council also urged the bishops, in the discharge of their teaching task, to use every effective means of communication in order to proclaim the gospel of Christ: "They should also strive to make use of the various media at hand nowadays for proclaiming Christian doctrine, namely, first of all, preaching and catechetical instruction which always hold the first place, then the presentation of this doctrine in schools, academies, conferences, and meetings of every kind, and finally its dissemination through public statements at times of outstanding events as well as by the press and various other media of communication, which by all means ought to be used to proclaim the gospel of Christ."[24]

Vatican II warned the laity against naïve expectations that the pastors of the Church will be able to give clearcut answers to all complex problems: "Let the layman not imagine that his pastors are always such experts, that to every problem which arises, however complicated, they can readily give him a concrete solution, or even that such is their mission."[25]

Because of the extraordinary developments in the field of communications resulting in the instant and widespread promulgation of doctrinal developments, many new pastoral problems present themselves to the bishops' attention. In union with other Christians and with all those who fulfill the teaching office of the Church in any way, the bishops must give prime concern to "the pastoral aspect of theological publication."[26]

Thus, the bishops have many special duties to perform as teachers in the Church. To prevent confusion, however, it must be noted that the bishops are not the only teachers in the Church, even though they are teachers in their own specific way. Teaching is an *analogous* term, and one kind of teaching competence must not be confused with another. Thus the bishops in their pastoral office of teaching the *faith* are not expected to master the analytical and methodological skills of the scientific theologian. Both bishops and theologians share a common concern for the integrity of the faith. Obviously, their distinct but complementary tasks should be executed in an atmosphere of mutual respect.

Object of the Magisterium

Doctrine of Faith or Morals. The First Vatican Council declared that the infallibility of the Church is directed to the revelation handed down by the Apostles.[27] The Church was to be, in Cajetan's phrase, the "ministra objecti" (steward of the deposit).[28] The object of this stewardship, according to the First Vatican Council, contains "doctrinam de fide vel moribus" (doctrine of faith or morals).[29] The meaning of "moribus" in this definition is not clear. In its long history the expression "faith and morals" has had varied meanings. At the time of Trent, "morals" included the practices and customs of the early Church as well as points of liturgy, doctrine and discipline.[30] The allegation that it means "the natural law" is novel; the multiplicity of natural law theories complicates any such assertion. Nor is it meaningful to allege, as some have, that the natural law is contained implicitly or virtually in the deposit of faith.[31]

These problems, however, should not obscure the fact that the Church has always felt that its Christian experience is truly relevant to morality. The Church has always felt impelled to speak to the moral problems of man and to attempt to show how the experience of truth which gave birth to the Christian people relates to those problems. Recent theology is concerned with giving an increasingly important role to the Church in the moral dialogues that take place in the human community. Thus, no one questions the obligations of the Church to operate in the sphere of moral education. There is a question, however, as to the certainty that the Church can achieve when it applies its moral vision to the specific complex moral questions of any particular time.

Specific Morality as Object of Infallibility. The question of infallibility in teaching specific issues of morality is largely academic since theology does not offer any examples of such teaching. Professor Richard McCormick notes that this issue has provoked considerable discussion and states that there is "a growing body of opinion on both sides of this question."[32] However, those who defend the possibility of infallibility in teaching morality do not produce specific historical instances in which such teaching has been promulgated. According to the guidance of Canon 1223, No. 3, of the Code of Canon Law nothing is to be considered defined *"nisi id manifesto constiterit"* (unless it is manifestly clear). There is no specific moral issue where this condition can be shown to obtain. There are no pronouncements on specific issues of morality that are defended as clearly infallible. Thus, in moral matters, the presumption is that the teaching is reformable and the possibility of licit dissent is logically contained in the notion of such inherently fallible doctrine. The question, then, of the moral *magisterium* involves the matter of authoritative, noninfallible teaching and the response due to such teaching.

It is clear in any event that the teaching of specific morality is not to be conceived of according to a juridical paradigm, as though teaching were understandable in terms of a legislative act.[33] Teaching is not "binding" because the teacher wills it to be binding but because it is convincingly true. The intellect is not bound by the will of another but by the appearance of truth presented in perceptible form.

*Vatican II and Specific Morality.*The Second Vatican Council teaches that those who fulfill the duty of teaching in the Church "should announce the gospel of Christ to men."[34] The Council urges further that the message of the gospel be applied to all the important issues of human life involving man's personal and social well-being. In general, it is recognized in the conciliar documents and in the general teaching of the Church that there is a specifically distinct ethical content in the Christian experience. This, however, does not mean that our traditional treasury of moral insight contains a detailed code for the regulation of all forms of human conduct. Many times, the genuinely Christian response to particular behavioral questions will be rather clear from the circumstances themselves. At other times, however, due to the mounting complexity of modern society, the problems will be marked by ambiguity and will appear to be open to diverse moral solutions. Vatican II acknowledges this in the *Pastoral Constitution on the Church in the Modern World*:

> Often enough the Christian view of things will itself suggest some specific solution in certain circumstances. Yet it happens rather frequently, and legitimately so, that with equal sincerity some of the faithful will disagree with others on a given matter. Even against the intentions of their proponents, however, solutions proposed on one side or another may be easily confused by many people with the Gospel message. Hence it is necessary for people to remember that no one is allowed in the aforementioned situations to appropriate the Church's authority for his opinion. They should always try to enlighten one another through honest discussion, preserving mutual charity and caring above all for the common good.[35]

In other words, though the Christian moral experience may be easily identifiable in its broad and generic outlines, the application of that vision to changing circumstances introduces great possibilities of variety. Even though certain generic moral principles may have a lasting value, they will not always apply in the same way in every case. According to the influential statement of Aristotle, "the more demonstration becomes particular the more it sinks into an indeterminate manifold, while universal demonstration tends to be simple and determinate."[36]

St. Thomas Aquinas also recognized, in accord with a strong scholastic tradition, that practical moral principles will not be found applicable in every type of case. Aquinas taught that practical moral principles are of such a nature that they are applicable *in pluribus* ("usually") but that they will be deficient and not applicable *in aliquo particulari* ("in some special situations").[37]

The Second Vatican Council shows that the problem of applying general moral doctrine to particular cases is becoming even more difficult in the modern world. The Council notes that we have moved to an evolutionary, dynamic view of the human situation; thus we are faced with ever new problems in the work of applying principle to context: "History itself speeds along on so rapid a course that an individual person can scarcely keep abreast of it. The destiny of the human community has become all of a piece, where once the various groups of men had a kind of private history of their own. Thus, the human race has passed from a rather static concept of reality to a more dynamic, evolutionary one."[38]

Indeed the Council was so aware of the new conditions of modern man that it said that "today the human race is involved in a new stage of history. . . . We can already speak of a true cultural and social transformation."[39] In this new evolutionary and rapidly changing world the Church must acknowledge the possibility of lawful diversity in matters where perfect clarity cannot be achieved: "Such a mission requires in the first place that we foster within the Church herself mutual esteem, reverence and harmony, through the full recognition of lawful diversity."[40] Vatican II also recognized the need for moral theology to take full account of the moral implications of the modern sciences. It urged moralists to blend modern science and its theories with the most recent discoveries in the area of Christian morality and doctrine.[41]

This inevitable diversity in the application of Christian wisdom to varying particular contexts means that usually there will be varying interpretations of what Christianity means in special cases. Everything that the Council has taught about the nature of this "new age" further emphasizes the need to keep debate open in complex issues. It means further that respectful dialogue is to be preferred to premature anathema.

The Magisterium and the Growth of Historical Consciousness

Historical Studies and the Proper Evaluation of Magisterium. The enlivened interest in historical studies in recent years has subjected many of the specific teachings of the Church to the scrutiny of sharp critical analysis. Historical studies have made theologians more aware of the many infelicitous specific teachings of the hierarchical magisterium in the past. These studies have not pointed out these errors and inadequacies in order to discredit the hierarchical magisterium but rather to make possible a realistic magisteriology that will properly reflect the true nature of the teaching and witnessing of the Church. It is the thinking of many theologians and historians today that it is necessary to understand fully the problems of the teaching Church in the past in order to develop a credible claim for a true teaching mission. The American Bishops, in their 1967 Pastoral Letter *The Church in Our Day,* point out that "those in apostolic office who violate the limits of their authority imperil the sense of community and diminish their effectiveness in echoing Christ authentically."[42]

Some Examples of Theological Dissent in Patristic and Medieval Periods

Among the many possible examples of theological dissent in doctrinal matters in the patristic and medieval periods, the following five have been chosen because of their value in illustrating both the possibility of dissent and, in varying degrees, the diverse manner in which such dissent has been expressed and made public to the affected community of believers due to the variation in the historical contexts.

The three patristic instances (the cases of Popes Liberius, Vigilius and Honorius) are unfortunately almost invariably considered in terms of the use that was made of them as classic arguments against the notion of papal infallibility. Although the proceedings of the First Vatican Council and subsequent historical research have demonstrated the inconclusiveness of those three incidents as arguments against the technical definition of infallibility, a somewhat narrow, apologetical approach has overlooked the significance of those cases as important moments in the history of Christian dissent. The two medieval examples to be described bear no such polemical overtones and thus may be approached more directly. It would seem that each of these cases involves the manual theology definition of ordinary papal magisterium.[43] The actual conclusion or solution of the following disputes is not as important as the essential action-reaction rhythm of papal intervention and subsequent manifest ecclesial dissent.

Case of Pope Liberius (352-66). During the tangled period of ecclesiastical and political altercation after the Council of Nicaea in 325, the triumph of the Emperor Constantius II over his rivals in 351 tipped the balance in favor of the anti-Nicene party. As a part of his pro-Arian campaign, Constantius exiled the hitherto obdurate Pope Liberius. Liberius was returned to his See in 358 upon agreeing to the condemnation of Athanasius, the cornerstone of Nicene orthodoxy, and upon ascribing to the Formula of Sirmium. Most probably, Liberius ascribed not only to the First Formula of Sirmium (351), an indeterminate creed which repudiated Nicaea by suggestion, but also to the Third Formula (358) as well, which made use of the term *homoiousion* (like the Father), rather than the Nicene term of *homoousion* (the same as the Father) in reference to the Son. He did not subscribe to the definitely heretical Second Formula of Sirmium drawn up in 357. The major weakness of the Pope's position, then, was a negative one: favoring the parties opposed to Nicaea by agreeing to a document which omitted the all-important *homoousion.*

The reaction in the West, still strongly pro-Nicaea, was immediate if not perduring due to the influence of imperial politics. The Synod of Rimini, meeting in July of 359, at first reaffirmed the creed of Nicaea and excommunicated the Arian leaders (it is interesting to note that Liberius did not take part in the Synod), but shortly thereafter bowed to the threats of Constantius and accepted another temporizing anti-Nicene creed. After the death of Constantius in 361, the creed of Nicaea gradually prevailed; it was solemnly redefined at the First Council of Constantinople in 381. Thus, although Liberius' Letters in favor of the Formula of Sirmium were a weakness typical of many during this confusing period, they provoked quite rapid dissent on the part of the orthodox parties.[44]

The Case of Pope Vigilius (540-55). For political reasons, the Emperor Justinian (527-65) was seeking reconciliation with the Monophysites, a group ardently opposed to the definition of the Council of Chalcedon (451) concerning the two natures in Christ. He felt that he could best do this by condemning the Antiochene theology which had been the source of Nestorianism, the error condemned at the Council of Ephesus (431), which the Monophysites felt had come to life again in the decisions of Chalcedon. Thus in 544 Justinian condemned the *Three Chapters* (three works of the Antiochene School): the person and writings of Theodore of Mopsuestia, certain writings of Theodoret of Cyrene and a letter of Ibas of Edessa. In 548 Justinian persuaded his protégé, Pope Vigilius, to issue a similar condemnation, the *Judicatum.* Since the reaction in the West was strongly in favor of Chalcedon and the *Three Chapters,* Vigilius persuaded Justinian to summon a Council to discuss the matter. On May 14, 553, Vigilius issued a document, the *First Constitutum,* which supported the Western view on the *Three Chapters,* but to no avail. The Second Council of Constantinople (553), under the control of Justinian, renewed the condemnation of the Chapters and excommunicated Vigilius. On February 26, 554, Vigilius issued a *Second Constitutum* in which he recalled his former document and approved the acts of the Council.

The reaction in the West was strong and fairly rapid, considering the disturbed state of communications due to the Gothic War then raging in Italy. Opposition to Vigilius' *Judicatum* was manifest among the deacons in Rome, but especially in Africa, where Bishop Facundus of Hermiane and others wrote defenses of the Chapters, and where a meeting of African Bishops in 550 declared Vigilius cut off from communion with the Church until he did penance. After the Council of 553, most of the West accepted the condemnation of the Chapters, but a schism did break out in northern Italy which was to last into the following century. The case of Pope Vigilius clearly illustrates that, even in matters of dogma as distinguished from morals, infallibility cannot be the note of every exercise of the papal magisterium and that theological dissent has expressed itself in rather strong terms at times.[45]

The Case of Pope Honorius (625-38). In this case the reaction to Papal error eventually led to the condemnation of heresies by Ecumenical Councils of the Church. Monenergism (one divine operation) and Monotheletism (one divine will) were the dialectical conclusions of the Monophysite movement, which had disturbed the East since the Council of Chalcedon. About the year 620, Sergius, the Patriarch of Constantinople, began to teach a doctrine of one divine operation and will in Christ. This position was attacked as being irreconcilable with the Decrees of Chalcedon, but Sergius appealed to Pope Honorius I. In 634 Honorius replied in two letters to Sergius which denied two contrary wills in Christ, refused to determine the question whether there were one or two operations in Christ and called for an end of discussion on the matter. Given the historical context and the tone of Honorius' first letter, there is a definite teaching character to the action of the Pope. Although Honorius' intentions may not have been heretical, he used expressions that were susceptible of an heretical interpretation, and his ban on further discussion would have prevented theologians from drawing correct theological deductions from Chalcedon.

Honorius' letters did not stop the debate. They were used to support the imperial program favoring Monotheletism (e.g., the *Ecthesis* of Heraclius in 638 and the *Typus* of Constans II in 648); but more importantly, a continuing protest in the tradition of Chalcedon brought to light the weaknesses of the position adopted by the Pope. This movement culminated in the Sixth Ecumenical Council held in Constantinople in 680-81. Here the Monothelite bishops were deposed and excommunicated and the intellectual leaders of the movement were anathematized and their writings burned; the letters of Honorius were also burned. The letters of Pope Leo II (682-83), and the Profession of Faith which each candidate for the papal throne during the Middle Ages was obliged to take, indicate papal acquiescence in this action. Clearly, in this instance, dissent beginning from theological reflection was not only notorious but achieved a notable magisterial effect.[46]

Pope Alexander III (1159-81) *and Twelfth-Century Christology.* The weaknesses of the Boethian definition of person (*naturae rationabilis individua substantia*: individual substance of a rational nature) caused difficulties in twelfth-century speculation on the manner of the union of two natures in Christ. Many theologians of the period felt that in order to maintain that Christ was one Person, the Divine Person of the Word, they would have to show that he was also one substance. In his *Book of Sentences,* Peter the Lombard had outlined three positions: (1) the *homo assumptus* (assumed man) theory: that Christ as man is both a person (*aliquis*: someone) and a substance (*aliquid*: something), but that man's substance becomes God in the Hypostatic Union; (2) that there are three substances (divinity, body, and soul) in Christ, but only two natures and one person; and (3) the *habitus* (habit) theory: that the relation of human nature to the Word is similar to the relation of a *habitus* to a substance, and not of a substance to a substance. Some held that the Lombard favored this last position when he said that Christ as man is not *aliquid,* i.e., a substance. This statement has sometimes been called "Christological Nihilism," but the name is a misnomer; the Lombard never asserted that Christ as man is nothing.

Roland Bandinelli, when a Master of Theology, had defended the third position stated by the Lombard, as did many other theologians of the day. Upon becoming Pope Alexander, Bandinelli changed his opinion and began an attempt to impose his new views upon the Church. At the Council of Tours (1163) he heard two propositions debated: (1) Christ is not *aliquis homo* (i.e., a human person) and (2) Christ as man is not *aliquid* (i.e., a substance). The Council reached no conclusion as to these propositions. Pope Alexander, however, condemned the latter opinion in two letters in 1170 (Epistulae *Cum in nostris* and *Eis qui*); he renewed the condemnation in 1171 (Epistula *Cum Christus*). These condemnations laid the groundwork for a papal condemnation of the third proposition articulated by the Lombard.

Historians of this controversy have spoken of "the remarkably stubborn opposition to his decision."[47] Until theologians could think their way past the Boethian definition of person in the latter part of the twelfth century, to say that Christ was a human substance seemed tantamount to saying that he was also a human person. Hence, there was a strong reaction on the part of those who adhered to the third position of the Lombard against the position adopted by Pope Alexander. The measure of this reaction can be gauged to some extent by the position of Peter of Poitiers favoring the third solution in his *In Sent.* IV, 10[48]—written at the heat of the controversy, c. 1175—and by the fact that, due to the remonstrances of the cardinals and bishops who agreed with this third position, Pope Alexander was compelled to remove the question from the agenda of the Third Lateran Council in 1179. In this case aggressive theological dissent delayed a papal intervention which could have been precipitous and dangerous had it come in advance of the necessary speculative groundwork.[49]

Thirteenth-Century Condemnations of Aristotle. By far the greater part of the works of Aristotle had been translated into Latin by the beginning of the thirteenth century. The philosophy of Aristotle, particularly as filtered through Arabic thought, raised certain problems for Christian theology, problems not always solved in the most felicitous fashion, as the errors of Amaury of Bene and David of Dinant at the beginning of the thirteenth century indicate. Because of implication with these views, Aristotle's *libri de naturali philosophia* ("books of natural philosophy," including some of his most important works, such as *Metaphysics, On the Soul,* etc.) were forbidden to be taught in the Faculty of Arts under pain of excommunication by the Council of Paris in 1210, a ban which was renewed by the Papal Legate, Robert of Courcon, in 1215. Nonetheless, the interest in Aristotle's works grew and even affected the Theological Faculty, as the letter of Pope Gregory IX to the Paris Theological Faculty in 1228 warning against the false use of philosophy in theology indicates. In 1231 Gregory once again forbade the use of the *libri naturales* until they could be purged of error, but the commission which he established for this work achieved nothing. The ban against these books was extended to the University of Toulouse by Innocent IV in 1245; as late as 1263, Urban IV confirmed the binding force of Gregory's Statutes of 1231.

The frequent repetition of the ban alone indicates that there was strong pressure against its observation. Documentary evidence clearly indicates infringements of the local bans of 1210 and 1215. The papal ban seems to have had effect in Paris for a period of some years, perhaps until approximately 1240 (though it had no effect in Toulouse then and never had effect in Oxford), but it is clear that dissent from it had become common and quite public by about 1245, e.g., Roger Bacon's *Commentaries on Aristotle* and Albert the Great's extensive use of Aristotle's works in his theological lectures. This dissent appears to have coexisted with a reaffirmation of the papal intervention, that of Innocent IV in Toulouse in 1245. By 1252, Aristotle's *De Anima* was listed as a required text, and Thomas Aquinas, with his heavy dependence on the Stagirite, was already lecturing on the *Sentences.* By 1255, the whole of the Aristotelian corpus was part of the Paris curriculum. Admittedly, the evidence is fragmentary and the exact extent of the ban is somewhat problematic, but in practice a continuing dissent seems to have confronted a continuing papal condemnation for over a generation. The dissent had magisterial effect: in 1366 Urban V's legates declared knowledge of the complete works of Aristotle to be necessary for the Degree of Licentiate of Arts.[50]

Issues concerning Which Authoritative Teachings Have Been Altered

Examination of the development of the magisterial position with respect to certain questions reveals the fundamental fact that the Church has changed its authentic teaching on central moral questions with the passage of time. In some instances the implication is clear that the change was necessary to correct a position that was wrong *ab initio*. The following examples of such changes are selected because they concern matters intimately related to truth, human life and the practical implications of man's social nature.

Church on War and Peace. Throughout history the Church has held a variety of conflicting positions with respect to the legitimate use of violence. Pre-Constantinian Christian literature took a strongly pacifistic position. Though this pacifism was untested for the most part and did not flow into practical pacifism in all situations, it revealed an extraordinary sensitivity to the horror of bloodshed. After Constantine, a new moral attitude toward war and military service developed. The sensitivity to military service, which was so remarkable in the early Church that Celsus thought that all Christians were pacifists, completely disappeared. By the fifth century, in fact, only Christians were permitted to serve in the army.

The theology of war that animated the crusading period, under the instigation of Pope St. Gregory VII and Blessed Urban II, sought to establish the kingdom of Christ, centered in Jerusalem, by means of the crusading sword. In the spirit of the Crusades, the *Decretum* of Gratian held that to die in combat against the infidel is to merit heaven. War and violence were also used to attack heresy in the history of the Church. The teaching of the hierarchical magisterium in these periods, as well as the *sensus fidelium,* is not compatible with the great papal and conciliar teachings on peace that have appeared in our day.[51]

Sexual Ethics. Pope St. Gregory the Great, in his prestigious *Pastoral Rule,* admonished couples that pleasure is not a fit purpose for intercourse and that if any pleasure is "mixed" with the act of intercourse, the married couple have transgressed the law of marriage; they have "befouled" their intercourse by "their pleasures."[52] St. Gregory also wrote to St. Augustine, the Archbishop of Canterbury, teaching that married couples could not receive communion after marital copulation. The Pope said in this letter, which had enduring pastoral consequences, that it was as impossible to have intercourse without sin as it was to fall into a fire and not burn. Only a miracle could save one in any case.[53] These teachings are no longer advanced by the hierarchical magisterium.

The imposition of celibacy upon the clergy during the Hildebrandine reformation was motivated by multiple appeals to Scripture and Tradition in order to prove the inherent unworthiness of the sexual act. This coincided with the gradual degradation of the marriages and spouses of clerics: "We may rightly call them not spouses but rather concubines or whores."[54] Pope Gregory VII was publicly opposed on the matter of clerical celibacy at the Synod of Paris (1074), the Synod of Mainz (1075), the Synod of Pavia (1076) and at Cambrai that same year. The opposition was a public dissent not only against the prudence of the rule but also contesting the truth of the reasoning. This same reasoning as a ground for the Church's rule of clerical celibacy today was firmly rejected by Pope Paul VI in the recent Encyclical, *Coelibatus Sacerdotalis.*[55]

In the twelfth century, Huguccio, Gratian's chief commentator, taught that coitus "can never be without sin."[56] Innocent III, an expert theologian in his own right, thought of this opinion as beyond question. By the twelfth century, the Augustinian doctrine about the need for procreative intention to free intercourse from sin was commonly accepted in the Church. It was affirmed strongly by the canonists and theologians of the thirteenth century and was not seriously contested in the fourteenth and fifteenth centuries. It was also commonly taught for centuries that intercourse during the time of menstruation was sinful. All of these opinions have since been challenged and abandoned. Until Vatican II, it was customary to refer to procreation and education of children as the primary end of marriage.[57] Due to advances in the appreciation of the other "ends" of marriage, this concession of primacy to one end was deliberately discontinued in Vatican II.

Condemnation of Interest Taking. The Council of Vienne (Fifteenth Ecumenical Council) condemned the taking of interest in very serious terms: "If anyone should fall into that error of pertinaciously presuming to affirm that interest taking is not a sin, we declare that he should be punished as a heretic."[58] Two other Ecumenical Councils lent their authority to this teaching, Lateran II and Lateran III; four popes also made clear statements in support of this teaching: Alexander III, Urban III, Eugene III, and Gregory IX.

Theological dissent was communicated to the affected community contemporaneously with the authoritative bans. The banking community invented various financing arrangements to circumvent the prohibition. The challenge to the usury doctrine culminated in the effort of two theologians in the sixteenth century, Dominic Soto and John Medina. One hundred years later a Roman congregation accepted their position; by the time of the great modern social encyclicals all scruples about taking legitimate interest had disappeared from the teaching of the magisterium.

Professor John T. Noonan, Jr., provided the Inquiry Panel with detailed information concerning the process of papal action and theological reaction in the question of interest taking (cf., pp. 536-549; 559-560, *Transcript of the Proceedings*). He emphasized the public dissenting role of the theologians with regard to specific Papal Bulls which condemned interest taking as a violation of divine natural and positive law (*Cum Onus,* 1569; *In Eam,* 1571; and *Detestabilis Avaritiae,* 1586). Although the communications media were limited, he testified that the ordinary medium of the time (public disputation) was commonly employed by theologians to discuss the question of interest taking and to debate the papal position. Furthermore, personal contact by the theologians with the community of the faithful directly affected by the papal teaching was common. Bankers consulted theologians and were informed of the various theological opinions concerning the question of interest taking. Sovereigns whose functions required them to frame laws on the subject of interest taking were advised of the theological positions on the subject. Apart from any rescinding of the papal position, Professor Noonan affirmed that theological dissent did effect a change in the teaching of the Church on interest taking. In addition, he indicated that, to his knowledge, no papal reactions were directed against the public *style* of dissent employed by theologians.

Moral Teaching concerning the Rights of the Accused. The Church also teaches by acting. In light of this, the following conclusion from a study by Patrick Granfield has considerable magisterial importance: "The ordeal, with its hot iron, molten lead, and boiling water, became commonplace. From the eighth to the thirteenth century, it was accepted by many local ecclesiastical courts with the approval of their bishops, who felt that it was a reliable way to discover the *judicium Dei* (judgment of God)."[59]

In 866, Pope Nicholas I had condemned legal torture as immoral. Subsequent practice and the *Ad extirpanda* of Pope Innocent IV, however, contradicted the teaching of Nicholas. Innocent IV accepted torture as a legitimate means for the interrogation of the accused. Until the publication of the Code of Canon Law, official Church teaching denied the right of silence or the right of non-self-incrimination (the American "Fifth Amendment" spirit) to the accused. With Canon 1743, No. 1, this doctrine was abruptly changed. Granfield suggests the explanation for this change: "It was the presence of a persistent, contrary theological opinion and a dramatic change in the civil law that finally influenced the Church."[60]

Religious Liberty. Progress in the moral teaching of the Church concerning religious freedom is easily illustrated. In his *Quanta Cura,* Pius IX condemned "that erroneous opinion which is especially injurious to the Catholic Church and the salvation of souls, called by our predecessor Gregory XVI *deliramentum* (derangement), namely, that freedom of conscience and of worship is the proper right of each man, and that this should be proclaimed and asserted in every rightly constituted society."[61] A striking change from this position is evident in the words of Vatican II: "The Council further declares that the right to religious freedom has its foundation in the very dignity of the human person. . . . This right of the human person to religious freedom is to be recognized in the constitutional law whereby society is governed and thus it is to become a civil right."[62]

Oriental Rites in the Church. Popes Clement VIII, Benedict XIV, Leo XII and Pius IX clearly and repeatedly taught the inferiority of the Oriental rites to the Latin rite. They were opposed, but opposition dissipated. The final rejection of Pius IX's invitation to the Orthodox hierarchy to attend the First Vatican Council was largely due to the fact that the Oriental Churches had been victimized by centuries of Latin disdain. This attitude has finally been changed in the Decree of Vatican II for the Oriental Catholic Churches.

No pope did more to impose Latinizations upon Orientals in union with Rome than did Pope Pius IX. He modified almost every aspect of their traditional customs, ascetical practices and canonical discipline. After making sweeping Latinizations in the Armenian rite, Pius IX condemned those who cried out to preserve their rites, calling them deniers of the Primacy of the Vicar of Christ.[64]

The Decree of Vatican II on the Oriental Catholic Church condemns the Latinizations of the past in the strongest terms and enjoins the Orientals to restore their authentic traditions.

Pope Gregory XVI: Encyclical Letter, Mirari Vos. Some of the teachings of Pope Gregory XVI in his Encyclical *Mirari Vos* have been clearly reversed in the current century. Vatican II's notion of Church reformation cannot be reconciled with Gregory's viewpoint to this effect:

> It is obviously absurd and most injurious to her [the Church] to demand some kind of "restoration and regeneration" as necessary for her existence and growth—as if it were possible for her to be subject to defect, to decay, or other such deficiencies.
>
> Now from this evil-smelling spring of indifferentism flows the erroneous and absurd opinion—or rather derangement—that freedom

of conscience must be asserted and vindicated for everyone. This most pestilential error opens the door to the complete and immoderate liberty of opinions, which works such widespread harm both in Church and state.

This passage, and Pope Gregory's references to "baneful liberty," "insolent liberty," "deleterious liberty," cannot be reconciled with Vatican II's teaching on the rights of conscience. For example, compare the following passages from *Mirari Vos* with the currently accepted notions of the rights of conscience and the complementary "right to know" in the Church:

> Here reference must be made to that deleterious liberty, which can never be execrated and detested sufficiently, of printing and of publishing writings of every kind, which some dare to demand and to promote with such insolence.
>
> Far different was the attitude of the Church in destroying the pestilence of evil books ever since the age of the apostles, for we read that they burned a large number of books publicly (Acts 19).

Boniface VIII's Unam Sanctam. Boniface VIII, in his *Unam Sanctam* (1302), taught that temporal authority should be subjected to the spiritual authority of the Church. He said: "We further declare, state, define, and pronounce as entirely necessary for salvation that every human creature be subjected to the Roman Pontiff."[65] It would be unhistorical to suggest that Boniface here was merely asserting the ecclesial dimension of grace, or some palatable modern conception. *Unam Sanctam* was based on the writings of Aegidius Romanus who said: "Totum posse quod est in Ecclesia reservatur in summo pontifice" (all the power in the Church resides in the supreme pontiff).[66] The concept of papal sovereignty taught in *Unam Sanctam* is no longer taught.

Jews in Public Life. Innocent III and the Fourth Lateran Council (1215) taught that it was absurd for a Jew to have authority over Christians and banned Jews from public office. Jews were also required by that Council to wear distinctive dress, a prescription that was later extended to heretics, prostitutes and lepers.

This teaching was very influential in shaping the attitude of Christian Europe towards the Jewish people, and it is now seen as a factor in some of the persecutions of Jews that followed. Such teaching has, of course, been abrogated by the clear pronouncements of Vatican II regarding the Jewish people.[67]

Pius IX's Syllabus or Summary of the Main Errors of Our Age (1864). Many of the teachings of the *Syllabus* have been contradicted. The following are examples of propositions *condemned* in the *Syllabus*:

"[That] the Roman Pontiff can and should reconcile and harmonize himself with progress, with Liberalism, and with modern civilization."[68]

Error 77: "[That] In our time it is no longer expedient to recognize the Catholic religion as the sole religion of the state, to the exclusion of any other forms of worship."[69]

Error 78: "[That] Hence it is laudable in certain Catholic countries to provide by law for the people immigrating thither to be allowed publicly to practice their own religion, of whatever form it may be."[70]

Error 79: "[That] For it is false that civil liberty for any kind of cult and likewise the full power granted to all of proclaiming openly and publicly any kind of opinions and ideas easily leads to corruption of the minds and morals of nations and to the propagation of the plague of indifferentism."[71]

The teaching office of the Church quite obviously no longer presses its condemnations of the foregoing propositions in light of Vatican II. It must be recognized that in the *Syllabus,* as well as in *Mirari Vos* and *Quanta Cura,* the Popes intended to condemn what they saw as dangerous trends: i.e., tendencies toward indifferentism, or attempts to justify outright denial of the truth. No doubt this explains the severe tone and approach of the documents. Nonetheless, the *Decree on Ecumenism* and the *Declaration on Religious Freedom* of Vatican II virtually contradict the foregoing citations word for word. Unquestionably, this indicates a definite development and advance in theological thinking on the questions of man's dignity and his freedom and a real change in the teaching of the Church on the question of religious freedom and on the other matters at issue.

Question of Membership in the Church. Pius XII, in *Mystici Corporis* (1943) and again with more emphasis in *Humani Generis* (1950), insisted that the mystical body of Jesus on earth was simply identical with the Roman Catholic Church. In *Humani Generis,* the Pope insisted that his teaching on the matter was to settle the discussion among theologians. Vatican II has produced a different teaching. The theology adopted by Vatican II acknowledges the ecclesial reality of other Christian churches, and does not exclude that the Church of Christ in some way exists in them and, therefore, that the mystical body of Christ cannot be simply identical with the Roman Catholic Church.[72]

Authoritative Teaching of the Biblical Commission. A *Motu Proprio* of 1907, issued by Pope Pius X, states: "All are bound in conscience to submit to the decisions of the Biblical Commission, which have been given in the past and which shall be given in the future, in the same way as to the decrees which appertain to doctrine, issued by the Sacred Congregations and approved by the Sovereign Pontiff."[73] Particular decisions of the Biblical Commission include scores of points, exegetical and doctrinal, which are completely repudiated by many Catholic biblical scholars today.

Reflection: Error, Dissent, Revision

Dissent from certain hierarchical teachings of the past is an accepted fact in the Church. The teaching of Pope St. Gregory the Great on sexual ethics, of Urban II on the relationship between Christianity and violence, of Boniface VIII on the power of the papacy, of a series of popes on the nature of usury, of Gregory XVI and Pius IX on freedom of conscience, of Innocent III on the treatment of Jews and of Innocent IV on the use of torture—all offer examples of positions seriously taught and since abandoned. Despite the different problems that existed at the time of the foregoing teachings and the different universe of discourse in which they were discussed, it is impossible to show that these teachings were "correct in their time." There were other views of the papacy when Boniface VIII wrote; there were other views on religious liberty when Gregory XVI produced his *Mirari Vos*. The vigor of repetition of many of the foregoing hierarchical teachings bears witness to the fact that other opinions were obtaining some contemporary prominence. These other views survived the papal condemnations to the extent that the Church at large now dissents from the papal teachings in question.

It would be gratuitous to assert that only the passage of time justifies dissent. The error should be corrected when it is detected. The passage of time may be a condition for dissent on issues that have not been adequately examined, but it would be a disservice to truth to insist on the passage of time to justify dissent with respect to issues that have had the advantage of extended and prolonged discussion.

In view of this history, therefore, normal hermeneutical and theological principles should be followed in assessing the value of a particular papal document. Thus, while the exact determination of the papal author's intention is an important hermeneutical factor, yet the manifest mind and will of the writer (in these cases, the pope) can never be the only criterion of truth. To consider the intentions of the pope as exclusively decisive of the truth and value of a teaching leads to an unrealistic positivism and a crass voluntarism. Indeed, since the pope does not teach other than what he thinks and wishes to be followed, making his "mind" and his "will" determinative of the possibility of legitimate dissent would virtually eliminate the distinction between fallible and infallible teaching contrary to Vatican I and II. The criterion of the "manifest" mind and will of the pope is properly employed to distinguish formal encyclicals from remarks at a papal audience, the former to be given great weight by the faithful, and the latter to be considered as simply relevant data.

Professor Noonan's testimony concerning the sixteenth-century controversy over interest taking illustrates the relative importance of the determination of the papal intention as a hermeneutical factor. Although the Papal Bulls of Saint Pius V indicate the Pope's conviction that he was performing an apostolic task by articulating the divine natural law and the positive law on the problem of interest taking, contemporary theologians disagreed with the papal assertion that this was a question of divine natural law. They asserted the question involved merely positive law and pointed to the nonacceptance of the papal condemnation as an indication of the positive law stance of interest taking. Professor Noonan's testimony indicated that although the papal intention was one important element in the interpretation of the papal position, it was not the decisive element in determining the status of interest taking as a question of natural law as opposed to positive law.

The Encyclical as a Genre of Magisterial Teaching

The Constitution on the Church does give great interpretive importance to the "manifest mind and will" of the Pope, but this is not the only, or completely independent, criterion of truth. "His mind and will in the matter may be known either from the character of the documents, from his frequent repetition of the same doctrine, or from his manner of speaking."[74] Consequently, analysis of papal teachings should include consideration of the nature of an encyclical, which is the type of document in which Paul VI enunciated his ban on artificial contraception.

A Recent Phenomenon. The papal encyclical, as known today, is a recent phenomenon. Although related to other ecclesiastical literary forms such as Bulls, Apostolic Constitutions and Papal Briefs, the encyclical is a distinct literary genre. Because it is a modern development, the issues raised by the encyclical form—its importance, its doctrinal character, its permanency—have become the objects of scholarly consideration only recently. Because the encyclical is an ecclesiastical literary form, the interpretation of a specific encyclical is subject to the canons of higher criticism as well as the general norms used to evaluate any magisterial document.

Origin and Development. Some find prototypes of papal encyclicals in antiquity, in the letters that Rome addressed to various churches, and in the "inaugural epistles" through which the patriarchs announced their election to one another. Etymologically, the encyclical suggests the idea of a "circular" (Greek: *en-kyklos*) addressed to a wide audience.

The present form and use of the encyclical originated in the eighteenth century. In 1728 Francisco Domenico Bencini published a treatise, *De litteris encyclicis,* in which he proposed the use of encyclical letters as a means to safeguard the unity and purity of faith and morals. He cited circular letters as an effective means whereby the primitive churches had been able to insure the antiquity, universality and unity of faith against innovations and novelties.

Bencini was a contemporary of Prospero Lambertini who, as Pope Benedict XIV (1740-1758), issued the first encyclical of modern times. Benedict's *Ubi Primum,* addressed to his "venerable brothers, Patriarchs, Primates, Archbishops and Bishops," reestablished the ancient custom of inaugural letters. In one way or another, the inaugural encyclicals, from *Ubi Primum* of Benedict to *Ecclesiam Suam* of Paul VI, stress the close ties between the See of Peter and the rest of the episcopate and emphasize the need for a common policy in governing the church and a united front against the errors of the day. Benedict XIV is responsible for another innovation: He had his encyclicals included in the register of official correspondence—the *Bullarium*—side by side with Apostolic Constitutions, Bulls and similar documents. In the example of Bencini, Pope Benedict explained that encyclical letters, addressed to his fellow bishops, were intended, as in ancient times, to safeguard the unity of faith and morals.

Although Benedict's immediate successors made some use of the genre, it was only in the 19th century that the flow of encyclicals became steady. Gregory XVI (1831-1846) and Pius IX (1846-

1878) published numerous encyclicals on a variety of timely topics, social as well as religious. Pointing out dangerous trends, their letters set down guidelines for the maintenance and restoration of a Christian society. The eighty-six encyclicals issued by Leo XIII (1878-1903), by all accounts, broke new ground for the Church in the modern world. His directives had a contemporaneity which those of his predecessors lacked. It is not to minimize the writings of Pius X or Benedict XV to give credit to Leo XIII, Pius XI and Pius XII for raising the encyclical form to its present level of prestige and importance. No one, cleric or lay, Catholic or otherwise, concerned with an application of Christian principles to contemporary issues can ignore them.

In the two centuries since Benedict's *Ubi Primum,* encyclicals have become more stylized, while at the same time varying widely in form, length and scholarship. A recent innovation first appeared in John XXIII's *Pacem in Terris*: besides addressing it to "patriarchs, primates, archbishops, bishops, and other local ordinaries in peace and communion with the Apostolic See, to the clergy and faithful of the whole world," as was customary, Pope John addressed it also "to all men of good will." Pope Paul VI used the same salutation in *Ecclesiam Suam* and *Humanae Vitae*.

If the audiences to whom encyclicals are addressed have expanded over the years, so have the topics they discuss. The encyclicals—with very few exceptions—have been issued to give guidance in almost every field of human endeavor. An unmistakable pastoral concern, found in all modern encyclicals, is probably their most distinguishing note. Although it is not always obvious to the general reader, it is almost axiomatic to the professional theologian and historian that passages in every encyclical are directed, however obliquely, to specific questions. There is genuine danger of distorting an encyclical if it is exegeted apart from the historical circumstances and context which brought it into being. *Humanae Vitae* is an obvious example.

Authority of Papal Encyclicals. Given the fact that the encyclicals represent a modern development, it is understandable that the question of their doctrinal import is also of recent origin.

Around the turn of the century in France, a minor controversy developed about encyclicals. Msgr. Perriot proposed that they represent dogmatic judgments and are, therefore, expressions of the infallible teaching authority of the Holy Father.[75] L. Choupin argued against extending the umbrella of infallibility to papal encyclicals.[76] A consensus has emerged.

One of the few monographs on encyclicals is by Dom P. Nau,[77] who is certainly no minimalist with respect to papal authority. He asserts that a majority of theologians do not consider encyclicals infallible statements. They are not *ex cathedra* definitions. Theologians are satisfied, according to Nau, to claim for them authority similar to that enjoyed by the decrees of the Sacred Congregations, that is, the duty of total compliance (*obéissance*) on the part of Catholics. Pope Pius XII addressed himself to the authority of encyclicals in an encyclical, *Humani Generis*: He allows that "in writing such letters the popes do not exercise the supreme power of their teaching authority. For these matters are taught with the ordinary teaching authority (of the popes)."[78]

It is commonly held in the standard texts (*auctores probati*) that papal encyclicals are statements of the ordinary magisterium. They are expressions of the teaching office carried on in normal circumstances, with varying degrees of reflection, scholarship and definitiveness. Historically, it is significant that the gradual explicitation of the distinction between the ordinary and extraordinary teaching of the pope coincides with evolution of the encyclical genre. It is significant, theologically as well as historically, that a direct quote from *Humani Generis,* which appeared in the original schema *De Ecclesia et de B. Maria Virgine* at Vatican II, was deleted in the final draft. In the text quoted in the first draft, Pius XII had asserted that once the pope goes out of his way to speak on a controverted subject, "this subject can no longer be regarded as a matter for free debate among theologians."[79]

While a practicing Catholic is expected to comply with papal teaching however it is communicated, his assent is, by definition, proportionate to the context and content of the pope's expression. The response due a solemn, infallible pronouncement is quite other than the adherence owed to a noninfallible (and, therefore, presumably a reformable) statement. There are authors who say that the pope might use an encyclical as a vehicle for an infallible, *ex cathedra* pronouncement, but Professor Lambruschini made it clear that *Humanae Vitae* is not such a pronouncement.

Reform and Development. Although papal directives have, over the years, closed off certain avenues of debate, they were never intended to forestall legitimate development, nor have they in fact impeded progress. G. K. Malone, in *The New Catholic Encyclopedia,* cites an address of Paul VI to a group of cardinals on June 23, 1964, to illustrate that even the popes themselves regard certain teachings pertaining to the ordinary magisterium as reformable.[80] Paul VI is quoted as saying that he felt some of the teachings of Pius XII were still valid until "he felt obliged to change them." If disagreement in practice or in preaching is to be labeled, in a limited vocabulary, a "dissent," then those "obligations" to truth which have moved, and which continue to move, popes and councils to alter or abandon former authoritative pronouncements must take their roots in what is called "dissent." Dissent founded on the search for truth is truly part of the magisterial process.

In conclusion, it is well to recall that the Church has always believed in the active presence of the Spirit of God. To discern the teaching influence of the Spirit, varying and contradictory criteriologies have developed in the history of the Church. At times there have been exaggerated claims for the reliability of the *sensus fidelium;* at other times, especially in recent centuries, excessive claims have been made suggesting an aggrandized teaching authority residing in councils and Church officers. In the face of this trend toward establishing an *exclusive* teaching prerogative in the hierarchy, recent historical studies have exercised a modifying influence by pointing out the presence of error in past papal and episcopal teaching and the correction of error by way of theological dissent. Dissent thus appears traditionally as one possible, responsible option in the theological task, and, in its own way, is an intrinsic element in the total magisterial function of the Church. The entire Church, as truly magistral, can never be contained simply and exclusively in what has become known as the *hierarchical* magisterium.

Notes

1. Vatican II, *Dogmatic Constitution on the Church* (*Lumen Gentium*), para. 25.
2. H. Vorgrimler and K. Rahner, *Theological Dictionary* (New York: Herder, 1965), p. 268.
3. Vatican II, *Dogmatic Constitution on the Church,* para. 12.
4. H. Küng, *Structures in the Church* (New York: Nelson, 1964), p. 207.
5. Y. Congar, "The Historical Development of Authority in the Church," in J. M. Todd, ed., *Problems of Authority* (Baltimore: Helicon, 1964), pp. 136–140; Congar, *Tradition and Traditions* (New York: Macmillan, 1967), pp. 134–137.
6. A. Weiler, "Church Authority and Government in the Middle Ages," in *Concilium,* vol. 7 (Glen Rock: Paulist Press, 1965), p. 131.
7. F. Suarez, *De Fide,* III, Sect. 2, n.11 in Vives edition of *Opera,* vol. 12, p. 100.
8. C. R. Billuart, *Cursus Theologiae,* Tract. De Regulis Fidei, Diss. II, a. 1; cf., *DTC,* XV, c. 1328.
9. J. B. Franzelin, *De Divina Traditione et Scriptura,* second edition (Rome, 1875), thesis XI.
10. L. Billot, *De Sacra Traditione contra novam Haeresim Evolutionismi* (Rome, 1904).
11. J. D. Mansi, *Sacrorum Conciliorum Nova et Amplissima Collectio,* ed., H. Welter (Paris-Leipzig, 1903), 52:764, 1213–14 (hereinafter cited as Mansi).
12. Mansi, *loc cit.,* esp. 1214.
13. *Ibid.*
14. *Ibid.*
15. *De Virg. Vel.,* 1 (P.L., 2, 889–890).
16. *Adversus Haereses,* IV, 26, 2 (P.G. 7, 1053–54).
17. Y. Congar, *Tradition and Traditions* (New York: Macmillan, 1967), p. 331.
18. *Ibid.,* pp. 119–37.
19. *Ibid.,* pp. 338–347; pp. 36, 49, 55, 203, 316.
20. R. Murray, "Collegiality, Infallibility and Sobernost," *One in Christ,* 1 (1965), pp. 19–42.

21. Vatican II, *Decree on the Bishops' Pastoral Office in the Church,* para. 2.
22. *Ibid.,* para. 12.
23. *Ibid.*
24. *Ibid.,* para. 13.
25. Vatican II, *Pastoral Constitution on the Church in the Modern World,* para. 43.
26. Cf. G. K. Malone, "Academic Freedom Revisited," *Chicago Studies,* 7 (1968), pp. 3–13.
27. Denz., 3069.
28. *In II–II,* q. 1, a. 1, nn. X and XII.
29. Denz., 3073.
30. J. L. Murphy, *The Notion of Tradition in John Driedo* (Milwaukee: Seraphic Press, 1959), pp. 292–300.
31. J. Reed, "Natural Law, Theology, and the Church," *Theological Studies,* 26 (1965), p. 55.
32. R. McCormick, "Notes on Moral Theology," *Theological Studies,* 26 (1965), p. 614.
33. Helpful for understanding the peculiar problems of the magisterium dealing with morality is the essay of J. G. Milhaven, "Towards an Epistemology of Ethics," *Theological Studies,* 27 (1966), pp. 228–41.
34. Vatican II, *Decree on the Bishops' Pastoral Office in the Church,* paragraph 12.
35. Vatican II, *Pastoral Constitution on the Church in the Modern World,* paragraph 43.
36. *Posterior Analytics,* I, 24, 86a, 4.
37. *Summa Theologica,* I–II, q. 94, aa. 4 and 5.
38. Vatican II, *Pastoral Constitution on the Church in the Modern World,* paragraph 54.
39. *Ibid.,* para. 4.
40. *Ibid.,* para. 92.
41. *Ibid.,* para. 62.
42. *The Church in Our Day* (Washington: U.S.C.C., 1968), p. 35.
43. Cf. e.g., F. A. Sullivan, *De Ecclesia, I: Quaestiones Theologiae Fundamentalis* (Rome: Gregorian University, 1963), pp. 343–44.
44. Cf. K. Bihlmeyer and H. Tuechle, *Church History,* vol. I: *Christian Antiquity* (Westminister: Newman, 1958), pp. 250–56; P. Hughes, *A History of the Church,* vol. I (New York: Sheed and Ward, 1947), pp. 208–13; Sullivan, *op. cit.,* pp. 331–32; E. Amman, art. "Libère," *DTC,* IX, c. 631–59.
45. Cf. Bihlmeyer-Tuechle, *op. cit.,* pp. 292–95; Hughes, *op. cit.,* pp.

278–85; Sullivan, *op. cit.*, pp. 332–35; E. Amman, art., "Affaire des Trois-Chapitres," *DTC,* XV, cc. 1868–1924.

46. Cf. Bihlmeyer-Tuechle, *op. cit.*, pp. 295–99; Hughes, *op. cit.*, pp. 292–302; Sullivan, *op. cit.*, pp. 336–37; E. Amman, art., "Honorius I," *DTC,* VII, cc. 93–132; B. Lonergan, *De Verbo Incarnato* (Rome: Gregorian University, 1961), pp. 184–96: 202–06.
47. N. Haring, "The Case of Gilbert de la Porreé, Bishop of Poitiers (1142–54)," *Medieval Studies,* 13 (1951), p. 39.
48. *P.L.,* 211, 1176.
49. Mansi, 22:458; cf., Haring, *art. cit.*, pp. 1–41, esp. pp. 26–39.
50. Cf. M. Grabmann, "I divieti ecclesiastici di Aristotele sotto Innocenzo III e Gregorio IX," in *Miscellanea Historiae Pontificiae,* V, fasc. I (Rome: Gregorian University, 1941); M. D. Chenu, *Towards Understanding St. Thomas* (Chicago: Regnery, 1964), pp. 31–39; F. Van Steenberghen, *Aristotle in the West* (Louvain, 1955), pp. 66–100; 108–11.
51. For a highly documented review of the diverse attitudes toward war and violence that have existed historically in the universal Church at large and in the teaching of the hierarchical magisterium, see R. Bainton, *Christian Attitudes Toward War and Peace* (Nashville: Abingdon, 1960).
52. *Regula Pastoralis,* 3:27; in *P.L.,* 77:102.
53. *Epistulae,* 11:64, in *P.L.,* 77:1196–97.
54. Peter Damian, in *Opusc.* XVIII, Diss. iii, c. 3.
55. M. Boelens, *Die Klerikerehe in der Gesetzgebung der Kirche* (Paderborn: Ferdinand Schoeningh, 1968), pp. 142–152.
56. *Summa,* 2.32.2.1.
57. *Code of Canon Law,* c. 1013, 1.
58. Denz., 906.
59. P. Granfield, O.S.B., "The Right to Silence: Magisterial Development," *Theological Studies,* 27 (1966), p. 404.
60. *Ibid.*, p. 420.
61. Denz., 1690 in older editions.
62. Vatican II, *Declaration on Religious Freedom,* para. 2.
63. W. DeVries, *Rom und die Patriarchate des Ostens* (Freiburg-Muenchen: Verlag Karl Alber, 1963); A. Petroni, "An sit ritus praestantior?" *Apollinaris,* 6 (1933), pp. 74–82.
64. Apostolic Letter, "Quo impensiore," May 20, 1870.
65. Denz., 875.
66. *De Ecclesiae Potestate* III, 9, ed., R. Scholz (Weimar, 1929).
67. Vatican II, *Declaration on the Relation of the Church to non-Christians,"* cf. commentary by J. Oesterreicher, in H. Vorgrimler, ed., *Com-*

mentary on the Documents of Vatican II, vol. 3 (New York: Herder, 1968), which also contains a bibliography on the vexed history of Jewish-Christian relations.

68. Denz., 2980.
69. Denz., 2977.
70. Denz., 2978.
71. Denz., 2979.
72. See C. Hay, "The Ecclesiological Significance of the Decree on Ecumenism," *Journal of Ecumenical Studies,* 3 (1966), pp. 343–53; P. Chirico, "One Church: What Does It Mean?" *Theological Studies,* 28 (1967), pp. 659–82.
73. Pius X., *Motu Proprio,* "Praestantia Scripturae," Nov. 18, 1907; Denz. 3503.
74. *Constitution on the Church,* para. 25.
75. Cf. *L'Ami du Clergé* (1903), pp. 196, 200.
76. L. Choupin, *Valeurs des Décisions Doctrinales et Disciplinaires du Saint-Siège* (Paris, 1907).
77. P. Nau, *Une Source Doctrinale: Les Encycliques* (Paris: Les Editions du Cedre, 1952), p. 59.
78. Pius XII, *Humani Generis* (Washington: NCWC, 1950), p. 10.
79. Cf. *infra.,* pp.
80. C. K. Malone, "Encyclicals," *New Catholic Encyclopedia,* vol. 5 (New York: McGraw-Hill, 1968), p. 332.

4

Contemporary Ecclesiological Awareness of Catholic Theologians

The Roman Catholic scholars who formulated their views on Pope Paul VI's Encyclical *Humanae Vitae* in the Statement of July 30, 1968, and made their views public by releasing and commenting on the Statement to the news media were convinced that *not* to have acted in such manner would have been positively irresponsible. The Statement itself expresses their conviction "that true commitment to the mystery of Christ and the Church requires a candid statement of mind at this time by all Catholic theologians." This conviction arises from responsible theological views on the ecclesiological and methodological imperatives under which the contemporary Roman Catholic theologian must work.

Questions of ecclesiology and methodology were intrinsically operative throughout the entire subject matter of the Inquiry. The scholars who subscribed to and publicized the Statement took "exception to the ecclesiology implied and the methodology used by Paul VI in the writing and promulgation" of *Humanae Vitae;* thus the Statement manifestly implied an ecclesiology and used a methodology at variance with those of Paul VI

The subject professors contend that their views regarding the ecclesiological and methodological shortcomings of *Humanae Vitae* are demonstrably within the pale of responsible Catholic theological judgment. They also suggest that such views relate intrinsically and necessarily to the question of "dissent" from one specific ethical teaching of *Humanae Vitae,* the absolute prohibition of all means of artificial contraception, as well as to the precise mode and manner in which this "dissent" was externally manifested and communicated. Consequently, some sense of the *ecclesiological context* out of which the Statement and related events arose is essential to this presentation. ("Ecclesiological context" is used to refer to the state of the Roman Catholic Church's self-awareness as a religious body looking both inward at itself and outward at all other persons, communities and events, as well as the state of that branch of scientific theology commonly designated as "theology of the Church.")

The presentation of this material will develop through four steps:

Modern Historical Development of the Church's Self-Awareness and of the Science of Ecclesiology;

Actual State of Ecclesiology and Ecclesial Self-Awareness: The Post-Conciliar Era;

Self-Awareness (or Ecclesiological Context) of the Catholic Scholar of the Sacred Sciences on July 29, 1968;

Ecclesiological Framework of the Exercise of the Interpretive Theological Function in the Instance of *Humanae Vitae.*

Modern Historical Development of the Church's Self-Awareness and of the Science of Ecclesiology[1]

The "Counter-Reformation" Ecclesiology. Responding to sixteenth-century events in a spirit of "Counter-Reformation," Roman Catholic theology of the Church evidenced:

a) A "hierarchology" which concentrated on the hierarchical element in the Church, concerning itself with the ruling, teaching and sanctifying power possessed by the apostles and their successors (bishops), most especially that of Peter and his successor (pope), and which practically excluded all broader-based considerations and realities, such as the notion of the laity as the basic and constitutive cause of the Church, the fellowship of believers and the presence of charismatic elements in the members of that fellowship;

b) A theology of the Roman Catholic Church over and against and to the exclusion of any other alleged "ecclesial" communities or realities outside it;

c) An articulation of self-awareness that was polemic and apologetic in method. The Church of Christ was considered as a visible ("perfect") society, its members being those who recognized the triple power (teach, rule, sanctify: *magisterium, regimen, sacerdotium*) and submitted themselves to it. The pneumatic or "mystical" aspect of the Church was not consciously suppressed, but was grossly neglected in the standard fare of ecclesiological treatises.

Counter-Reformation and, in the early twentieth century, anti-Modernist ecclesiology prevailed in seminary, manualistic and general catechetic and homiletic expressions until very recently. In fact, the authors commonly used in Roman Catholic seminaries until and even during Vatican II, e.g., Hervé, Pesch and Tanquery, are prime examples of the counterreform and anti-Modernist presentation which had such a great impact on the general ecclesial consciousness of Roman Catholicism. Since the social and communal context in which salvation itself is mediated to man is basic to all further theological considerations, the science of ecclesiology ("What is the church?") is of fundamental importance in Catholic theology. The typical textbook approach of the manualists, however, contained and communicated all the dominant characteristics of counterreform and anti-Modernist methodology. It had a distinctly bureaucratic cast.[2]

The manner in which the science of ecclesiology was cast *both reflected and reinforced the actual life-style of the Church itself.* Simple observation of the day-to-day workings of the Roman Catholic Church (worldwide, national, diocesan and parish) confirms the fact that the foregoing *conception* of the Church approximated the *reality* of Church life on all levels. Characteristically, "Church" was seen to mean the pope and his direct agents (Roman Curia, bishops and even local parish pastors). The notion, *Roma locuta est, causa finita est* (Rome has spoken, the issue is closed) extended to include anything and everything emanating from the "Holy See" or the local Chancery office.[3] Both the scientific *concept* and the actual *reality* of the Church of the Counter-Reformation era and spirit are perhaps suitably described in terms of a *pyramidic structure*. The pope stands at the top; through him all hierarchical power is transmitted since he stands as the personal vicar of Christ Himself. He alone possesses the plenitude of priesthood and jurisdiction. The episcopate is viewed atomistically: Each residential bishop is independent of the others, limited only by the pope and the papal curial officials. Below the bishops are priests, whose power of jurisdiction is limited and subject to approval and control of the local bishop. Then come the faithful, who form the solid base of the pyramid. They obey their pastors (the "Church"), and attend services where prayer is offered in their name by persons consecrated for this purpose (Mass and Sacraments). The faithful ("laity") are also expected to assist their hierarchical pastors in whatever tasks might be assigned.[4]

Expanding Notions of the Church in the Nineteenth and Twentieth Centuries. A reaction against counterreformation ecclesiology and the correlative life-style of the Church was voiced through the writings of a small minority of Catholic theologians, beginning in the nineteenth century with the Tübingen scholar, J. A. Moehler, along with M. J. Scheeben, and evidenced in the first four or five decades of the twentieth century by persons such as K. Adam, E. Mersch, H. de Lubac, C. Journet and M. Schmaus. These men and a few others resuscitated the "mystical body" motif. It is worthy of note that the draft schema presented to, but never adopted by, the First Vatican Council (1869-1870) echoed this nineteenth-century attempt at an ecclesiological revival. However, the Vatican I definition regarding the pope, together with the nonaction of Vatican I on the necessary balancing doctrines, only served further to reinforce the "hierarchological" thrust of ecclesiology and Church life.[5] In fact, the action of Vatican I regarding the role and prerogatives of the pope and the subsequent "Modernist" crisis solidified *Ubi Petrus ibi Ecclesia* (the Church is where Peter is) as the primary and almost exclusive motif of Catholic ecclesiology and "papo-centrism" as the dominant feature of Catholic life.

This nineteenth- and twentieth-century minority movement (co-existing with the dominant hierarchological style) planted the seed for a massive and effective ecclesiological and ecclesial renewal.

In the twentieth century, the distinct and "official" recovery of a broader-based ecclesiology under one biblical image was brought about by the encyclical *Mystici Corporis* of Pius XII (1943). This Encyclical marked an important stage in the development of ecclesiology—the end of one era (taking up the findings and themes of over a century of minority theological work) and the beginning of another era. Ecclesial life-style, however, was not significantly changed by the issuance of *Mystici Corporis*. However, almost immediately it was recognized that the doctrine and limits of the 1943 Encyclical and the use of solely the "mystical body" image were inadequate to articulate properly an authentic churchly self-awareness, both domestically in terms of the internal componency and life-dynamics of the Church, and especially in respect to other Christian communities outside the Roman communion.[6]

After 1943, and with increasing intensity up to the Second Vatican Council (1962-1965), ecclesiology developed many biblical and speculative motifs which began to seriously influence churchly self-awareness and set the proximate context for the accomplishments of Vatican II. A parallel and intertwining series of "movements"—especially biblical, liturgical, patristic, ecumenical and lay apostolate—dramatically influenced the Catholic theology of the Church and the Church membership at large. The seminary textbooks and the catechetic and homiletic fare within the Roman Catholic Church retained the characteristics described above as "counterreformation" and "anti-Modernist," with at times only the mildest acknowledgment of newer dimensions and emphases. Nonetheless, the "people of God" motif, the "pilgrim church" motif, other broader-based and more flexible motifs (largely drawn from biblical imagery and paradigms), questions concerning the relationship between the Roman Catholic Church and separated Christian bodies and between the Church and modern society, and other similar strands of scholarship and even popular awareness started to make themselves heard and felt by the eve of Vatican II.

Conceptual and Practical Tensions on the Eve of Vatican II. During the first session of Vatican II (Autumn, 1962), the tension and diversity within the Council halls among the bishops themselves, and in evidence throughout the whole Church, could be described in a schematized form of two "fundamentally different" conceptions of the Church. This schema is helpful in developing an appreciation of the somewhat "schizophrenic" situation which prevailed at that time and which perdures even now within Catholicism. It likewise provides a convenient reference point for evaluating the final acts of Vatican II and the postconciliar status of Church life and ecclesiology. The image of the "pyramidical structure"[7] is contrasted with the "concentric circles" model which begins with the faithful.

All, including pope, bishops, priests, all clergy and laity, belong to the faithful who, by virtue of their common baptism, are members of the one people of God. Together they form the royal and priestly people whose inner coherency is assured by the grace of the indwelling Spirit. This one people of God is at the same time the Mystical Body of Christ.

Within this one people and one Body, there are certain persons who, by virtue of special Ordination, receive a further consecration and consequently deputization to the function of exercising special witness and authority, of ministering unto the sanctification of all in a special way. This consecration is ultimately divine; it is not communicated by the pope but by Christ Himself acting in the Sacraments. The practical and concrete exercise of these specially ordained ministries may and indeed must be ordered by jurisdictional authority in the Church for the good of the whole community. But the precise manner in which they are ordered at any given point in the Church's historical pilgrimage is the function of circumstances, cultures and local conditions.

The consecration or ordination to the special Christian ministry does not make its recipients essentially superior to ordinary believers; they remain believers just like the others; but it does, in the name of Christ and in the power of His Spirit, give them a valid *mission,* a real and efficacious *function* in the Church, especially in the realm of the Word of God and of the Sacraments. It is within this context that the collegiate espiscopate may be understood. For these specially ordained ministers are primarily the bishops joined together as the successors of the Apostoles in a "college." This aspect of collegiality is a vital structural element in the Church. It is not a question merely of independent atoms, indirectly bound to one another through their common bond with the pope, or through a contingent contract to collaborate pastorally in a specific area. Episcopal collegiality is simply not derived juridically from the pope; its roots run much deeper into the very nature of the Church itself. The idea of collegiality was absolutely evident in the early centuries and was expressed by the manifold forms of "communion" between the local churches in various parts of the world, and between the bishops of these churches personally. ("Priests" are collaborators or coadjutors of the bishops individually and collegiately.)

Within the episcopal college the Bishop of Rome, successor of St. Peter, holds a special place. He has received from this historical succession a special mission and function of unification and authentication of the Christian community.

The "concentric circles" image provided a fresh framework within which to approach the science of ecclesiology; it likewise has had profound impact on the broad-based ecclesial self-awareness of the Roman Catholic Church. By the eve of Vatican II, it seems, the *pyramid* image was about to be superseded.[8]

The Eccesiology of Vatican II. Vatican II (1962–1965) constituted a highly significant, if not revolutionary, state in the continuing development in ecclesial self-awareness and self-expression and contributed many substantially new data to the science of ecclesiology. The ecclesiological accomplishment of Vatican II is so enormous that it cannot be adequately summarized herein.[9] Certain particular developments in the Council, however, are specifically relevant to the issues in the Inquiry.

By characterizing the Church principally as "mystery" (i.e., although it is a community of men on earth and a structured society, nonetheless the Church is the special *locus* of God's ineffable merciful action among men, and, in and behind and through the visible community, is the encounter with the transcendent God Himself), the Council set a context not reflected theretofore in standard ecclesiological reflections.[10] By abundant use of biblical imagery, the Council broadened, diversified and recognized as flexible the pilgrim itinerary which the Church must wend. The "people of God" motif found its place as the dominant characterization of Church—fellowship, familial service and witness are the chief attributes of the salvation community; full churchly status is accorded *all* the faithful, quite antecedent to any consideration of *special* offices or ministries, such as those of bishops and priests.[11]

Vatican II certified, beyond further question, in explicit terms (with reference to bishops vis-à-vis the Bishop of Rome and equivalently with respect to the entire Church community), the collegial (rather than pryramidic or monarchical) nature of the Church.[12] The nonidentification of "Church" and "hierarchical office" is abundantly clear and consistently emphasized in the Council documents.[13] Vatican II recognized the "laity" as constitutive of the Church; recognized their prophetic, regal and priestly identity and roles; and affirmed the facts that *all* are the Church and that *all* are concerned with and responsible for the totality of the Church's life.[14]

Vatican II affirmed the true (although in some sense defective) ecclesiality or churchliness of the Christian communities from whom the Roman Catholic Church is presently separated. This is an extremely significant assertion, which McNamara calls "a truly major development and clarification in Catholic theology of the church."[15] Developing the meaning of this recognition in terms of worship, witness and magisterium of separated Christian communities is one of the major tasks of postconciliar theology.[16]

The Council expressed its consciousness that the Church is essentially *dialogic*: with separated Christian communities, with Judaism, with other non-Christian religions, with unbelievers, with society and the world at large, with technology and contemporary culture and with all men of good will.[17] The full implications of the Church's self-awareness as an essentially *dialogic* community must be developed in the postconciliar era. Pope Paul VI, in his Encyclical *Ecclesiam Suam,* signalled a distinctly new era for the "relational" or "dialogical" Church.[18]

Vatican II adopted the theoretical and working principle of *renewal and reform* as the touchstone of *every* act in and of the Catholic Church today: the way we say things (*doctrinal* renewal and reform), the way we do things (*structural* renewal and reform) and the way we live (*personal* and *communitarian* renewal and reform).[19] This principle is succinctly enunciated in the Council documents and papal statements themselves: e.g.,

> All (Catholics) are led to examine their own faithfulness to Christ's will for the Church and, wherever necessary, undertake with vigor the task of *renewal and reform*. . . . But their primary duty is to make an honest and careful appraisal of whatever needs to be renewed in the Catholic household itself, in order that its life may bear witness more loyally and luminously to the teachings and ordinances which have been handed down from Christ through the Apostles. . . . Christ summons the church, as she goes her pilgrim way, to that *continual reformation* of which she always has need, insofar as she is an institution of men on earth. . . .[20]

> If the influence of events or of times has led to deficiencies in moral conduct or in church discipline, or even in the way that church teaching has been formulated—to be carefully distinguished from the deposit of faith itself—these should be set right at the opportune moment in the proper way.[21]

The words of Pope John at the opening of the first session of Vatican II evidence the same perspective: "The deposit of faith is one thing, the way that it is presented is another; for the truth preserved in our sacred doctrine can retain the same substance and meaning under different forms of expression. . . ."[22]

The *concentric* conception of Church generally prevails throughout the total acts of Vatican II; the *pyramidic* conception has been transcended in principle. This is not to imply that Vatican II's ecclesiology is completely homogeneous or consistent. Certainly, some, even many, residual elements from past formulations and positions are in evidence; but sufficient new dimensions and emphases are in evidence to justify the claim that Vatican II was truly a "revolutionary" accomplishment.

The Place of Vatican II Documents in Catholic Church Life and Theology. The achievements of Vatican II have been sufficiently extolled to be taken for granted in this presentation. Truly, revolution was wrought in Roman Catholic conciliar history; truly, the official acts, and the by-products of these acts, as well as the unofficial surrounding events of the total Vatican II period have made a significant impact on the Church. The basic conciliar teachings and commitments concerning the collegiality of bishops, the position of laymen in the Church, the nature of divine revelation and the imperative of full religious liberty have provided strong support for the sincerity and conviction that underlie the Council's explicit mandate for the future. The ecclesiological development supporting, surrounding and resulting from the Council is overpowering. However, simply to analyze and assimilate the Church's self-awareness expressed in the *Dogmatic Constitution on the Church* and the fifteen satellite documents is a consuming task. Nor would that be sufficient. The Roman Church's self-awareness expressed in Vatican II marks the end of an ecclesiological era and the inauguration of a new one. With all reverence, theologians recognize that the documents of Vatican II were "dated" on the first day after solemn promulgation. The mandate given to Catholic theologians extends beyond conciliar exegesis, just as the mandate given to all the Catholic faithful far exceeds a rote memorization of, and literalist conformity to, the conciliar teachings and directives.

Catholic ecclesiology presently runs the risk of a pejorative "post-Vatican II" mentality, just as the Council of Trent led to a rigid "post-Tridentine" Roman Catholicism. The *spirit* of Vatican II might be ignored in favor of the letter and limitations of officially promulgated formulations. Reference in the future to the letter of the pronouncements of Vatican II as the final norm for evaluating theological data would effectively bring Roman Catholic ecclesiological progress to a halt. This is not because the Vatican II formulations are unsuitable; rather, it is because they are intrinsically limited to what the Council Fathers intended them to be—formulations which express, for the most part, the maximum capacity of that time but which do not preclude future, ongoing developments beyond the categories of Vatican II itself.

The Vatican II documents, especially the *Dogmatic Constitution on the Church,* require a *dynamic* interpretation. "One must not ask himself solely what exactly this or that single phrase says or means; rather, at the same time, he must ask what constructive possibilities from now on are offered by this doctrinal decision of the church."[23]

As Paul VI reminds us: "The conciliar decrees are not so much a destination as a point of departure toward new goals. The renewing power and spirit of the council must continue to penetrate to the very depths of the church's life. The seeds of life planted by the council in the soil of the church must grow and achieve full maturity."[24]

Actual State of Ecclesiology and Ecclesial Self-Awareness: The Postconciliar Era

Since the closing session of Vatican II, theologians have been occupied with the task of properly discerning and assimilating the conciliar teachings;[25] of locating and articulating the deficiencies as well as the strengths and acquisitions of the conciliar teachings and setting them in proper and total theological and historical context;[26] of making inital attempts at formulating a completely new ecclesiology which would incorporate all the acquisitions of Vatican II in proper perspective, supply its deficiencies, *develop* themes contained in or suggested and implied by the Vatican II accomplishment, build upon Vatican II and go beyond it to achieve contemporaneity and meet furture needs;[27]

and of striving to translate speculative postconciliar ecclesiology into new structures and *ways-of-being-church.*[28]

The developments of the postconciliar era implicate the whole Church. The science of ecclesiology and the broad ecclesial self-awareness of all Catholics are being affected by the postconciliar theological themes. The theologian must take the measure of this developing churchly self-awareness; in the process, his awareness of his own role will assume new dimensions.

The Self-Awareness (or Ecclesiological Context) of the Catholic Scholar of the Sacred Sciences on July 29, 1968

Awareness of General Theological Development. First of all, the Catholic scholar of the sacred sciences was *aware* of all the foregoing developments discussed. He was intensely aware of his own proper role and function in the Church fellowship. He was rightly preoccupied with the dominant new acquisition and dimensions of emphasis emerging from the Vatican II period. Particuarly, he was concerned with the themes of *collegiality* and *co-responsibility* in the Church; with due recognition in theory and practice of the proper Christian witness of *laity* in spheres of their competence, both scientific and experiential; with due recognition in theory and practice of the authentic ecclesial witness of separated Christian communities; with giving full import to modern scientific and technological advances; and with a proper understanding and exercise of "authority," both administrative and doctrinal, in the Church.

He was intensely conscious of the implications of the work of his colleagues. For example, he knew that the postconciliar Church was, or should have been, in the process of renewal and reform. He was aware of the thematic principles of reform in contemporary ecclesiology: the *divine-human* principle; the principle of *historicity;* the *pneumatic-charismatic* principle; the principle of the fundamental *equality* and *co-responsibility* of all

Christians; the principle of *fellowship;* the principle of *diakonia* (service); the principle of *dialogue;* and the principle of *subsidiarity.*

He was aware of the biblical paradigm as duly *normative* for Christian church life, and familiar with the questions arising from contemporary biblical studies on "church order": e.g., he was aware that church structures appear in a *variety* of forms and have undergone periods of *development* (seeing this variety enables one to avoid absolutizing present forms and arguing *only* from *present* structures); that authority, though expressed in individuals, has a special relationship to the community; that *human weakness* of the officeholder is a conscious biblical theme; that the officeholder exercises his authority in virtue of a special relationship to the *teaching of tradition.*[29]

He was conscious of the contemporary recovery of the sense and recognition of *charismata* in the Church and the diversities of functions or roles within the community—all, each in its own way, serving the whole.[30] He was conversant with the present discussion of authority, magisterium and obedience in the Church.[31] He was in "dialogue" with the persons, institutions, currents of thought and "movements" of the world (ecclesial and otherwise) in which he lived.

Awareness of the Need to Reinterpret the Relationship between the Hierarchical Magisterium and the Theologian, and the Need to Develop This Reinterpretation through Co-responsive Dialogue. The Roman Catholic theologian was aware that a new view of the magisterium had quite inevitably followed upon the advances in ecclesiology which occurred in Vatican II and which were continuing in the postconciliar period. Many scholars are in full agreement with Robert Murray, S.J., who writes: "The magisterium is not above or outside of the community of believers."[32] Vatican II includes the ingredients of an advanced ecclesiology. Since the notion of magisterium is intimately related to the notion of Church, it may be expected that the theology of the magisterium will also show important changes in this period of development. The new images of the Church, such as "people of God" and "the pilgrim Church," and the recognition of the ecclesial reality of non-Catholic Christian bodies have significant implications for any treatment of the magisterium today.

The theology of the magisterium does not exist in isolation; it is representative of recent developments in this area. Today's theologians are familiar with the contemporary theological literature which has deepened his understanding of magisterium under the influence of recent advances in ecclesiology stemming from Vatican II. For example, Gregory Baum has developed the idea of the magisterium as a ministry with inevitable limitations and has made several suggestions as to how the magisterium might function in the modern world.[33] He also discussed the magisterium in the light of history and the development of thought, stressing the "negative potential" in the Church, that it might obscure the light of the gospel due to the presence of sin.[34]

Ernest Kaesemann and Raymond E. Brown have discussed the development of New Testament ecclesiology and offer corrections for the usually oversimplified review of this phenomenon.[35] John T. Noonan, Jr., has expanded upon his familiarity with the usury and contraception questions and shows from history how these issues have served to illustrate the nature of authority in the Church.[36] Piet Fransen has treated the authority of the Councils as illustrative of the teaching authority of the Church.[37] Quentin Quade and James Rhodes have examined the question of teaching authority with a view to how that authority affects the experts in various fields. These authors contend that a Catholic should consult the Church's teachings on all matters of morals and indeed follow it when he sees no other principles in conflict. They insist, however, that the concept of Church authority does not make a priori decisions possible, nor does it substitute for moral prudence.[38]

George Dejaifve has taken a position on the relationship of the believing Church to the hierarchical magisterium as this problem appeared in the *Acts* of Vatican I. He illustrates that Vatican I, in spite of its strong hierarchical emphasis, was not unaware of the positive role of nonhierarchical Christians in matters of teaching and belief.[39] John C. Bennett has written lucidly on the Protestant view of authority in the Church.[40] Yves Congar has contributed monumental work on the development and historical conditioning of authority in the Church.[41]

Vatican II also instigated a rethinking and reinterpretation of the working relationship between the theologian and the hierarchical magisterium. That rethinking is of course prerequisite to a renewed interpretation of the "right of dissent." The model for the relationship of hierarchical magisterium and theologians must presuppose certain distinctions which have become the accepted assumptions of hierarchies and scholars alike since Vatican II.

It is agreed that theologians and the hierarchical magisterium (bishops, including the pope) have related but distinct and different functions in the Church. As the American Bishops noted in their 1968 Pastoral Letter: "These (bishops and theologians) have their diverse ministries in the Church, their distinct responsibilities to the faith and their respective charisms."[42] Bishops and theologians exercise distinct but related and mutually helpful roles.

The *truth* which is the object of proper theological inquiry is not synonymous with the *faith* by which the theologian's intellect is illumined to begin with, nor is it synonymous with the "revelation" or the *doctrina de fide vel moribus* which the bishop (or priest) as pastoral minister must proclaim and celebrate. Whereas theologians "respectfully acknowledge a distinct role of hierarchical *magisterium* (teaching authority) in the Church of Christ," they are also aware that "Christian tradition assigns theologians the special responsibility of evaluating and interpreting pronouncements of the *magisterium* in the light of the total theological data operative in each question or statement."[43] The teachings of the hierarchical magisterium are part of the total data which the Catholic theologian must integrate into his work; he must be aware of these teachings, evaluate their weight, give them their proper significance and interpret them.

The hierarchical magisterium as such and per se (and a fortiori an individual bishop or a regional or national group of bishops as such and per se) is incompetent in theology as such and per se.

The magisterium is not to be viewed as a refuge from the discipline of theology. Rather, the propounding and explanation of the *faith* involves a theological task, and is subject to the interpretations and evaluations of theological science. As the theologian is dependent on the magisterium as the touchstone of *faith,* the hierarchical magisterium depends on theology for the full articulation of Christian meanings. This position does not imply that one must be a scientific theologian to teach in the Christian Church, or that one must be a theologian to be a bishop. However, it must be acknowledged that when one seeks to explain the *faith,* he employs specific theological forms and patterns of thought and language (Scripture itself contains varying *theologies*). Any use of such forms or patterns should be subject to the scrutiny of theological science, just as theological science influences the presentation and explanation of *faith* itself.[44]

Pope Paul VI's talk in 1966 to the International Congress on the Theology of Vatican II[45] suggests an understanding of the pertinent distinctions. Theology and the magisterium, he states, have different functions (*officia*), are endowed with different gifts. The office of bishop and the office of theologian are distinct but related functions in the Church. (Immediately the *charismata* discussed at length by St. Paul in I Corinthians 12-14 should be recalled: special gifts and ministries which are to serve the whole community.) Theologians occupy a mediating position between the faith of the Church and the teaching office of bishops, as they seek to discover how the Christian community might translate its faith into practice and try to grasp the truths, opinions, questions and trends which the Holy Spirit stirs up in the people of God (". . . what the Spirit says to the Churches," Rev. 2:7). Using the method and principles proper to their specialty, *theologians must evaluate* the faith of God's people as actually lived, and their aims, in order to bring them into harmony with the Word of God and the doctrinal heritage faithfully handed down by the Church, and in order to propose solutions to questions which arise when this faith is compared with actual life, with history and with human inquiry. Without the help of theology, Pope Paul VI notes that the teaching office of bishops could certainly guard and teach the faith, but that it would have great difficulty in reaching the deep and full understanding of faith which it needs for the adequate fulfillment of its own function. The teaching office of bishops knows that it does not have the charism of revelation or of inspiration, only that of the assistance of the Holy Spirit. Deprived of the efforts of theologians, the teaching office of bishops would lack one of the "tools" whereby to achieve the purpose of its existence—which is directly pastoral, not academic. Theology is unquestionably recognized as an essential science *in* and *for* the Church.

Theology and the hierarchical magisterium, therefore, stand in a healthy, ongoing, dialectical and dialogical relationship. As evidenced in the history of the theology-magisterium relationship, an interplay of the two adequately manifests the totality of the Christian quest for fuller expression of the truth.

Awareness of the Latitude and Limits of the Roman Catholic Faith-Commitment. It has already been noted, in a preliminary manner, that Catholic theologians must "respectfully acknowledge a distinct role of hierarchical magisterium (teaching authority) in the Church of Christ," and that theologians hold "the special responsibility of evaluating and interpreting pronouncements of the magisterium in the light of the total theological data operative in each question or Statement."[46] Furthermore, it has been noted immediately above that the relationship between theologians and hierarchical magisterium must be one of co-responsive dialogue, each according to a proper and distinct role in and for the Church. Since, however, both hierarchical magisterium *and* theologians must always function *within* the context and according to the claims of the Roman Catholic faith-commitment, it is appropriate here to delineate the precise nature of the *faith*-commitment to which all are equally bound: what is it and how is it determined in terms of human discourse?

This question, beyond its obvious theoretic importance, assumes a specific practical importance for the investigation of the responsibility of public dissent from *Humanae Vitae*. Some persons, including hierarchical members of the Board of Trustees of Catholic University, have suggested that the subject professors, by their actions and declarations in regard to *Humanae Vitae,* violated the Catholic *Profession of Faith* which is a statutory requirement of all Catholic faculty members at the University.[47]

The subject professors have made it quite clear in chapter two of this presentation that, with the First Vatican Council,[48] they affirm the essential role of *faith* in the proper functioning of the Roman Catholic theologian. In fact, their description of the theologian is simply unintelligible in the "no-faith" hypothesis, since the fundamental note of theology is precisely *"ratio fide illustrata"* ("reason enlightened by faith").[49] Obviously, the description herein insisted upon is of a Catholic *theologian* in the fullest, and therefore narrowest, sense of the term. Perhaps in the face of the present complexities of the task, no one person alone actually verifies the fullest sense of the term, since he usually cannot enjoy in his own right the enormous scope of required expertise. Except in the most extraordinary instance, the full description of Catholic theologian is more often verified of a collaborating group rather than of any single individual. By its very nature, theology in the Church is a collegial enterprise; today it is collegial also by sheer force of human necessity. The subject professors are prescinding, therefore, from the necessity of faith in the proper functioning of a "theologian" in any of the broader or auxiliary senses not accounted for by the descriptions of Catholic theology and the Catholic theologian contained in chapter two of the present work.

In the received classical idiom of Vatican I, the *faith* which is essential to the proper functioning of the Roman Catholic theologian is the assent to or belief in divinely revealed truth because of, and solely because of, the authority of God revealing.[50] In a contemporary idiom, *faith* is the intimate and abiding *relationship,* in the very depths of a person's being, to God communicating Himself to man through Christ in His Holy Spirit—which relationship is accepted by a man's personal, free and fundamental option of response to God calling him. In either idiom, *faith* as such is "invisible," "inaudible," and cannot be gauged by any human instrument. Faith, however, is ordered to be expressed and professsed and to have a transforming impact on persons, human society and the course of history. It is at the same time an *ecclesial* commitment for the Roman Catholic. The expression and reinforcement of faith is usually through sharing in the sacramental life of the Church; the profession (or "confession") of faith usually takes the form of symbols or creeds or other formulae constructed and guaranteed as authentic by the very life and tradition of the Church itself, especially by the hierarchical magisterium; the transforming impact of faith is something for which Catholics must account to the judgment of both mankind and God Himself. It is the *profession* ("confession") *of faith* that has particular pertinence here, since by it the criteria for judging the faith-commitment are set in intelligible human discourse.

The profession of faith usually takes the normative form of expressed adherence to *articles* of faith properly so-called. Articles (or *dogmas*) of faith are described by the First Vatican Council[51] and by the present Code of Canon Law[52] in the following way: Truths which are contained in the Word of God, whether written or handed down (*"in verbo Dei scripto vel tradito"*), *and* are proposed by the Church to be believed *as divinely revealed,* either in solemn judgment (papal or conciliar definition) or through the ordinary and universal magisterium. In regard to articles (dogmas) of faith strictly so-called, whether they are proposed in solemn form or in everyday ordinary and universal form, the believer enjoys the guarantee of *infallibility* inherent in the Church's proposal of them *as divinely revealed.*

The scope of *Divine and Catholic Faith,* therefore, is an extremely well delimited and readily discernible category for the Roman Catholic, whether he be theologian or nonacademic. In a final analysis, and granting that all "hermeneutical" problems have been accounted for and equalized, to deny or reject an article of Divine and Catholic Faith is heresy in the classical sense of the term and cuts one off from the community of believers which is the Church. However, the *total* faith-commitment of the Roman Catholic goes beyond the narrow scope of assenting to articles of divine faith strictly so-called. It includes a further commitment to at least two other distinct levels of normative Church teaching.

Some truths, although not of Divine and Catholic *Faith* strictly so-called, are so intimately connected (by presupposition or by consequence) with a dogma of the faith that to deny them would be necessarily reducible to denying the dogma of faith itself. Should such a truth be the object of a solemn definition by either the papal or the universal episcopal magisterium, the believer is provided with an infallible certitude in his assent to the truth. His overall faith-commitment absolutely does not permit him to deny or equivocate on such an infallibly defined truth in any way. We prescind here from the very necessary contemporary debate about infallibility as such.

There are, however, other teachings of the hierarchical magisterium, whether papal or universal episcopal, which are neither dogmas of the *faith* nor infallibly defined but are *authoritatively* proposed. It is to this category of hierarchical teaching that the Church requires a "religious assent" which is neither the absolute assent of Divine and Catholic *Faith* nor the absolute theological assent due to other infallibly taught truths but is the *conditional* assent to the teaching as only presumptively true, as described in the manualists' tradition above.

The total faith-commitment of the Roman Catholic is accounted for in the official formula for the *Profession of Faith* currently prescribed by the Vatican Congregation for the Teaching of the Faith. On May 31, 1967, that Congregation issued a new formula to be used according to law, in place of the Tridentine formula and the Oath against Modernism, whenever a Profession is prescribed. The new formula reads as follows:

> I (name) with firm faith believe and profess each and everything contained in the symbol of faith, namely: (There follows the Nicene-Constantinopolitan Creed, called the "Nicene Creed," familiar from liturgical use.) That is followed by this additional statement:

I also embrace and retain each and everything regarding the doctrine of faith and morals, whether defined by solemn judgment or asserted and declared by the ordinary magisterium, *as they are proposed by the Church,* especially those things which concern the mystery of the holy Church of Christ, its Sacraments, the Sacrifice of the Mass, and the Primacy of the Roman Pontiff.[53]

This formula analytically is composed of two parts. The first part, whose object is the Nicene-Constantinopolitan symbol, is to be believed and professed by firm faith (*firma fide credo et profiteor*). The second part, whose object is an all-inclusive category of teachings, is to be firmly embraced and retained (*firmiter . . . amplector et retineo*), as they are proposed by the Church (*prout ab ipsa proponuntur*). Thus, the second part of the Profession of Faith formula itself implicitly acknowledges the several levels of teaching and diverse binding force of each. The phrase, "as they are proposed by the Church," makes it clear that the hierarchical magisterium intends a binding force proportionate to the level and quality of each particular teaching. Some teachings are to be believed by *divine faith* since they are proposed by the Church, whether through an infallible definition or by the ordinary universal magisterium, *as divinely revealed*; some teachings are to be held under an absolute binding force since they are *infallibly* proposed, although not of divine faith strictly so-called; other teachings are to be held by that "religious assent" which is due to authoritative noninfallible pronouncements. (The Encyclical *Humanae Vitae* was promulgated and universally received as an authoritative, fallible pronouncement of the papal magisterium.)

The sincere and full adherence to the Profession of Faith by no means excludes the right of responsible dissent from authoritative, noninfallible teachings by competent persons under certain qualifications. The confessional commitment, or "faith-commitment," attested to by the Profession of Faith, may be preserved intact even in the instance of responsible dissent from noninfallible teachings of the papal or episcopal ordinary magisterium. The relevant question is whether, under the circumstances, public dissent from a particular authoritative, noninfallible pronouncement of the papal magisterium is within the pale of supportable Roman Catholic theological options. The Profession of Faith attests that a person intends to remain within the pale of responsible Roman Catholic theological options and implies nothing by way of further limitation on his theological views. (It is the position of the subject professors that a determination of whether a theologian is or is not within the faith-commitment is clearly within the capacity, competence and province of his peer group of Roman Catholic theologians.) It is clear, therefore, that the subject professors retain the integrity of their total faith-commitment and Profession of Faith in the same way that the fathers of Vatican II could retain the same integrity in approving the final text of *Lumen Gentium,* n. 25, which, according to the *Modi,* antecedently provides for the "right to dissent" from authoritative, noninfallible pronouncements of the papal magisterium as described by "*auctores probati.*"[54]

Awareness of the Response Requested by Paul VI in Humanae Vitae, and of the Need to Reinterpret the Reference Points of His Request. Theologians accept as part of the relevant theological data Paul VI's exhortation in paragraph 28 of *Humanae Vitae* that priests should observe "loyal internal and external obedience to the teaching authority of the Church." "That obedience, as you well know," Paul VI continues, "obliges not only because of the reasons adduced, but rather because of the light of the Holy Spirit, which is given in a particular way to the pastors of the Church in order that they may illustrate the truth." A footnote at this point refers to paragraph 25 of the *Dogmatic Constitution on the Church* (*Lumen Gentium*), where the Second Vatican Council teaches:

> Religious allegiance of the will and intellect should be given in an entirely special way to the authentic teaching authority of the Roman pontiff, even when he is not speaking *ex cathedra;* this should be done in such a way that his supreme teaching authority is respectfully acknowledged, while the judgments given by him are sincerely ad-

hered to according to his manifest intention and desire, as this is made known by the nature of his documents, or by his frequent repetition of the same judgment, or by his way of speaking.[55]

Thus, *Lumen Gentium* calls for a "religious allegiance of the will and intellect" to be given to pronouncements of the papal magisterium which are authentically authoritative but noninfallible. Paul VI, in *Humanae Vitae,* refers to this passage in *Lumen Gentium* to specify the response he expects to the teachings contained in the Encyclical.[56] That it is to this statement about *religiosum voluntatis et intellectus obsequium* that Paul VI is referring in *Humanae Vitae* (and not to other statements of the same paragraph 25 of *Lumen Gentium*) is clear from Paul VI's own manner of speaking in the Encyclical and from the remarks of Professor Ferdinando Lambruschini in presenting and interpreting the Encyclical to the mass media of communications on July 29, 1968.

The dissenting professors were aware that the official supporting acts of Vatican II itself note that paragraph 25 of *Lumen Gentium* should be read in the light of the presentations of the ordinary *magisterium* in "approved [theological] authors," both with respect to the possibility in which an educated person *(eruditus quidam)* cannot, for solid reasons, give the type of assent normally expected, and with regard to the quality of the adherence of mind and intellect required, viz., nonabsolute in respect of nonirreformable teachings. These same official, supporting acts of Vatican II acknowledge that freedom for further investigation and for doctrinal progress are by no means excluded by paragraph 25 of *Lumen Gentium.*

Since paragraph 25 of the *Dogmatic Constitution on the Church* states what response Paul VI himself was seeking to the teaching contained in *Humanae Vitae,* and since this same paragraph 25 has been widely used by others to identify the response sought, e.g., in the American Bishops' Pastoral Letter, *Human Life in Our Day,* issued November 15, 1968, and in many diocesan pastoral letters of initial comment on *Humanae Vitae*, it would be useful to examine the background or "legislative history" of this text from the official acts of the Second Vatican Council.[57]

The original *Schema De Ecclesia et de B. Maria Virgine* (*Draft on the Church and The Blessed Virgin Mary*), presented to the Council at the first session in 1962, contained the following section dealing with the ordinary teaching authority of the pope:

> To the authentic teaching authority of the Roman pontiff, even when he is not speaking *ex cathedra,* religious allegiance of will and intellect should be given; this should be done in such a way that his supreme teaching authority is respectfully acknowledged, while the judgment given by him is sincerely adhered to according to his manifest intention and desire, as this is made known by the nature of the documents, by his frequent repetition of the same judgment, or by his way of speaking. The intention and desire of the Roman pontiffs is made manifest especially through those doctrinal acts that they address to the whole Church, such as certain Apostolic Constitutions or Encyclical Letters or their more solemn addresses; for these are the principal documents of the ordinary teaching authority of the Church; they are the principal ways in which it is declared and formed, and what is taught and inculcated in them often already belongs, for other reasons, to Catholic doctrine. And when the Roman pontiffs go out of their way to pronounce on some subject which has hitherto been controverted, it must be clear to everyone that, in the mind and intention of those pontiffs, this subject can no longer be regarded as a matter for free debate among theologians.[58]

In support of the general obligation of assent, the text referred to the First Vatican Council, Pius XI's *Casti Connubii,* the Code of Canon Law and Leo XIII's *Sapientiae Christianae.*[59] A second footnote identified the last lines of the passage as a direct citation from Pius XII's *Humani Generis.*[60]

The first *schema* on the Church was rejected by the Council at the first session. Between the first and second sessions a second *schema* was elaborated which was presented to the second session and accepted as a basis for discussion. In the second *schema,* the paragraph on the teaching office of the Church (no. 19) was entitled, *"De Episcoporum munere docendi"* (*On the Teaching Role of Bishops*), and formed part of the new chapter III, *"De Constitutione Hierarchica Ecclesiae et in specie de Episcopatu" (On the Hierarchical Constitution of the Church and on the Episcopate in Particular).* The section on the ordinary magisterium of the people is the last part of paragraph 19 and is, except for very minor differences, the same text cited above from *Lumen Gentium.*[61] In the second *schema* the explanation of the concrete mode of exercise of the magisterium and the warning against continued public theological discussion are both omitted. Apparently the warning was not dropped without opposition, for among the suggested *emendationes* distributed along with the second *schema* was that of five bishops who ask that the statement from *Humani Generis* be replaced in the text.[62] This suggestion was not accepted, nor was that of Bishop Cleary, who proposed that the text include a statement about freedom of investigation.[63]

The concluding stage in the history of paragraph 25 of *Lumen Gentium* was the presentation and acceptance of the revised second schema at the third session. Very slight changes were made in the text of the section on the ordinary magisterium of the pope (paragraph 25); but its position in the paragraph was changed, so that, as it was explained, "it might be clearer that the discussion of the teaching office of the Roman Pontiff was being carried on *in the context of the teaching office of the entire college of bishops,* which is the subject of this paragraph."[64]

These *modi* (proposed emendations) for paragraph 25 were presented to the Doctrinal Commission. The *modi* and the answers they received are important for our purpose:

Modus 159 was the suggestion of three bishops who "invoke the particular case, at least theoretically possible, in which an educated person (*eruditus quidam*), confronted with a teaching proposed noninfallibly, cannot, for solid reasons, give his *internal* assent." The response of the Commission was: "For this case *approved theological explanations* should be consulted."[65]

Modus 160 was the proposal of three bishops that the text read, in respect of the pope: "and that the judgments given by him are sincerely adhered to, *although not with an absolute and irreformable assent.*" The reason for the addition was to make clear the distinction between the response owed to the infallible magisterium and that owed to the authoritative but noninfallible magisterium.[66] The reply of the Commission was: "The ordinary teaching office often proposes doctrines which already belong to the Catholic faith itself; so that the proposed addition would itself have to be completed. Therefore, it is better to refer to the *approved authors.*"[67]

Finally, *modus* 161 was the proposal of one bishop that an addition be made indicating the freedom to be permitted for further investigation and for doctrinal progress. The reply of the Commission was: "The observation is true, but does not need to be brought in at this point."[68]

These three *modi* and the reasons given by the doctrinal commission for their rejection indicate that paragraph 25 of the *Dogmatic Constitution on the Church* should be read in the light of the presentation of the ordinary magisterium given by the *auctores probati* (approved authors). An examination and reinterpretation of the "approved authors," especially the standard manualists, will show the scope of the "right to dissent" which is affirmed in the "legislative history" of paragraph 25 of *The Dogmatic Constitution on the Church.*

Awareness of the Developing Theological Reinterpretation of the Exercise of Right to Dissent

Emanations from Vatican II and Post-Vatican II Ecclesiology. The ecclesial self-understanding of Vatican II and the postconciliar Church requires, as has been noted, a reinterpretation of the "right of dissent" taught by the older "manualist" authors. The "manual" tradition, which taught the possiblity of "dissent" from teachings of the authoritative, noninfallible hierarchical magisterium, was operating in an ecclesiological framework that was heavily hierarchical and markedly juridical in tone and content. Nevertheless, in spite of these ecclesiological weaknesses which have since been largely corrected, these respected and tested works arrived at an appreciation of the possibility and, in some circumstances, necessity of responsible and proper dissent. The

Catholic scholar in July of 1968 would recognize that this traditionally recognized interpretive possibility known as dissent, if it were to be exercised contemporarily, must be exercised according to the demands of the contemporary ecclesiological context, not limited by specifications laid down within an ecclesiological era long since surpassed. The American Bishops, in their Pastoral Letter of November 15, 1968, clearly recognized that we are in a new era. After noting that there exist norms of licit dissent, they affirm that: "Since our age is characterized by popular interest in theological debate and given the realities of modern mass media, the ways in which theological dissent may be effectively expressed in a manner consistent with pastoral solicitude should become the object of fruitful dialogue between bishops and theologians."[69]

Even before the issuance of *Humane Vitae* Catholic theologians were aware of developing reinterpretations of the "right to dissent" as proposed in the manuals, which was obviously based on the newly developing theological contexts. Thus, the possibility of public dissent was accepted by some of the more contemporary Catholic theologians writing explicitly on the question. For example, S. E. Donlon maintained that where "there is still room for modification of the Church's position, voiced dissent would not involve a denial of the Church's right; nevertheless, the one invoking freedom should realize that the Church will generally regard the traditional viewpoint as enjoying a strong presumption of truth, and that a personal concern for the faithful will urge the Church to exact from the one claiming freedom patience, sobriety in expression of a newer viewpoint, and circumspection in propounding his views."[70]

Bruno Schueller, S.J., clearly perceived the needed contemporary reinterpretation:

> An interesting example of emphasis is found in a monograph called *When the Popes Speak* by F. Gallati (F. Gallati, *Wenn die Paepste Sprechen,* Vienna: 1960). He talks of when one is "allowed" to withdraw one's submission to a judgment of the authentic magisterium, thereby inferring that one *need* not! Yet the conditions he gives involve "clear and convincing" grounds for thinking that the magisterium

is in error. Such grounds should make withdrawal of submission strictly *obligatory!* Further on, Gallati takes as self-evident that, even in such a case, one may not *publicly dispute* the judgment. Actually, there would seem to be an obligation to correct the error, unless a greater evil would ensue. Hitherto the faithful's loss of confidence in the authentic magisterium would have seemed to most a greater evil—but what of the case where a mistaken decision causes widespread and agonizing conflict of conscience, and puts on many burdens beyond their strength to bear? Would not a delay in retracting such a decision work against the credibility of the magisterium in the long run? And so against the Church of which the magisterium is part?

Finally, if the faithful were educated as to the significance of the distinction between infallible and merely authentic magisterium, then the danger of their losing confidence in the Church's teaching would be greatly reduced.[71]

Karl Rahner discussed public dissent in the context of an article on demoncracy in the Church:

This does not mean, however, that there can be no serious theological differences of opinion in the Church, nor that the case would, from the outset and in principle, be excluded, in which a Christian appealing to his conscience, refuses obedience to a —well-intended to be sure— particular command of one who holds an office in the Church, the reason being that this Christian despite the "good faith" of the office-holder, has to judge this command to be incompatible with justice or love. We must become accustomed to such dissonances in the Church. We must learn to understand that tensions do not have to destroy the unity of confession, the will to obedience and love. Both sides must become accustomed to this: The official leadership, which must not think that in the Church calm or silence is the first and last "civic duty"; the laity, who must not think that, because of the fundamental possibility of theological differences of opinion and because of the possibility of withholding obedience in a particular case, an arbitrary stance in theological matters and a fundamental revolutionary hostility toward the official leadership are the ideal attitudes.[72]

Within the last decade there has also been a somewhat publicized debate even in the more popular press about the obedience required of Catholics to the pronouncements of the noninfallible hierarchical magisterium, particularly in the form of encyclicals. The occasion for the debate was the Encyclical of Pope John XXIII, *Mater et Magistra,* issued in 1961. This controversy began with a number of editorials in the *National Review* (beginning in the July 29, 1961 issue) and with the inclusion of the now famous *"Mater, si; Magistra, no"* in the collection of miscellaneous items under the heading "For the Record" in the July 29, 1961 issue of the same publication. The controversy continued for more than a year in such other popular Catholic publications as *America* and *Ave Maria.*

In 1964, Professor Gary Wills published *Politics and Catholic Freedom,* which reviewed the controversy over *Mater et Magistra* and considered in a popular manner the question of individual conscience and the assent due to the noninfallible papal teaching, especially in the form of encyclicals.[73] The very first words in this volume, from the Foreword by Professor Will Herberg, are most interesting in light of subsequent events:

> The encyclical *Mater et Magistra,* issued by Pope John XXIII in 1961, captivated world opinion by the breadth and generosity of its appeal. It also raised some questions, and initiated a controversy, that, in the long run, may prove as significant as the substantive content of the message. The questions raised related to the nature and extent of the assent required of believing Catholics to a Papal encyclical and its various parts. The controversy over these questions flared up for a brief moment, and then appears to have subsided. But the appearance is surely deceptive. . . .[74]

Post-Vatican II ecclesiology contemporizes the classic "right to dissent" in a dialogic context. There is, first of all, the very experience of the Council. The conciliar documents did not descend full-grown from above but were arrived at only after long and sometimes bitter debate. If we believe the Spirit to have presided over Vatican II, it remains true that the Spirit guided its course precisely through the human dialectic of disagreement, discussion and compromise. Nor was this dialectic a closed debate among members of "the teaching Church"; it involved consultation with theologians, with the non-Catholic observers present, and even, through the press, with the non-Christian world. Whatever progress was made at the Council was in varying measures due to all these factors; it would be presumptuous to restrict the working of the Spirit to any single one of them.

Secondly, there is the perspective in which Vatican II discussed the infallibility of the Church. The *Dogmatic Constitution on the Church* deliberately refrained from speaking of the infallibility of the Church *in credendo* (in believing) as a "passive" thing, deriving from the "active" infallibility of the magisterium as an effect from a cause.[75] The Council Fathers did indeed speak of the Church's "faithful obedience" to "the guidance of the sacred teaching authority," but they did so in a context in which it had also been explained to them that respected post-Tridentine theologians saw no danger to the hierarchy in arguing "from the faithful to the hierarchy," or from infallibility *in credendo* to infallibility *in docendo* (in teaching).[76]

Along the same lines, the Council insisted (in the *Dogmatic Constitution on the Church*) on the freedom and responsibility of the laity to make known to Church authorities their needs, desires and opinions.[77] In the *Pastoral Constitution on the Church in the Modern World,* the Council referred to that assertion in the *Dogmatic Constitution on the Church* to indicate that "all the faithful, clerical and lay, possess a lawful freedom of inquiry and of thought, and the freedom to express their minds humbly and courageously about those matters in which they enjoy competence."[79] Such comments are not without connection with conciliar statements on charisms in the Church.[80]

In such statements the Council may be considered to be thematizing its own experience. Another indication to the same effect can be found in the Council's acknowledgment that the forces leading towards the growth of the Church's understanding of itself and of its mission and message proceed not only from within the Roman Catholic Church. God's grace and truth also exist outside the Roman Catholic community in non-Catholic Christians and their communities,[81] in non-Christian religions[82] and in the world.[83] From dialogue with non-Catholics, the Church grows in its self-knowledge and self-criticism.[84] With the world and aided by it, the Church, which does not have solutions to all men's problems, commits itself to search for them.[85] From the world which she helps, the Church has, in her turn, derived abundant and various helps in preparing the way for the Gospel[86] and even in her presentation of the knowledge of God.[87]

The Second Vatican Council, while restating the place and role of the teaching office in the Church, at the same time recognized and emphasized the activity of the Spirit in many and differing ways in the Church and in the world. It is from all these workings of the Spirit that the Church grows in its understanding and accomplishment of its mission, and it may be suggested that by all these workings the Spirit might operate for the correction of mistaken teachings.

Dissent as Interpretation in the Contemporary Theological Context. When transposed to the contemporary theological context, therefore, the traditional "right to dissent" is but an aspect of the wider and deeper question of theological interpretation or hermeneutic. It is merely one way to assure the genuine development of doctrine and to assure that doctrinal vocabulary does not lose its underlying truth-value (as involved with *mystery*). Such would happen whenever doctinal formulae become overly clear and distinct and overly literalized or are frozen in an older thought pattern and language structure (the constant temptation of an age with little or no historical sense).

The theologian's task of interpretation and his responsibility to assure genuine development, at times, in the history of theology, have put him in a very uncomfortable position. It is regrettable but understandable that the major theologians who are recognized as the most fruitful reinterpreters of Catholic tradition were often distrusted in their own age by those entrapped in another conceptual framework and thereby unable to appreciate the possibilites of development within their own tradition. The experiences of such now revered figures as Lagrange, Congar, de Lubac and Teilhard de Chardin are recent examples of this problem. In former ages the episcopal condemnations of St. Thomas

Aquinas and the persisting suspicion surrounding the theological career of Cardinal Newman are ample indications of this difficulty.

Within the pluralism of interpretive possibilities within the Roman Catholic theological tradition, the only positions which may be considered theologically responsible are those which, whether they seem "conservative" or "liberal," reject any extrinsicist interpretation of the relationship of the theologian to his tradition by recalling always both the reality of tradition and its need for theological interpretation and by developing adequate theological interpretive tools for that task. What was classically understood as "dissent" may properly be understood only in the wider context of the interpretation task of the theologian, as it was affirmed in the "approved authors" and in Vatican II, and as it has achieved a yet deeper recognition and expression in the developmental context of genuinely Catholic theology.[88]

The nature of contemporary theology is intimately related to the pastoral concern of the Church and cannot be scientifically separated from it. The classical distinction between speculative and practical intellect is no longer adequate to the study of the constitutive meaning-possibilities of the contemporary context. Part of the significant data which the contemporary theologian must investigate is the contemporary situation itself. He must become more familiar than his classical counterpart with the seemingly external cultural factors, especially those transforming-meaning factors, concerning his discipline. Moreover, the theologian must himself be involved in the attempt to thematize those transforming possibilities; he cannot ignore the "existential" (practical, pastoral) consequences of his work without violating his co-responsibility to the community-church which sustains him, gives him his meaning and rightfully expects him to find ways to mediate the meaning he has discovered for critical evaluation and "existential" aid. Indeed, the theologian's relationship to his faith-community and the demands put upon him to dramatize the constitutive meanings of the Christian vis-à-vis contemporary culture in turn require of him responsible speech to those concrete ("pastoral," "existential," "practical") situations wherein his competence lies; the gravity of a particular situation may impel him to speak.

Given the recognized "right to dissent," reinterpreted more accurately to signify the right to interpret the traditional data in a different manner with respect to authoritative noninfallible pronouncements of the Roman Catholic tradition, the demands put upon the theologian to speak as theologian ("conscious of his duties and his limitations") with respect to a concrete situation where his competence is clear will fall under the general rubric of his duties as an academician committed to interpreting the Roman Catholic tradition by the best scientific methods of his day. He cannot responsibly withdraw himself from the life of the very church-community which he serves.

Ecclesiological Framework of the Exercise of the Interpretive Theological Function in the Instance of Humanae Vitae

Ecclesiology Implied and Methodology Used by Paul VI in the Writing and Promulgation of Humanae Vitae. The Catholic scholars of the sacred sciences who subscribed to the statement had a duty to interpret the Encyclical.[89] An examination and evaluation of the "ecclesiology implied and methodology used by Paul VI in the writing and promulgation of the document"[90] was undertaken, with constant reference to the presently developed state of ecclesiological science and ecclesial self-awareness. Sufficient serious reasons appeared to these scholars to "take exception" to the ecclesiology implied and the methodology used by the Pope in this act of magisterium.

From an ecclesiological viewpoint alone, the issuance of *Humanae Vitae* suggested a preconciliar style of exercise of papal authority. The ecclesiological presuppositions of the Encylical are a controlling influence on the theological methodology and argumentation employed. The ecclesiology of *Humanae Vitae* tends to be decisively hierarchical and does not evidence warranted appreciation of the *magisterial* significance of separated ecclesial communities and of the many Catholic spouses whose experience has led them to other conscientious conclusions. The Encyclical's rejection of solutions to the contraception question "which departed from the moral teaching on marriage proposed with constant firmness by the teaching authority of the Church,"[91] seems to reflect on the witness of spouses, theologians, scientists, doctors and members of the papal birth control commission, particularly in its assertion that "men of good will" must come to accept the conclusions of the Encyclical. It appeared that Pope Paul treated the witness of previous popes as exclusively decisive. This is particularly indicated by the footnote citations. Aside from the quotations from Scripture (none of which are apposite to the contraception issue), there are 33 references to popes, 14 to Vatican Council II, 3 to the Catechism of the Council of Trent and one to the Code of Canon Law. Only one reference is made to only one theologian, St. Thomas Aquinas. *Lumen Gentium, Gaudium et Spes* and the *Decree on Ecumenism* of Vatican II articulate an ecclesiological atmosphere that differs basically from the rather hierarchological character of *Humanae Vitae*.

The Encyclical's usage of the term "the Church" suggests that the Church is considered equivalent to the hierarchy and, occasionally, to the pope.[92] There is also a tendency to equate the magisterium with the papal office: "That commission . . . had as its scope the gathering of opinions on the new questions regarding conjugal life . . . so that the magisterium could give an adequate reply to the expectation not only of the faithful, but also of world opinion."[93] Near the end of the Encyclical, the Pope asks for acceptance of his teaching because the Spirit of God "assists the magisterium in proposing doctrine. . . ."[94]

Vatican II urged that Christian morality be in greater dialogue with the findings of "the secular sciences."[95] The mood of this exhortation was one of dialogue and openness to the moral significance of the sciences. *Humanae Vitae* approaches scientists less in a framework of dialogue than in a directive and instructive mood.[96]

Such ecclesiological considerations and their methodological implications alone would engender caution and reserve in evaluating any specific ethical teaching issuing therefrom. Ecclesiology and theological methodology are necessary and intrinsic to the proper understanding and evaluation of the question of "dissent" from the specific ethical teaching of *Humanae Vitae* on the absolute prohibition of the use of artificial contraception.

Some Ecclesiological Implications of a Critical Interpretation of Humanae Vitae. If Humanae Vitae does not *require* assent, is there any teaching of the ordinary papal magisterium which must be considered as *requiring* assent? A serious equivocation and a dangerously simplistic mentality may be implied by such a question. The "required" assent to an authoritative, noninfallible papal teaching is not taught in the Church to be unconditional or unqualified; it should never be equated with the assent of *divine faith* properly so-called, nor even with the assent given to solemn and infallible definitions of other matters not directly of *divine faith*. In fact, the assent "required" by the very nature of *Humanae Vitae* was, or should have been, known as a matter of condition or qualification regarding a teaching that is *presumptively,* but only presumptively, true. In the final analysis the presumption can be weakened or effectively rebutted by serious reasons to the contrary.

Assent to *Humanae Vitae* can be suspended only because serious, personally convincing reasons lead a person to believe that the general presumption is not verified in the instance. Furthermore, depending on the weight of authority operative in each case, any other authoritative teaching of the magisterium also requires assent and can be dissented from only for reasons that are similarly sound and convincing. This analysis asserts nothing that is not implicit in the recognition that such teaching is fallible. If it is fallible, it may be mistaken. If it may be mistaken, absolute unqualified assent need not be given. If it is mistaken, it has no claim on assent. If a person is convinced that it is mistaken, then he may, indeed he must, suspend assent to it. This is the teaching of the manuals and the teaching presupposed by

Lumen Gentium and implicitly referred to in *Humanae Vitae* itself.[97] It does not undermine papal teaching authority to maintain that in one or another, even in one very serious case, it has been wrong. The authors of the manuals considered that very possibility without suspecting that they were thereby undermining the papal teaching office.

If the Encyclical is possibly wrong about contraception, then it is possible that for many centuries the Church has been giving incorrect moral guidance. Some theologians will believe it impossible for the Spirit to let the Church fall that seriously into error. It is risky, however, to try to predict how much of evil (whether the evil of sin or the evil of error) God might permit to creep into the Church.[98] There are cases in which the hierarchical magisterium has been wrong in the past (some indicated in the Statement), and there are no a priori grounds on which it can be demonstrated that it could not be wrong again. The reformable teaching of *Humanae Vitae* requires assent only to the extent that it is objectively true; thus, although one may be required to obey a *law* that one may believe to be incorrect, no one can be required to assent to a *teaching* he believes to be incorrect. The possibility cannot be excluded a priori that the Spirit may make his will known independently of the pope; it cannot be demonstrated a priori that it is not the Spirit who is leading individuals to dissent in this case; and therefore it cannot be excluded a priori that the Spirit may be using such dissent to correct more quickly than would otherwise be possible a teaching that is, as all agree, at least reformable and possibly incorrect.

These ecclesiological implications of a critical interpretation of *Humanae Vitae* are consistent with the self-understanding of a "pilgrim" church which is in constant process of renewal and reform, and just as they are consistent with the implications of the teaching of Vatican II itself, they are antecedently provided for by long-term and conventional ecclesiological science.

Clearly, the ecclesiological context out of which the Statement of Theologians of July 30, 1968 and related events arose is an essential and intrinsic consideration in any judgment of responsible theological activity. A sense of the modern historical development of the Church's self-awareness and of the silence of ecclesiology, from the counterreform era to the present post-Vatican II period, sets a general context within which the contemporary Catholic theologian views his task of interpretation and reinterpretation. Specifically, he knows that "dissent" from non-infallible teachings of the hierarchical magisterium is, and has always been, nothing more than one of many interpretive options open to him when sufficient reasons exist to exercise this right. Finally, the contemporary Catholic theologian is intensely aware of the veritable ecclesiological imperatives operative today whenever he is called upon by his very role in the Church to function in a particular instance.

Notes

1. Cf. K. McNamara, "From Moehler to Vatican II: The Modern Movement of Ecclesiology," in K. McNamara, ed., *Vatican II: The Constitution on the Church, a Theological and Pastoral Commentary* (Chicago: Franciscan Herald, 1968), pp. 9–35.
2. Cf. P. Fannon, S.M.M., "The Council and The Bible: The Church," *The Clergy Review,* New Series, 48 (1963), pp. 696–708.
3. Cf. *Ibid.*
4. Cf. P. Fransen, "The Theological Implication of the Discussions of the Liturgy at The Second Vatican Council," *The Scottish Journal of Theology,* 16 (1963), pp. 5–6.
5. Cf. J. Hamer, "The Meaning and Implications of the Encyclical 'Mystici Corporis,'" in *The Church is a Communion* (New York: Sheed & Ward, 1964), pp. 13–25.
6. For brief expansions of this matter, see K. McNamara, *art. cit.;* J. Hamer, *op. cit.;* and J. O. McGovern, *The Church in the Churches* (Washington: Corpus Books, 1967), pp. 19–38.
7. P. Fransen, *op. cit.,* pp. 5–6.
8. Cf. *Ibid.,* pp. 6–9.
9. For a précis on the *new* acquisitions of Vatican II, see E. Schillebeeckx, *The Real Achievement of Vatican II* (New York: Herder, 1967), pp. 27–43; 46–52. Schillebeeckx has noted that the "new" achievements of Vatican II possibly represent "how much has been officially

accepted of what may well have been alive among the faithful—theologians and others—long before the Council but could, at that time at least, neither appeal to the Church's teaching authority nor look to the hierarchy for support," p. 27.

10. G. Baum, "The Constitution on the Church," *Journal of Ecumenical Studies,* 2 (1965), pp. 1–19.
11. *Ibid.,* pp. 8–9.
12. See chapter two of the *Constitution on the Church;* Cf. G. Baum, op. cit.; E. Van Antwerp, "Collegiality in the Constitution on the Church," *Guide,* 199 (1965), pp. 7–14; L. Cardinal Seunens, *Co-responsibility in the Church* (New York: Herder, 1968), chap. one.
13. Cf. *Constitution on the Church* and apposite commentaries.
14. D. Worlock, "The Layman in the Church," *The Clergy Review,* 50 (1965), pp. 836–843.
15. K. McNamara, *art. cit.,* p. 35.
16. Cf. P. Chirico, "One Church: What Does It Mean?" *Theological Studies,* 28 (1967), pp. 659–682; C. Hay, "The Ecclesiological Significance of the Decree on Ecumenism," *Journal of Ecumenical Studies,* 3 (1966), pp. 343–353.
17. Cf. Vatican II documents and commentaries: *Decree on Ecumenism; Declaration on the Relationship of the Church to Non-Christian Religions; Pastoral Constitution on the Church in the Modern World.*
18. E. Schillebeeckx, "The Church as a Sacrament of Dialogue," in *God, the Future of Man* (New York: Sheed & Ward, 1968), pp. 117–40.
19. Cf. especially Vatican II, *Decree on Ecumenism,* paras. 4 and 6.
20. *Ibid.*
21. *Ibid.,* para. 6.
22. 54 *AAS* (1962), 792.
23. Cf. H. Ott, "The Reformed Theologian of Basel," in G. Barauna, ed., *La Chiesa del Vaticano II* (Florence: Vallechi, 1966), p. 1227.
24. Letter to International Theological Congress at Rome, September 21, 1966, *cf. L'Osservatore Romano, s.d.*
25. Cf. E. Schillebeeckx, *op. cit.;* L. Suenens, *op. cit.,* pp. 15 ff.
26. Suenens, *loc. cit.*
27. Cf. *e.g.,* H. Küng, *The Church* (New York: Sheed & Ward, 1968), as an example of a fresh postconciliar ecclesiology; also, R. Reuther, *The Church Against Itself* (New York: Herder, 1967).
28. J. C. Murray, "Freedom, Authority, Community," *IDO–C,* 67–1 (January 15, 1967); F. Klosterman, "Principles of a Structural Reform," *IDO–C,* 67–23 (July 16, 1967).
29. Cf., E. Kaesemann, "Unity and Diversity in New Testament Ecclesiology," *Novum Testamentum,* 6 (1963), 290–97; J. Ratzinger, "Office and Unity of the Church," *Journal of Ecumenical Studies,*

I (1964), pp. 42–57; H. Küng, *op cit.*, pp. 388–413, 428–29, 456–65; M. Bourke, "Reflections on Church Order in the New Testament," *Catholic Biblical Quarterly*, 30 (1968), pp. 493–511; R. Schnackenburg, *Church in the New Testament* (New York: Herder, 1965), pp. 22–35, 74–77, 94–102, 126–132.

30. H. Küng, "The Charismatic Structure of the Church," *Guide*, 227 (1968), pp. 7–11; K. Rahner, "Dynamic Element in the Church," *Quaestiones Disputatae*, 12 (New York: Herder, 1964); W. Koupal, "Charism: a Relational Concept," *Worship*, 42 (1968), pp. 539–45.
31. Cf. J. L. McKenzie, "Reflections on the Church's Teaching Authority," *Catholic World*, 203 (1966), pp. 86–90; *Ibid.*, *Authority in the Church* (New York: Sheed & Ward, 1966); J. C. Murray, "Freedom, Authority, Community," *IDO–C*, 67–1 (January 15, 1967).
32. R. Murray, "Collegiality, Infallibility and Sobernost," *One in Christ*, I (1965), p. 21.
33. G. Baum, "The Magisterium in a Changing Church," in *Concilium*, vol. I, n. 3 (January 1967), (London: Burns and Oates), pp. 34–42.
34. G. Baum, "The Christian Adventure—Risk and Renewal," *The Critic*, 23 (April-May 1965), pp. 41–53.
35. E. Kaesemann and R. Brown, "New Testament Ecclesiology," *Theology Digest*, 13 (1965), pp. 228–233.
36. J. T. Noonan, Jr., "Authority, Usury, and Contraception," *Cross Currents*, 16 (1966), pp. 55–79.
37. P. Fransen, "The Authority of the Councils," in *Problems of Authority*, ed., John M. Todd (Baltimore: Helicon, 1963), pp. 43–78.
38. Q. Quade and J. Rhodes, "What Can the Church Demand?" *The Catholic World* (December 1966), pp. 162–169.
39. G. Dejaifve, "Infallibility and Consent of the Church," *Theology Digest*, 12 (1964), pp. 8–13.
40. J. C. Bennett, "A Protestant View of Authority in the Church," *Theology Digest*, 11 (1963), pp. 209–219.
41. Y. Congar, "The Historical Development of Authority in the Church: Points for Christian Reflection," in J. M. Todd ed., *Problems of Authority* (Baltimore: Helicon, 1962), pp. 119–156.
42. American Bishops' Pastoral Statement, *Human Life in Our Day* (November, 1968), Washington: U.S.C.C.
43. *Statement by Catholic Theologians* of July 30, 1968, para. 1.
44. R. A. MacKenzie, "The Function of Scholars in Forming the Judgment of the Church," in L. K. Shook, ed., *Theology of Renewal*, Vol. II (New York: Herder, 1968), pp. 118–132.
45. Paul VI, Address to the International Congress on the Theology of Vatican II, *The Pope Speaks*, 11 (1966), pp. 351–352.
46. *Statement*, para. 1. Cf. *supra*, chapter 3, *passim*.

47. Cf. e.g., Trustee (Cardinal) McIntyre's motion in the special session of the Board, September 5, 1968, and the curious post-Inquiry writings of Trustee (Archbishop) Dwyer writing in *Twin Circle,* May 18 and May 25, 1969.
48. Denz., 3016 ff.
49. The words of the First Vatican Council, *ibid.*
50. Cf. Denz., 3008.
51. Cf. Denz. 3011.
52. *Codex Iuris Canonici,* n. 1323.
53. *AAS,* Vol. LIX, p. 1058; emphasis added.
54. Cf. immediately *infra.* Note that in this section the exposition of the faith and especially of infallibility follows the teaching generally proposed in the manuals. The subject professors are aware of the contemporary discussion about infallibility, but that discussion stands beyond the scope of this section which merely intends to show that neither the Roman Catholic faith-commitment itself, nor the juridic formula of the *Profession of Faith* is violated from authoritative, noninfallible papal teaching.
55. Vatican II, *Constitution on the Church,* para. 25.
56. *Humanae Vitae,* para. 28.
57. Here the subject professors again acknowledge their indebtedness to Professors Joseph Komonchak and Harry McSoley for their valuable research into the Acts of Vatican II. Cf. J. A. Komonchak, "Ordinary Papal Magisterium and Religious Assent," in C. E. Curran, ed., *Contraception: Authority and Dissent* (New York: Herder, 1969), pp. 101–126.
58. *Schemata Constitutionum et Decretorum de quibus disceptabitur in Concilii sessionibus: Series Secunda, De Ecclesia et de B. Maria Virgine* (Vatican Press, 1962), pp. 48–49.
59. *Ibid.,* p. 57.
60. *Ibid.*
61. *Schema Constitutionis Dogmaticae De Ecclesia:* Pars I (Vatican Press, 1963), p. 30.
62. *Emendationes a Concilii Patribus scripto exhibitae Constitutionis Dogmaticae De Ecclesia,* Pars I (Vatican Press, 1963), pp. 43–44.
63. *Ibid.*
64. *Schema Constitutionis De Ecclesia* (Vatican Press, 1964), p. 96; (italics in the original text here and elsewhere unless otherwise indicated).
65. *Schema Constitutionis Dogmaticae De Ecclesia: Modi a Patribus conciliaribus propositi a commissione doctrinali examinati, III: De constitutione hierarchica Ecclesiae et in specie de Episcopatu* (Vatican Press, 1964), p. 42.

66. *Ibid.*, p. 42.
67. *Ibid.*
68. *Ibid.*
69. *Human Life in Our Day* (November, 1968), Washington: U.S.C.C., p. 18.
70. S. Donlon, S.J., "Freedom of Speech," *The New Catholic Encyclopedia*, Vol. 6, p. 123.
71. B. Schueller, S.J., "Remarks on the Authentic Pronouncements of the Magisterium," 16 *Theology Digest* 330–31 (Winter 1968). This article is a précis of "Bemerkunger zut authentischen Verkundigung des kirchlichen Lehramtes," 42 *Theologie und Philosophie* 534 (1967).
72. K. Rahner, "Demokratie in der Kirche," 182 *Stimmen der Zeit* (July 1968), pp. 1–15.
73. G. Wills, *Politics and Catholic Freedom* (Chicago: Henry Regnery Co., 1964).
74. *Ibid.*, p. ix.
75. *Schema Constitutionis De Ecclesia* (Vatican Press, 1964), p. 46.
76. *Ibid.*
77. Vatican II, *Constitution on the Church*, para. 37.
78. Vatican II, *Pastoral Constitution on the Church in the Modern World*, para. 62.
79. Cf. the use of this text in the first draft of the doctrinal report of the Synod of Bishops: "As far as doctrine is concerned, we must distinguish between truths infallibly defined by the magisterium of the Church and those which are authentically proposed but without the intention of defining. While preserving that (*sic*) obedience to the magisterium, 'the just freedom of research for faithful aid clerics, as also freedom of thought and of expressing their opinion with courage and humility in those matters in which they are competent.' . . ." P. Hebblewaithe, *Inside the Synod: Rome, 1967* (New York: Paulist Press, 1968), pp. 132–33.
80. Vatican II, *Constitution on the Church*, para. 12.
81. Vatican II, *Decree on Ecumenism*, paras. 3, 20, 21; *Constitution on the Church*, paras. 8, 15, 16; *Pastoral Constitution on the Church in the Modern World*, para. 40.
82. Vatican II, *Declaration on the Relations of the Church to Non-Christian Religions*, paras. 1–2.
83. Vatican II, *Pastoral Constitution on the Church in the Modern World*, paras. 22, 26, 34, 36, 38.
84. Vatican II, *Decree on Ecumenism*, paras. 4, 9.
85. Vatican II, *Pastoral Constitution on the Church in the Modern World*, paras. 10, 11, 33.
86. *Ibid.*, nn. 40, 44, 57.

87. *Ibid.*, n. 62.
88. Especially as expressed by E. Schillebeeckx, "Toward a Catholic Use of Hermeneutic," in *God, the Future of Man* (New York: Sheed & Ward, 1968), pp. 1–49.
89. Cf. *supra,* Chapter 2, on the nature and function of theology and theologians.
90. *Statement,* para. 3.
91. *Humanae Vitae,* para. 6.
92. Cf. *Humanae Vitae,* para. 4 with note 4; para. 6; para. 11 with note 12; para. 14 with note 15; para. 15 with note 19; paras. 16, 17, 18, 20, 25 and 28.
93. *Humanae Vitae,* para. 5; cf. note 5 which refers to the papal allocution of June 23, 1964 in which Paul VI promised a decision on the birth control question.
94. *Humanae Vitae,* para. 29.
95. Vatican II, *Pastoral Constitution on the Church in the Modern World,* para. 62.
96. *Humanae Vitae,* para. 24.
97. It should be recalled that a prohibition of further public discussion after a papal pronouncement included in the first draft of the *Schema de Ecclesia* at Vatican II, was dropped in the second *Schema;* cf. supra, pp. II–34 and III–27 to 30.
98. Cf. J. Cameron's criticism of Charles Davis for failing to place ecclesiastical failure and sin against the larger background of the enormous evils that exist in the world but do not shake our belief in God's existence or providence, *New Blackfriars,* 49 (1968), p. 333.

5

Public Dissent in and for the Church

In chapter two, theologians representative of the manualist tradition were cited as clearly teaching the possibility of dissent from authoritative noninfallible teachings of the hierarchical magisterium. One or another of them imply that this "possibility" may become an obligation for someone who perceives such cogent contrary reasons that to maintain assent would be a perversion of his rational faculties. On the question of *public* dissent or disagreement, however, most of the manualists maintained that one who suspends his internal assent still must keep a *silentium obsequiosum* and present his difficulties privately to the hierarchical authority itself. It has already been noted that some contemporary Catholic theologians, such as Schueller, K. Rahner and Donlon, writing before the issuance of *Humane Vitae,* explicitly recognized the limited horizon of the manualists' restrictions and openly taught that *public* dissent might well be called for in some instances.

In the teaching of the manualists there are, nonetheless, elements which definitely argue for a futher development of the question; in fact, a contemporary rationale for "external" dissent seems quite continuous with some of the underlying principles and values which can be gleaned from the manualists themselves.

For example, all the manualists agree that noninfallible teaching calls for a *conditional* assent, not an absolute and irrevocable one, since the ultimate possibility of error is inherent in the very nature of fallible teachings. The pope, they acknowledged, might feel it helpful to the Church to "permit" public discussion to confirm the truth of a teaching, or to prepare the way for an infallible statement. At least one manualist saw several potential results from continued inquiry: acceptance of a teaching by the whole Church, or possible detection of error! Further discussion and inquiry, then, could either confirm the truth or discover a mistake. But in either case, the Church would be served.

The fact that many of the manualists do not allow for public dissent cannot be taken, therefore, as an *absolute* norm always obliging in all conceivable circumstances. The controlling value in all cases appears to be the good of the Church. Service of the Church is the enduring value which pervaded the manualist tradition on this point, and should constitute the dominant concern of every approach to the contemporary question of public manifestation of dissent in the Church; dissent *in* the Church must always be dissent *for* the Church.

It is well to recall here also that the question of dissent in the manualist tradition is properly cast in the category of the interpretive function of the theologian. Theological dissent is itself a part of the theological tradition which must constantly be reinterpreted! The following considerations, in addition to those in chapter four, attempt to summarize some of the more pertinent elements which bear upon such work of reinterpretation, both in theory and in the everyday reality of the life of the Church. In effect, they constitute truly ecclesiological presuppositions and implications of interpretive dissent from *Humanae Vitae.*

The Teaching of the Church on Information, Communication and the Use of Mass Media

Any discussion of responsible public expression today of a dissenting theological interpretation must take careful account of the Church's teaching on communications and the use of the mass media. Precisely because the extent and the power of the mass communications media is a relatively recent phenomenon, the attitude of the Church to these matters did not receive full expression until the twentieth century.

In *Mater et Magistra,* John XXIII characterized our epoch as one of "socialization" (*rationum incrementa socialium*), an age of "the growing interdependence of men in society giving rise to various patterns of group life and activity." John XXIII goes on to say:

> It is clear that many benefits and advantages flow from socialization thus understood. It makes possible, in fact, the satisfaction of many personal rights, especially those of a socio-economic nature. The right to the indispensable means of human subsistence, to health services, *to instruction at a higher level, to more thorough professional formation,* to housing, to employment, to suitable leisure and to decent recreation are typical examples. In addition, through increasing systematization of modern media of mass communications—press, motion pictures, radio, television—it becomes possible for *individuals to participate, as it were, in human events even on a world-wide scale.*[1]

The recognition of the complexities of modern life has led the Church to weigh the moral aspects involved. John XXIII's Encyclical, *Pacem in Terris,* recognizes that "by the natural law, every human being has the right to respect for his person, to his good reputation, *to freedom in searching for truth and—within the limits laid down by the moral order and the common good—in expressing and communicating his opinions,* and in pursuit of art. *He has the right, finally, to be informed truthfully about public events.*"[2]

The right to be truthfully informed, and also to search freely for the truth and express one's opinions, is clearly affirmed, and this right is taken up again in the *Decree on the Media of Social Communications* promulgated by Vatican Council II.[3] The conciliar fathers claim that the announcing of the good news of salvation is to be done also with the help of the media of social communications. The use of the media for such a purpose is indeed an "inherent right" of the Church, and "it is the duty of Pastors to instruct and guide the faithful so that they, with the help of these same media, may further the salvation and perfection of themselves and of the entire human family." The Decree recognizes the usefulness and the need of information in contemporary society, and it goes on to say:

Therefore, in society men have a *right to information,* in accord with the circumstances in each case, *about matters concerning individuals or the community*. The proper exercise of this right demands, however, that the news itself that is communicated should always be true and complete, within the bounds of justice and charity. In addition, the manner in which the news is communicated should be proper and decent. This means that in both the search for news and in reporting it, there must be full respect for the laws of morality and for the legitimate rights and dignity of the individual.[4]

Paragraph 11 of the document states that the "principal moral responsibility for the proper use of the media of social communications falls on newsmen, writers," and others of similar vocation. But at the same time it is recognized that *"all* must strive, through these media as well, to form and spread sound public opinion."[5]

Concretely, how are these principles to be worked out? The emphasis on the moral responsibility of newsmen is quite proper, but the education of these men in various fields of knowledge must also be assured. The ecclesiastical hierarchy has recognized this need at Vatican Council II, and at regional episcopal conferences, by establishing press panels for the instruction of reporters and writers.

Pope John XXIII was acutely aware of this need; in his address to the journalists covering the Council (October 13, 1962), recalling to his audience the fact that prejudices against the Church exist, he stated:

These prejudices rest most often on inaccurate or incomplete information. People attribute to the Church doctrines which she does not profess; they blame her for attitudes which she has taken in definite historical circumstances and which they unjustifiably generalize without taking into account their accidental and [contingent] character.[6]

Speaking to the members of the Catholic Press Association on May 17, 1968, Bishop James Shannon, in the same vein, asserted that "we have made secrecy into a way of life in the Catholic Church." He recognized that "we have a long way to go in the Catholic Church before we can convince ourselves that we have an obligation to share more and more information with all of the media of communication. . . . It has been a revelation to the general press to find out that we do have differences of opinion within the Catholic Church, that on a given matter which is not *de fide* there are heated discussions among the bishops, among the editors, and among official spokesmen for the Church."[7]

On the occasion of World Communications Day (May 4, 1967), the United States Bishops' Committee for Social Communications issued a statement that underlined man's right to information:

> Man's right to be informed is a natural, inherent right. It is given him by God himself. It is not a privilege conferred by any authority. . . . By the same token, this right to information places important demands upon both those who have a duty to inform as well as those who are the professional communicators. To be sure, the circumstances in each case demand a great deal of prudence, taking into consideration those twin pillars of the moral order, justice and charity. The right to information, however, we firmly believe must be stressed today because only a true and complete knowledge will enable society and man as an individual to stand secure in an age of intellectual and moral turmoil. Moreover, the corollary of the right to information is the right to full expression.[8]

The bishops observed that the Church opposed totalitarianism because of the dignity of man, and that one aspect of man's dignity is his freedom:

> History affords us many examples of the fact that freedom suffers the moment man's inherent right to information begins to be curtailed. Thus we reiterate this fundamental right, not only because it is necessary for the freedom that the Church expects from the State, and rightly so, but also because it is man's constant defense against the suppression of his own birthright of freedom.[9]

Indeed, in all quarters today it is recognized that public opinion is of vital importance in society. This is true also in the Church society, as was recognized by Pope Pius XII in his address to the Third International Congress of the Catholic Press on February

17, 1950. The Pope defined public opinion as "a natural echo, a more or less spontaneous common resounding of acts and circumstances in the mind and judgment of people who feel they are responsible beings, closely bound to the fate of their community." His words about public opinion "within the bosom of the Church" are particularly important:

> Finally we should like to add a word regarding public opinion within the bosom of the Church (naturally, with respect to matters left to free discussion). This consideration can surprise only those who do not know the Church or know her only poorly. Because the Church is a living body, something would be wanting in her life if public opinion were lacking—and the blame for this deficiency would fall back upon the pastors and the faithful.[10]

Cardinal Cushing developed this thought further in his pastoral letter of Good Shepherd Sunday, 1963, *The Church and Public Opinion,* when he wrote:[11]

> For us, public opinion may be described as the beliefs, attitudes and judgments held by members within the Church, and especially those views which are expressive of the usual working of the Spirit, making ever more manifest the divine truth within it. This will include an expression of views concerning those contemporary areas of life and action where the Church's teachings need to be applied more fully or with greater precision. A further element will also show itself in public opinion as a reaction to abuses which, through human frailty, may at any time be developing within the Church as an institution. Public opinion then is an existent and visible force within the Church which consists in the confluence of many individual opinions on those matters which touch upon the Christian life. The more mature the society and the more committed its members become to the implications of their faith, the more sure are we to have a living ferment of Christian thought among us.[12]

These hierarchical teachings in the Roman Catholic Church on the right to know, the duty to inform, the right to free self-expression, the role of public opinion and the use of communications media are clear and contemporary. They are also significant *ecclesiological* factors intrinsic to any adequate articulation of the nature of Church life, both within its own household and in relationship to the several communities with which the Church is in dialogue.

Responsibilities of Theologians in and for the Church: Communities to Which They Owe a Duty of Communication

The obligations and responsibility of the contemporary theologian are manifold. He has a responsibility to *truth* to make his interpretation known in such a manner that the truth may best be served. The theologian has an obligation to the *whole Church as the people of God,* who are constantly striving to "do the truth in love" (Eph. 4:15). Truth above all is respected in the Church. Such truth must not be sought in a way that would heedlessly destroy or lessen the fellowship of love uniting the members of the Church in the unity of the whole Christ. Scandal should be avoided as far as possible. However, the pilgrim Church will always know the tension of trying to do the truth in love; such tension can never be totally eliminated. Thus, prudent judgments will be required in each instance to determine the best way to search out and to communicate the truth to minimize the risk of harm which must be accepted.

The theologian has an obligation to *the pope and other bishops* of the Church in their hierarchical and magisterial role. The theologian has an obligation to supply to the hierarchical pastoral office in the Church the necessary theological data so that bishops can properly make pastoral judgments and doctrinal pronouncements.

The theologian has an obligation to his *fellow theologians* to express his views in such a manner that other theologians can appraise such views in their continual and communal searching for the truth.

The theologian has an obligation of interpretation to the *individuals directly touched* by the particular point in question. These are the people most in need of assistance, especially in terms they themselves can assimilate and understand. The Encyclical created a grave crisis for many people torn between their personal convictions on birth control and their loyalty to the Church. They had a right to know that the position that one may dissent from authoritative, noninfallible teaching without cutting himself off from the Church of God is a responsible, *Catholic* possibility.

The theologian has an obligation to the *priests* of the country who have been trained to look for theological opinions and judgments from theologians. Priests were quickly confronted with questions about the papal document and conscientiously wanted to respond to such requests, but they needed theological advice and direction to respond. This obligation of theologians to priests was especially incumbent upon the faculty of The Catholic University of America. The unique position of the University and its unique character give a special obligation and responsibility to those who are invited to teach on its faculty. Furthermore, as academicians, the subject professors would have an added obligation to inform their former students of continuing and important developments in their own fields of competency. The former students who have received their theological training at The Catholic University of America now reside in all parts of the country and abroad.

The theologian has an obligation to his *university community*. Psychology, sociology, biology and many other sciences are in dialogue with theology. In addition, the professional schools of law, nursing and social work frequently need and expect theological interpretations.

The theologian has an obligation to the *public communications media*. Recent popes have spoken eloquently about the obligation of the press to express the truth to its readers. The media expressed a great interest in the issue of birth control, and many stories were devoted to the Encyclical. Reporters, writers and editors generally lack the requisite theological competency to interpret theological statements and even fail to realize the existence of the accepted Catholic teaching allowing dissent from authoritative, noninfallible teachings under certain conditions. There was a great danger that through the press the issue would be so polarized that many people would feel a conflict between their personal conviction on birth control and their loyalty to the Roman Catholic Church. Only a properly informed press could fulfill its dignified mission and obligation to the truth. The theologian must provide this necessary background and interpretation for the press.

The theologian also has an obligation to *non-Catholics in general,* especially through his contacts with theologians and leaders in other churches. (Many of the subject professors, sometimes as official representatives of the Roman Catholic hierarchy in the United States, have been in ecumenical dialogue with non-Catholics with the express purpose of interpreting Catholic theology to them and searching together in dialogue for the truth.) At times such as those following the issuance of a long-awaited papal pronouncement, the need for such interpretation is even greater.

The theologian has an obligation to *all men of good will.* In Catholic theology itself a universalism, which was strong in the teachings and writings of Pope Pius XII, became even more explicit in the encyclicals of John XXIII, which were also addressed for the first time to "all men of good will." *Humanae Vitae* is likewise addressed by Paul VI to all men of good will. Thus all men of good will were also in need of the interpretation of the Encyclical. Likewise, Catholic theologians have the obligation to show the credibility of the Church to all mankind. This becomes more necessary in our own day when even some Catholics have attacked the credibility of the Church. This obligation to make the Church and the teachings of the Church more credible is the work of interpretation. However, dissent itself can also serve the credibility of the Church, especially among those who incorrectly understand the Church as an authoritarian institution denying true freedom and, in particular, freedom of discussion in theological matters.

They frequently fail to realize that the Church has traditionally allowed for such freedom of discussion by theologians in areas of noninfallible teaching.

The responsible theologian must be cognizant of all these diverse obligations which are incumbent upon him. To neglect any of these responsibilities would be irresponsible. The manifold responsibilities of the theologian to truth, to the whole Church, to the bishops, to fellow theologians, to the individuals directly involved, to priests generally, to his academic community, to the communications media, to non-Catholics and to all men of good will provide the constant factors with respect to which the theologian must evaluate his declarations and actions. The interpretive possibility of public dissent must be weighed with respect to all the foregoing factors in the light of prudence. Thus, the existing norm of public dissent consists not in a simple, verbal formula in the former manualist style but rather in the prudent balancing of the accepted values represented by each of the foregoing constant constituencies of the theologian.

In the contemporary ecclesiological context, therefore, theologians are conscious of their co-responsibility for the entire Church and their many different relationships with the other people of God. Contemporary ecclesiology is conscious of the different roles and functions in the Church which work together to build up the whole body of Christ. The hierarchical office and function, though necessary for the Church and of great importance, is not the only functioning role in the Church.

In the contemporary understanding of the modern age of communications, theologians realize that there are abundant and effective means available for the communication of theological interpretations. On other questions the subject professors themselves have often been asked to appear on radio and television programs and to grant interviews to the press. Requests for such communication of theological interpretations have come from the University itself and from official agencies of the United States Catholic Conference under the auspices of the American bishops.

Ecclesiology and the modern communications media have made both theologians and the magisterium aware of the function of public opinion in the Church. Pope Pius XII asserted the role of public opinion in the Church, even though at times an earlier generation rejected such a notion. Theologians, taking their lead from Pius XII, have developed the notion and place of such public opinion in the Church.

Also, as already noted, in the last few years, some theologians writing about the mode of dissent in the light of some of the developing theological context admit the possibility of *public* dissent.[13]

Thus the Roman Catholic theologian has a responsibility and an obligation to interpret the teachings of the Church even to the point of dissenting from "authoritative, noninfallible teachings of the magisterium when sufficient reasons for so doing exist."[14] Such dissent must be expressed in a responsible manner, which for the Roman Catholic means a way in which the good of the Church is ultimately helped and not hindered.

Public Nature and Practical Urgency of the Issue

The fact that *Humanae Vitae* concerns a matter that is not speculative and not practically indifferent such as, for example, subsistent relations in the Trinity, or the quality of Adam's original justice, but rather a matter of immediate and urgent practical consequence for millions of persons, both Catholic and non-Catholic, placed the subject matter, of its very nature, into the forum of public concern. It thus involves the "right to know," and the correlative "duty to inform," pertaining to a category of persons coextensive with the audience of the mass communication media. The class of persons vitally interested in *Humanae Vitae* is so vast that the ordinary channel of communication with such persons would be the mass communications media. Perhaps in recognition of the urgency of this question, theological interpretations approving the Encyclical's ethical conclusion have been made public to and through the mass communications media, beginning with Professor Lambruschini's press conference on July 29.

The possibility of mistake in papal teaching on this urgent matter, however, raises the question, in turn, of whether theological interpretation critical of the Encyclical should be communicated to the same public by the same means. Catholics believe eventually that the truth or error of the papal teaching will emerge. The process of confirmation or of correction could take a critically long time, however, if the necessary dialogue is conducted in private. Although the Church might not suffer if the process of *confirmation* of *Humanae Vitae* were to be prolonged, it would be most difficult to maintain that values protected by private discussion outweigh the harm that could be done to the Church if the process of *correction* were unduly prolonged, especially in this issue of immediate, urgent and practical consequence for the daily lives of millions of persons. If there is a *real possibility* of error, furthermore, the Church has nothing to fear from public discussion! If the teaching is correct, Catholics believe that the Spirit will confirm their teaching. If the teaching is incorrect, it can best be corrected if the freedom to consider the matter further is enjoyed by hierarchical magisterium and theologians alike.

Since collaboration and communication is a necessary part of the theological endeavor, the exercise of such freedom can hardly remain "private." No theological journal is so abstruse and no language so arcane as to prevent *immediate* (not merely *eventual*) publication of critical theological views of the Encyclical by the modern press, which was even able to obtain the *papal* statement days ahead of the official release. It is not certain that one can even speak of "private" theological discussion on such critical issues. In fact, the mass media began disseminating information throughout the world concerning *Humanae Vitae* and its content on July 27, two days before its official release to the public press at the Vatican, from an official English translation. The news media were not hesitant to give their own untrained "interpretations" of the normative significance of the Encyclical for Roman Catholics. These facts at least make clear that theological discussion, in these days of the pervasive presence of the press, cannot be confined quietly to the "speculative" pages of scholarly journals. The communications enterprises of today subscribe to such journals, and when an issue for speculative inquiry has dynamic effect on the lives of millions, the mass journals will be quick to expose and analyze significant scholarly opinion. Theologians must recognize this possibility if they are to prevent the scandal which may result from a misinterpretation of their own or others' scholarly views by well-meaning but not necessarily well-trained media reporters. Any notion that scholarly theological opinion written in journals can generally be quietly confined to private distribution is today a myth. In the face of the reality of likely exposure of his scholarly views on topical issues, the theologian acts with prudence when he chooses to issue a candid statement of legitimate views on his own motion, lest his position be misconstrued by press interpretation.

Respect for Hierarchical Teaching Authority. Responsible theological interpretation is not disrespectful to the hierarchical teaching authority. Nor will the laity lose respect for the teaching authority of the Church if such "dissenting" interpretation becomes generally known, if the faithful have generally and accurately been taught the respective and mutual roles of teacher and believer in the Church, that generally all pronouncements on religious matters are not of equal authoritative weight and that the responses they owe differ accordingly.[15] Danger of scandal and disrespect in the wake of public dissent would be considerably mitigated by accurate and adequate instruction on the nature and function of the papal teaching office. It was the strong recommendation of the Vatican Synod of Bishops in 1967 that "clearly and in ways adapted to the contemporary mentality" the faithful be taught their responsibilities before the magisterium.[16] A clear and intelligent explanation of the various responses a Catholic owes to the various exercises of the Church's teaching office, including a discussion of the circumstances under which it is quite legitimate and even necessary for a Catholic to suspend his assent, is an exercise of theological responsibility recognizing an existing "need to know" in the Church.

Public Dissent as a Balance of Values

Development in the science of theology, the methodology practiced by contemporary theologians and the ecclesiological insights of Vatican II and postconciliar theology contribute to a full theological understanding of the "right of dissent" which was articulated in a limited context by the manualist authors. In the era of mass communications, in the context of a co-responsible Church and in respect of moral issues with immediate practical consequences for millions of persons, the propriety of publication of "dissenting" theological opinion cannot be judged by inference to a fixed general formula in the manualist style. That is not to say that one's right to publish dissent is as broad as *his* opinion requires. The interpretative task of the theologian requires him not only to eschew simplistic formulas but also to identify the factors that must be weighed and balanced to determine whether publication of dissent is proper in a particular case. Thus, the theologian exercises the right to dissent in the living context, taking into consideration the substance and impact of the views in question as a key factor, but not the only factor, determining the manner in which such dissent should be expressed.

Each factor he identifies will represent a value to be protected. Some of the relevant factors and values with respect to the question of dissent from *Humanae Vitae* have been indicated in the foregoing paragraphs. The ultimate judgment on the balance of the factors and values becomes a question of practical prudence.

Prudence as Practical Wisdom

In the Christian tradition, prudence is practical wisdom that reduces the abstract and general principles of moral theory to particular practice. It is not a virtue that stands by itself, but one that enters into the practice of all the other virtues. Imprudence characterizes moral actions that are ill-advised, reflect careless judgment or are negligent. Prudence is the practical wisdom that conditions reason to right action. Any human action involving morality, and therefore, prudence, is virtuous not because of good intention or subjective honesty but because the action itself is good.[17]

Concerning the public communication of theologians' "dissenting" interpretation of an authoritative papal teaching addressed to the entire world, theologians must ascertain: (1) if the dissent among them is of a character and dimension that makes the dissent itself significant for the general interpretation of the papal document; (2) if the public at large is entitled to a knowledge of the fact of this dissent; (3) how their dissent is to be communicated so as to serve the good of the Church and of the public at large; and (4) if the public expression of dissent will result in good for the Church and for its image among the public at large that will outweigh the evil that may conceivably result from it.

The steps involved in the public expression of dissent among theologians are matters of *practical judgment*. The validity of such judgments cannot be scientifically established, but nonetheless can (and must) be based on reasonably sound knowledge in the practical order. Such knowledge is part of the professional equipment of theologians, gained in the practical execution of their responsibility as theologians. It is their task to be familiar with the paramount issues in the thought and life of the Church at any given time, to ascertain the opinions, points of view and attitudes of their professional colleagues, to be aware of the sentiments, moods and actual decision-making on such issues within the Church, the influences that produce them, and their theological implications; and, finally, to be alert to the degree of conflict within the Church on a given issue, to the likely impact of a papal decision on the issue and of the reasons offered for that decision, and to the impact of the papal decision in the world outside the Roman Catholic Church itself. Since the entire process of the public communication of dissent involves a series of practical judgments, there will be dissenters to the dissent; what is at issue is "practical wisdom," an area of human activity in which unanimity is rarely achieved, especially on issues that are complex.

Intraecclesial Dialogue and Magisterial Process

The necessity of dialogue between teaching and believing Church and, in this instance, the possibility that the teaching of *Humanae Vitae* may be incorrect, indicate the desirability of broadly based intraecclesial dialogue. Dialogue has always played a major role in the development of Church teaching in the past, as the most casual reading of the history of the councils makes abundantly clear. Within the people of God, furthermore, public opinion is necessary in order that total understanding and unity can be fostered. In a matter that is not *de fide,* all voices should be heard, for the sake of mature theological results.

Extraecclesial Dialogue

The Roman Catholic Church proclaims and attempts to live a sincere and full dialogic relationship to the several other communities which, together with the Church, comprise the totality of the worldwide human family: separated Christians, Jews, other non-Christians, "unbelievers" and "secular society," or the world at large. *Humanae Vitae* is itself addressed to "*all* men of good will" and treats issues which affect *all* persons in the practical as well as theoretical order; it has special words for governments, scientists, physicians, priests and spouses. The "addressees" of the Encyclical can "respond" in dialogue to the Roman Catholic Church only if they know whether there exist responsible alternate options within full Catholic hierarchical and eucharistic fellowship.[18]

Testimony of Expert Witnesses

Contemporary, living expertise and testimony is an essential element in the theological work of reinterpretation, especially in the instance of a responsible public dissent from the position taken by the papal magisterium in *Humanae Vitae*. Such expert testimony was, in fact, delivered before the Catholic University Inquiry Panel.

The Reverend Walter J. Burghardt, S.J., Editor-in-Chief of *Theological Studies,* and Professor of Patristic Theology, Woodstock College, testified that the Statement by Catholic Theologians could not have been confined within technical theological journals, given the current circumstances, including subscription to theological journals by major news media and the popular interest in the Encyclical.[19] Furthermore, even if dissent from the Encyclical could have been confined to technical theological journals, it should not have been. According to Professor Burghardt, the majority of theologians would hold that the task of the theologian ordinarily involves going beyond what can be found in magisterial statements. The theologian has a real relationship with the faithful which makes it necessary for him, with increasing frequency, to deal immediately with large groups of the faithful, and a theologian, since Vatican II, can no longer disregard the impact of magisterial statements on non-Catholics.

Professor Burghardt further testified that, in view of the responsible reasons for a public response of theologians to the Encyclical, and in view of the three or four years of serious theological study and controversy that had been going on before the Encyclical was promulgated, the response set forth in the Statement by Catholic Theologians was not excessively quick in the circumstances. Professor Burghardt affirmed that the common teaching of the "manualists" regarding dissent from authoritative, noninfallible magisterial teachings permitted such dissent if done in a semiprivate manner; the changed communications and education situation within the Church, however, allows theologians to take from the manualists the right to dissent and determine in the present changed circumstances the prudentially appropriate manner of expressing such dissent; the manualist restriction of the manner of dissent to "semiprivate" no longer applies. If other factors justified a public dissent in the circumstances, the impact of dissent on the "authority" of the magisterium would not be a sufficient reason to refrain from public dissent.

Professor Burghardt concluded his testimony with the proposition that any scandal, in the sense of placing an obstacle into the development of the life of a Christian, possibly caused by the Statement by Catholic Theologians, was permissible because of the greater good to be achieved by the immediate issuance of the Statement. It would have been even more scandalous if later it became known that hundreds, if not thousands, of theologians had been convinced that dissent from the Encyclical was possible but had kept silence. He testified that his obligations as a member of a Pontifical Faculty to sincerely acknowledge the authority of the Pope and to present the doctrine of the Encyclical as the official and authoritative doctrine of the Church in teaching and preaching were in no way compromised or violated by his subscription to the Statement by Catholic Theologians.

Professor Burghardt himself was a subscriber to the Statement by Catholic Theologians, and shortly after April 1, 1969, it became a public fact that he had testified in support of public dissent at the Catholic University Inquiry. Nevertheless, on April 30,1969, Pope Paul VI named him a member of the thirty-man international panel of theologians to evaluate new trends in theology.

Kenneth Woodward, Religion Editor of *Newsweek,* explained the methods and practices of the religion department of *Newsweek* magazine in obtaining, formulating and selectively publicizing matters of general theological interest or concern.[20] He testified that expert and representative theological views are actively and constantly solicited by his worldwide staff; that a large number of technical and semitechnical theological and religious periodicals are subscribed to and read by *Newsweek,* and that editors and publishers of scholarly theological works spontaneously supply him with advance notice or copies of "interesting" writings precisely so that they may be communicated popularly to the widest possible audience. In his expert view, it is virtually impossible today to conceal a significant theological view from the public. A sudden "silence" by American theologians after the issuance of *Humanae Vitae* would have been inexplicable, and would have itself given rise to a *Newsweek* story speculating on the reasons for silence. Even if the Statement by Catholic Theologians of July 30, 1968, had never been made, the *Newsweek* story immediately pursuant to the release of *Humanae Vitae* would have been substantially the same, gleaned from European and worldwide theological spokesmen. He further testified that, in any event, large-scale "private" dissent on the part of American theologians from the specific ethical conclusion of the Encyclical would have quickly and inevitably become "public."

The Reverend John Coleman Bennett, President, Union Theological Seminary, testified that the concept of the responsibility of the theologians found in the prepared written testimony of the subject professors was an admirable formulation, and that theologians might be guilty of withdrawal from responsibility if they hesitated to make public a responsible theological point of view (within the context of their own faith-commitment) merely because such a point of view represented a challenge to traditional formulations.[21] He thought that suppression of such public disagreement might lead to even more confusion than the statements made initiating the dialogue.

Professor Bennett further testified that the Statement by Catholic Theologians was enormously helpful to the Protestant community in mitigating the appearance of the Roman Catholic Church as a monolithic institution, and that, specifically, the dissent of professors at Catholic University has created a favorable impression of the University in ecumenical circles because it showed that there is academic freedom at the University, and that theologians at the University are able to speak as scholars and thinkers.

Reverend John H. Hotchkin, Associate Director, Bishops' Committee for Ecumenical and Interreligious Affairs, National Conference of Catholic Bishops, testified that, given the ecumenical commitment of the Catholic Church since Vatican II, and given the concern among a number of Protestant officials as to whether or not there was a retrenchment within the Catholic Church in its ecumenical relations, the calibre of responsible dissent within the Catholic Church evidenced in the Statement by Theologians subscribed to by the subject professors had a positive ecumenical value. Specifically, the Statement made it possible for non-Catholics to be more muted, more calm and more patient in the face of a teaching on birth control whose method and content was disagreeable.[22] He testified that a dissent from the Encyclical disguised in any other style would not have had the same positive ecumenical effects.

Developing theological and ecclesiological insights show that the possession of responsible, interpretive theological views by Roman Catholic scholars demands of them appropriate external manifestation and communication of such views. This is equally true when the specific, responsible interpretive views include a responsible dissent from authoritative, noninfallible teaching of the hierarchical magisterium.

Appropriate external manifestation and communication, in principle and from the very nature of the Church itself, require that all persons who have the right to know such responsible, interpretative theological views be apprised of them as quickly, candidly and efficiently as possible. Such appropriate external manifestation and communication in actual fact today requires the effective use of the ordinary means of mass social communications media, when "all persons who have the right to know" is a category which is coextensive with every person who would have access to and be dependent on such media.

Notes

1. John XXIII, *Mater et Magistra,* para. 61 (emphasis added).
2. John XXIII, *Pacem in Terris,* para. 12 (emphasis added).
3. Vatican II, *Decree on the Media of Social Communications,* para. 3.

4. *Ibid.*, para. 5 (emphasis added).
5. *Ibid.*, para. 8 (emphasis added).
6. John XXIII, Address to the Journalists covering the Council, October 13, 1962. NCWC News Service.
7. Bishop James Shannon, Address to the Catholic Press Association, May 17, 1968, NCWC News Service.
8. American Bishops' Committee for Social Communications Statement on the Occasion of World Communications Day, May 4, 1967, NCWC News Service.
9. *Ibid.*
10. Pius XII, Address to the Third International Congress of the Catholic Press on Feb. 17, 1950, NCWC News Service.
11. R. Cardinal Cushing, Pastoral Letter of 1963, *The Church and Public Opinion,* NCWC News Service.
12. For an expansion of these materials, and specific application to the life of the Church, cf., P. Granfield, "Ecclesial Cybernetics: Communication in the Church," *Theological Studies,* 29 (1968), pp. 662–78.
13. Cf. *supra,* pp. with notes 70–72.
14. *Statement,* n. 8.
15. Unfortunately, American Catholics did not receive clear teaching on such matters in 1967; cf., American Bishops' Pastoral Letter of 1967, *The Church in Our Day* (Washington: U.S.C.C., 1969), pp. 69–73.
16. Cf. P. Hebblewaithe, S.J., *Inside the Synod: Rome 1967* (New York: Paulist, 1968), p. 155.
17. T. Gilby, O. P., "Prudence," *New Catholic Encyclopedia,* vol. 11 (New York: McGraw-Hill, 1968), pp. 925–28.
18. See P. D. Morris, *Ecumenical Dialogue as An Operative Principle in the Christian Unity Movement* (Doctoral Dissertation, unpublished), Washington: School of Theology, The Catholic University of America, 1967.
19. Transcript of Proceedings, Catholic University Board of Inquiry, pp. 388–441.
20. *Ibid.*, pp. 655–89.
21. *Ibid.*, pp. 482–510.
22. *Ibid.*, pp. 579–609.

6

The Reasonsibleness of Reponsible Dissent from One Particular Ethical Teaching of the Encyclical

The Statement by Theologians takes exception to the absolute ban on artificial contraception proposed in *Humanae Vitae* primarily because of an "inadequate concept of natural law" which serves as the basis of the proposed ethical conclusion of the Encyclical. This chapter will explicitly point out the defects in such an understanding of natural law and also develop in more detail the specific shortcomings in the moral methodology implied in the Encyclical. There is no detailed development of a particular line of reasoning which would argue against the absolute condemnation of the Encyclical. This chapter only intends to point out the different approaches which have been used by some Roman Catholic theologians in coming to conclusions which admit the need of artificial birth control in some circumstances.

The historical development of the teaching on contraception will be summarized to show how historical and cultural factors do influence a particular moral teaching. In particular, the history of the growing dissatisfaction among Catholic thinkers with the teaching on contraception as it has developed since *Casti Connubii* in 1930 will also document the reasonableness of dissent from the specific conclusion of *Humanae Vitae*. The Statement by Theologians concludes "that spouses may responsibly decide according to their conscience that artificial contraception in some circumstances is permissible and indeed necessary to preserve and foster the values and sacredness of marriage." But in the context of the whole Statement, this cannot be construed as a simplistic argument based on the universal rights of conscience. The Statement maintains that in certain circumstances artificial contraception is not wrong and that the conscience of the couple must decide when this is a valid ethical judgment, after considering all the values which are present, in much the same fashion as an older Catholic theology taught about the personal conscience decision to use rhythm.

Natural Law and Humanae Vitae

DEVELOPMENT IN NATURAL LAW THEORY RECOGNIZED BY CONTEMPORARY THEOLOGIANS

Pluralism of Natural Law Theories. Not all thinkers have meant the same thing by the term "natural law." Nor are all natural law theoreticians in agreement concerning which actions are opposed to the natural law.

Aristotle considered nature as the intrinsic principle in every living organism which is teleological, dynamic and specific. Whereas Aristotle stressed the individual substance as the principle of intelligibility, the Stoics looked upon the universe as a whole as the principle of intelligibility. For the different Stoic theoreticians, natural law had merely a generic meaning, much like our "morality." Roman law (per Ulpian) defined the natural law as that which is common to man and all the animals, as distinguished from the *ius gentium* which is proper to man because of his reason. Gratian, the monk who codified the laws of the Church in the twelfth century, described the natural law in an historical perspective as that "which is contained in the law and the Gospel."

Thomas Aquinas, in citing these and other definitions of the natural law, thus illustrates the ambiguity and pluralism existing in the theory of natural law. Aquinas himself struggled with the characteristics of the natural law: universality, immutability and indispensability. In theory, he admitted that the general principles of the natural law (e.g., good is to be done; act according to right reason) are always binding. However, he held that the conclusions of the common principles (e.g., what is owed must be returned) oblige only generally (*ut in pluribus*), because other considerations could change the validity of the conclusion as the analysis becomes further removed from the first principles. Contemporary Thomists similarly advance their own different approaches to the question of natural law. They emphasize that natural law is right reason and condemn overly legalistic approaches to natural law.[1] Thus, for the greater part of the history of the Church, natural law has not signified a coherent philosophical system with an agreed body of ethical content.[2]

Catholic Moral Theology and Natural Law. Since natural law is not a monolithic philosophical system with an agreed-upon body of ethical content, Catholic moral teaching cannot be said to be based on the natural law. The greater part of Catholic moral teaching on particular points was arrived at long before Thomas Aquinas articulated his theory of natural law in the thirteenth century. His theory merely explained in a coherent way the already existing moral teaching on a number of particular points.

Generally, only in the last hundred years has Catholic teaching in the hierarchical magisterium been explicitly based on natural law reasoning, particularly in respect to medical morality and social ethics. However, the *Pastoral Constitution on the Church in the Modern World* of Vatican II appears purposely to avoid the term "natural law," which occurs only twice in this long document devoted to social ethics.[3]

The moral teaching of the Church, *de iure,* can never be tied to any one philosophical system and understanding of man. The sovereign freedom of the Word of God can never be totally dependent on any one philosophical approach.

Danger of Physicalism: Biological and Physical Aspects as Primary Determinants of Morality. Catholic moral theology generally avoids identifying the morality of an act with the physical structure of the act itself. For example, the physical act of killing is not always wrong, whereas the moral act of murder is always wrong. To identify the moral act totally in physical or biological terms seems to be a distortion of morality. Historically, there are two main sources of this aberration. As noted, Ulpian, in the third century, defined the natural law as that which is common to man and all the animals. He differentiated the natural law from the *ius gentium,* the law proper to man because of his reason. To him, the word nature meant those things which are common to man and all the animals. Consistent with this terminology, Thomas Aquinas and the other scholastics employed the word nature to describe actions totally in biological terms. For instance, in the matter of chastity, Thomas divided all sins into two categories: sins against nature—those in which the biological process of the depositing of male semen in the vagina of the female is not observed (masturbation, homosexuality and bestiality), and sins according to nature—those in which the biological process is perfect, but a specifically human element is missing (fornication, adultery and sacrilege). The anthropology underlying such analysis considers man as a layer of rationality atop a layer of animality: the animality retains its own structure and finality and cannot be interfered with in the name of rationality. The teaching that procreation is the primary end of marriage (a teaching no longer maintained in recent statements of the hierarchical and papal magisterium) is logically connected with the approach of Ulpian, since procreation is common to man and all the animals, whereas the love-union aspect of marriage is proper only to men.

In a more primitive understanding of reality in a nontechnical and nonscientific society, happiness was truly found by conforming oneself to nature and the laws of nature. This attribute of a nonscientific culture was definitely reflected in the natural law theory of the Stoics. However, scientific and technological man has the power to interfere with nature precisely to make human life more human.[4]

The Shift from Classicism to Historical Consciousness and Its Effects in Moral Theology. The classicist world view sees reality in terms of eternal, immutable and unchanging reality. The historical world view sees reality more in terms of growth, change and development. Two different methodologies correspond to these two different perspectives:

The classicist methodology emphasizes the abstract, the a priori and the deductive.

Historically conscious methodology emphasizes the concrete (it does not deny the absolute need for metaphysics, but pays more attention to the concrete, the particular and the historical), the inductive and the a posteriori.

The documents of Vatican II reflect both tendencies, but for the first time there is an emphasis on an historically conscious methodology. This is illustrated in the call to begin reading "the signs of the times"; in the understanding of the Church as a pilgrim Church constantly in need of reform and change; and in the call for dialogue with other Christians, non-Christians and even atheists in the continual, ongoing search for truth.

The differences between the approaches of classicism and historical consciousness are further evidenced in the following areas:

A more historically minded approach realizes the need for change without canonizing every change possible.

An historically conscious approach stresses inductive reasoning, the empirical sciences and the experience of Christian people in moral matters.

A classicist approach makes absolute certitude the ideal; the more historically minded approach realizes that man must be satisfied with a lesser degree of certitude.

A classicist approach considers the magisterium's pronouncements somewhat abstracted from historical circumstances, whereas the historically conscious approach views the teachings of the magisterium as limited by their historical and cultural circumstances and open to further growth and change.

A classicist approach sees reality primarily in terms of essences and substances, whereas the historically conscious approach sees reality more in terms of relationships and development.

An historically conscious approach realizes that "subjectivity" enters into "objectivity" itself. Transcendental methodology sees objectivity not merely in terms of "the object out there" but in terms of the objectivity of the human knowing process itself.[5]

Newer Approaches in Catholic Ethical Theory. The traditional teaching on natural law enshrines two important values that Catholic moral theology must retain. There is a source of ethical wisdom and knowledge, apart from the explicit revelation of God in Christ in the Scriptures, which Christians share with all mankind. Also, morality cannot be based on an individual's whims or fancies. However, many contemporary Catholic theologians have expressed dissatisfaction with the concept of natural law as found in the manuals of moral theology.

There have been many developments in Catholic theology and philosophy in the last few decades and these newer insights necessarily have theoretical and practical consequences for a proper understanding of natural law. From a theological perspective, the need for a "theology of compromise" is shown by the danger of making an ideal into an absolute norm for all and by a consideration of the reality of sin and its effects on man's actions.

From a philosophical perspective, differences between a substantialist approach and a more relational approach, as illustrated by the example of lying and the changed understanding of the reason for its malice, would result in different practical conclusions. The new viewpoint which does not define the moral action in terms of the physical or biological structure of an action seen merely in itself, apart from the vital relationships surrounding it, will have many practical repercussions. Differences between the notion of objectivity in the older approaches and the notion of objectivity in the transcendental philosophy which is being proposed by many Catholics today (e.g., Rahner, Lonergan, Coreth)[6] will also affect concrete ethical judgments. The current literature in moral theology (e.g., Johann, Simons, van der Marck, Boeckle and Schueller) illustrates such newer approaches and different conclusions.[7]

There exists a plurality of different philosophical understandings of man and his actions. On the specific question of contraception, these different philosophical understandings—personalism, a more relational approach and transcendental method—would arrive at solutions different from the absolute condemnation of artificial contraception contained in *Humanae Vitae*.

Natural Law as Employed in the Encyclical Humanae Vitae[8]

Pope Paul's Encyclical *Humanae Vitae* explicitly employs a natural law methodology to arrive at its particular moral conclusions on the licit means of regulating births. The Encyclical admits that the teaching on marriage is a "teaching founded on natural law, illuminated and enriched by divine revelation" (*Humanae Vitae,* paragraph 4). The Encyclical then reaffirms that "the teaching authority of the Church is competent to interpret even the natural moral law" (*Humanae Vitae,* paragraph 4).

The conclusions of the Encyclical receive their force, according to the Encyclical, both from the reasoning on which they are based and from the teaching authority of the Pope, which enjoys the special assistance of the Holy Spirit. In paragraph 12 the Encyclical states: "That teaching, often set forth by the magisterium, is founded upon the inseparable connection, willed by God and unable to be broken by man on his own initiative, between the two meanings of the conjugal act: the unitive meaning and the procreative meaning. Indeed, by its intimate structure, the conjugal act, while most closely uniting husband and wife, capacitates them for the generation of new lives, according to laws inscribed in the very being of man and of women. . . . We believe that the men of our day are particularly capable of seizing the *deeply reasonable and human character of this fundamental principle*." (Emphasis added.)

Though, in paragraph 28, priests are reminded "that obedience, as you know well, obliges not only because of the reasons adduced, but rather because of the light of the Holy Spirit, which is given in a particular way to the pastors of the Church in order that they may illustrate the truth," nonetheless, natural law argumentation was employed in the Encyclical; and such argumentation contains certain defects.

Failure to Admit Plurality of Natural Law Theories. The reasoning in the Encyclical does not admit that there is a pluralism in understandings of the natural law and in the conclusions which can be derived from different natural law theories. The impression lingers in *Humanae Vitae* that the natural law is a coherent philosophical system with an agreed-upon body of content.

Physicalism. The notion of natural law employed in the Encyclical appears to involve a "physicalism" in identifying the moral act with the physical and biological structure of the act itself. (Note that the fact that the moral aspect of the act may coincide with the physical structure of the act is not denied in this presentation.) The core practical conclusion of the Encyclical states: "We must once again declare that the direct interruption of the generative process already begun, and above all directly willed and procured abortion, even if for therapeutic reasons, are to be absolutely excluded as licit means of regulating birth" (*Humanae Vitae,* paragraph 14). "Equally to be excluded . . . is direct sterilization . . . . Similarly excluded is every action which, either in anticipation of the conjugal act, or in its accomplishment, or in the development of its natural consequences, proposes, whether as an end or as a means, to render procreation impossible" (*Humanae Vitae,* paragraph 14). The footnotes in this particular paragraph refer to the *Catechism of the Council of Trent* and the utterances of more recent popes. Reference is made to the Address of Pius XII to the Italian Catholic Union of Midwives in which direct sterilization is defined as "that which aims at making procreation impossible as both means and end."[9] The concept of "direct" is thus described in terms of the physical structure and causality of the act itself.

The moral conclusion of the Encyclical forbidding any interference with the conjugal act is based on the "intimate structure of the conjugal act" (*Humanae Vitae,* paragraph 12). The "design of God" is written into the very nature of the conjugal act; man is merely "the minister of the design established by the Creator" (*Humanae Vitae,* paragraph 13). The Encyclical acknowledges that "it is licit to take into account the natural rhythms immanent in the generative functions." Recourse to the infecund periods is licit, whereas artificial contraception "as the use of means directly contrary to fecundation is condemned as being always illicit" (*Humanae Vitae,* paragraph 16). "In reality there are essential differences between the two cases; in the former, the married couple make legitimate use of a natural disposition; in the latter, they impede the development of natural processes" (*Humanae Vitae,* paragraph 16). The natural law theory employed in the Encyclical thus identifies the moral and human action with the physical structure of the conjugal act itself.

Classicist World View. The Encyclical appears to operate within the horizon of a classicist world view and does not take into consideration the more historically minded world view which is now perfectly acceptable, indeed more acceptable, to contemporary Catholic theologians.

In its methodology, *Humanae Vitae* well illustrates a classicist approach. The Encyclical admits that "changes which have taken place are in fact noteworthy and of varied kinds" (*Humanae Vitae,* paragraph 2). These changes give rise to new questions. However, the changing historical circumstances have not affected the answer or the method employed in arriving at concrete conclusions on implementing responsible parenthood. The primary reason for *Humanae Vitae*'s rejection of the majority report of the Papal Commission was "because certain criteria of solutions had emerged which departed from the moral teaching on marriage proposed with constant firmness by the teaching authority of the Church" (*Humanae Vitae,* paragraph 6).

Rationale Excessively Deductive. Since the Encyclical adopts a classicist world view and methodology, the natural law methodology employed in the Encyclical is excessively deductive and does not leave enough room for the inductive.

The Encyclical specifically acknowledges the fact that there are new signs of the times, but it is questionable whether sufficient attention has really been paid to such changes. The footnotes to the Encyclical are significant even if the footnote references alone do not constitute conclusive argument. The footnotes include only random scriptural texts (none of which pertain to the specific teaching of the Encyclical), one citation of Thomas Aquinas, and references to earlier pronouncements of the hierarchical magisterium. A more inductive approach would be inclined to give more importance and documentation to the signs of the times. The footnote references contain no indication of any type of dialogue with other Christians, non-Christians and the modern sciences. The Encyclical describes certain social consequences of the use of contraception (*Humanae Vitae,* paragraph 17), but no documentation is given for what appear to be unproven assumptions. Since the methodology describes the human act in physical terms, the practical moral conclusion is the absolute condemnation of means of artificial birth control. The Encyclical thus betrays an epistemology that has been rejected by many Catholic theologians and philosophers today. In addition, the document does not explicitly take into consideration what the *Pastoral Constitution on the Church in the Modern World* regarded as a fact based on induction: "But where the intimacy of married life is broken off, it is not rare for the faithfulness to be imperiled and its quality of fruitfulness ruined" (*Gaudium et Spes,* paragraph 51).

Outdated Biological Conceptions. The assumptions of the Encyclical seem to be based on an outdated biology. Biology in general, and the understanding of the physiology of human reproduction in particular, have changed greatly in the last century. It is quite possible that much of the earlier reasoning against contraception was based on what is now known to be inadequate. Only within the current century, and particularly in the last few decades, has man come to a better understanding of the process of conception. Conception cannot occur unless the sperm is able to fertilize an ovum. However, a fertilizable ovum is present in the female only during a comparatively short time of the menstrual cycle. From a biological viewpoint, many acts of sexual intercourse are not truly open to procreation since there is no ovum present. Perhaps, as one author suggests, the natural law in this matter would call for a randomness of sexual acts, a principle which would be specifically violated by rhythm.[10]

Single Act Analysis. The Statement maintains that "many positive values concerning marriage are expressed in Paul VI's encyclical." Among the positive values is the insistence on the unitive and the procreative aspects of marriage and human sexuality, so that marriage is seen in terms of a union of love in the service of life. The Encyclical, however, views these two characteristics as being inseparably connected with each and every conjugal act (paragraphs 12 and 13). Modern biology, however, tells us that every act of sexual intercourse is not open to procreation. Should not the insistence be on the fact that sexual intercourse does have a relation to procreation, at least to the extent that it takes place within a procreative union? The danger exists today of many people forgetting the two inseparable meanings of marriage and sexuality, but one must also avoid the overreaction of stating that these two meanings are inseparably connected in each and every conjugal act.

Insufficient Attention to Demographic Questions. The Encyclical does not seem to give sufficient attention and weight to one of the most talked-about signs of the times—the question of overpopulation. The demographic problem is mentioned particularly in paragraphs 2 and 23. However, the Encyclical does not seem to accord this matter the same urgency as other Catholic scholars have attributed to it. No explicit mention is made of the fact that there are, even in the teaching of the Encyclicals, acceptable means of responsible parenthood to be utilized in an effort to come to grips with the demographic problem. Experts seem to agree that "economic and social progress" is in itself not enough to overcome the demographic problem as it is existing in some countries. The Encyclical could have disputed such assertions, or at least recognized them and offered more positive approaches towards their solution. Thus the Encyclical is open to the charge of failing to give sufficient attention to this very perplexing problem.[11]

Other Acceptable Approaches

Different approaches to natural law and ethical theories currently employed in Catholic theology today would come to different conclusions on the matter of contraception. Three such perspectives could be described as: a more personalist approach; a more relational approach; and a transcendental method.

A More Personalist Approach. A more personalist approach has characterized much of contemporary ethics. For the Christian, the biblical revelation contributes to such an understanding of reality. A personalist approach cannot be something merely added on to another theory. A personalist perspective will definitely affect moral conclusions, especially when such conclusions have been based on the physical structure of the act itself. Personalism always sees the act in terms of the person positing the act and does not determine morality merely by an examination of the structure and finality of a given organ or faculty viewed apart from the person. The *Pastoral Constitution on the Church in the Modern World* realized that objective standards in the matter of sexual morality are "based on the nature of the human person and his acts." (See paragraph 51.) Bernard Haering has shown how such a personalist approach would deny an absolute condemnation of artificial contraception.[12]

A More Relational Approach. A more relational understanding of morality stems from a different view of man. The natural law approach as found in the manuals of theology views nature as a principle of operation within every existing thing. Thus, man should act according to the design of God inscribed in his very nature, which is unfolded in his life and actions. Notice that the Encyclical adopts such a view of man. However, many thinkers today view man not as a substantial entity existing in himself, with his own nature as the complete guiding principle of his life embedded within him, but rather as a person existing as a being with others in a network of relationships. Man is not a being totally programmed by the nature he has. Rather, man is characterized by openness, freedom and the challenge to make himself and his world more human in and through his many relationships. The human person is actually constituted in and through these relationships. Relationality thus characterizes man and his existence. Phenomenological and existentialist approaches view man as a being for and with others who is described in terms of intersubjectivity. A philosophy of *process* proceeds somewhat further in the direction of a more relational and historical approach to reality.

On the particular question of contraception, a more relational approach would not view the person or a particular faculty as something existing in itself. Each faculty exists in relationship with the total person and other persons within a universal community. Morality cannot merely be determined by examining a particular faculty and its physical structure or a particular act in itself. The changed ethical evaluation of lying well illustrates the point. Manuals of moral theology have generally accepted the Augustinian definition of lying as speech against what is in the mind (*locutio contra mentem*). The malice of lying thus consists in violating the purpose of the faculty of speech. Recently, Catholic theologians have proposed a different understanding of lying which actually corresponds more with the thinking of the earlier Augustine before he arrived at his famous definition. In this recent formulation, the malice of lying consists in the violation of the neighbor's right to truth. Falsehood is the physical act of speech which is contrary to what is in the mind; but lying as an immoral act consists in the violation of my relationships with my neighbor and the community. Both Johann and van der Marck have employed a more relational approach to argue on behalf of the ethical value of, and need for, contraception in certain circumstances.[13]

A Transcendental Method. A third philosophical approach to man espoused by a growing number of Catholic thinkers today is a theory of transcendental method. Transcendental methodology owes much to the neo-Thomist, Joseph Marechal, and is espoused today in varying forms by Bernard Lonergan, Karl Rahner and Emerich Coreth.

In general, transcendental method seeks to go beyond the

object known to the structures of the human knowing process itself. According to Lonergan, the intrinsic objectivity of human cognitional activity is its intentionality.[14] Lonergan's ethics is an extension of his theory of knowing. Moral value is not an intrinsic property of external acts or objects; it is an aspect of certain consciously free acts in relation to man's knowledge of the world. Man must come to examine the structures of his knowing and deciding process. Lonergan uses as a tool the notion of horizon analysis. Basic horizon is the maximum field of vision from a determined standpoint. This basic horizon is open to development and even conversion. Lonergan posits four conversions which should transpire from the understanding of the structures of human knowing and deciding: the intellectual, the moral, the religious and the Christian. Ethics must bring people to this Christian conversion so that they can become aware of their knowing and doing and flee from inauthenticity, unreasonableness and the "surd" (absurdity) of sin. Thus, Christian ethics is primarily concerned with the manner in which an authentic Christian person makes his ethical decisions and carries them out. However, such a meta-ethics must then enter into the realm of the normative, all the time realizing the provisional value of its precepts which are limited by the data at hand. Donald Johnson has said of Lonergan's ethic, as applied to moral theology: "The distinct contribution of the moral theologian to philosophical ethics would consist in clarifying the attitudes which are involved in man's responding in faith to the initiative of a loving God who has redeemed man in Christ." Thus a transcendental method would put greater stress on the knowing and deciding structures of the authentic Christian subject. Such a theory would also tend to reject the Encyclical's view of man and his generative faculties.[15]

Conclusions Regarding Humanae Vitae and Natural Law. The notion of natural law has been under reconsideration in recent Roman Catholic theological research. The concept of natural law as employed in the Encyclical *Humanae Vitae* seems to be inadequate from a number of viewpoints. Other ethical theories or varieties of natural law thinking which have been proposed by

Catholic theologians in the last decade would come to different conclusions about the absolute immorality of contraception. Thus the natural law basis of the argument presented in the Encyclical is not convincing, and many Roman Catholic scholars have admitted as much, both before and after the issuance of the Encyclical.

The Morality of Contraception
Historical Development of the Argument against the Morality of Contraception[16]

Hebrew Scriptures. The Genesis accounts of creation (chaps. 1 and 2) evidence both the unitive and procreative aspects of the man-woman relationship as the ancient Hebrew writers viewed the ideal in the mind of Yahweh-God: "two in one flesh" and "increase and multiply" set a basic, double theme which recurs with varying emphasis and intermittent distortions throughout the entire course of salvation history. Immediately, within Genesis itself, the predominant value in human sexuality became procreation, especially for the feminine sex.

In a patriarchal society, woman encountered religious and social disabilities and was regarded as subordinate to man. Polygamy and slave concubinage were permitted. An unmarried man who had intercourse with an unmarried girl was to be fined and forced to take her as a wife, but if a girl had secretly been unchaste, she was to be stoned (Dt. 22:13-29). Divorce could be obtained only by a husband (Dt. 24:1-4).

"Woman as temptress" was a consistent theme. Woman embodied an attraction which might cause disaster. Eve and Dalia were temptresses to sin (Gn. 3:1-17, Jgs. 16). Bathsheba was the occasion of David's fall; Tamar, of Amnon's (2 Sam. 11-12, 2 Sam. 13). In the Psalms, sexuality was occasionally associated with sin. Ritual purification was necessary for man after emission of seed and for woman after menstruation and childbirth (Lv. 5:16, 18, 16:28, 12:1-8).

"Immortality through generation" was also consistently stressed.

The salvation of the Jews, whether individually or collectively considered, was to come through generation. Their historical destiny could be achieved only if their race continued to flourish. This emphasis on procreation and the contempt for sexuality characterized the pre-Christian biblical view of sex.

There were explicit post-Exilic legislations against homosexuality, bestiality and temple prostitution (Lv. 8:22, 20:13, 20:15-16, Dt. 23:18), but no law against contraception. In the absence of clear prohibition, the Jewish people would have believed that *coitus interruptus* or the use of contraceptives was not immoral. However, Onan was condemned for *coitus interruptus* with his sister-in-law. Some theologians attributed his condemnation to his contraceptive intention; Pope Pius XI, in his *Casti Connubii,* paragraph 55, cited this interpretation: "As St. Augustine notes: 'Intercourse even with one's legitimate wife is unlawful and wicked where his conception of the offspring is prevented. Onan, the son of Juda, did this and the Lord killed him for it.' " However, modern exegetes reject this interpretation. The reason for Onan's condemnation could have been his disobedience to his father, violation of Jewish law or lack of family feeling.[17]

Christian Scripture. The teaching of Christ placed special emphasis on human behavior on love. However, the New Testament writers carried over many of the Old Testament notions of woman and human sexuality into Christianity. Likewise, the New Testament writers tended to accept uncritically some of the cultural assumptions of their own times, e.g., the inferiority of women. The understanding of sexuality in the writings of the New Testament can be summarized in the following themes: the value of virginity; the institutional goodness of marriage; the sacral character of sexual intercourse; the value of procreation; the significance of desire as well as act; the evil of extramarital intercourse; the unnaturalness of homosexuality; the connection of Adam's sin with the rebelliousness of the body; and the evil of "medicine."

The Gospels inculcate virginity as a great value when undertaken in view of the Kingdom of God. Procreation in marriage is emphasized less in the Gospels than it is in the Old Testament.

There is no passage in the Gospels dealing explicitly with contraception. St. Paul's *Epistle to the Romans* (1:24-27), which speaks of "unnatural acts," could be interpreted as referring to one form of contraceptive conduct. Most exegetes conclude, however, that St. Paul was condemning homosexual and lesbian acts, not contraceptive acts. In his Epistle to the Galatians, St. Paul condemns *pharmakeia* (potion, medicine), and Apocalypse (9:21, 21:8) describe the punishments of *pharmakoi* (medicine men). However, it is not clear at all whether contraceptive drugs were condemned.

Conclusion from Scripture. There is no conclusive evidence in the Hebrew or Christian Scriptures that contraception is morally wrong. Note that the Encyclical *Humanae Vitae* offers no scriptural basis for its conclusions.

Early Fathers. The Church Fathers' attitude toward human sexuality is characterized by a low estimate of the nature of woman. From St. Paul's admonition "it is good for a man not to touch woman," they reasoned that it must be bad to touch a woman. Methodius thought woman must be by nature "carnal and sensuous," the "irrational half of mankind." St. Jerome called woman "the devil's gateway . . . a scorpion's dart . . . ." St. Clement of Alexandria told woman that "it is shameful for her to think about what nature she has." Tertullian told woman to make herself ugly, since her beauty "is dangerous to those who look upon it." St. John Chrysostom, St. Cyril of Alexandria, St. Ambrose and Pope St. Gregory all considered woman to be naïve, unstable, mentally weak and in need of an authoritative husband.

The most influential of the Church Fathers in regard to marriage and contraception is St. Augustine. His threefold good of marriage, *proles, fides* and *sacramentum,* had been accepted by theologians until recent times. His writings on contraception unfortunately reflected a violent reaction against the Manichees' belief that all procreation was evil (since in conception the particles of light of the Father were imprisoned). St. Augustine maintained the opposite extreme: every intercourse must be procreative either in fact or in intent. One exception could be allowed when the conjugal debt was involved, but even in this respect positive interference (which would have included the "rhythm" method in his frame of reference) for contraceptive purposes was equally forbidden.

Injunctions against contraception are also found in the writings of Caesarius, Bishop of Arles (470-543), St. Martin of Braga (d. 579) and Gregory the Great, all former monks. Caesarius' condemnation is based primarily on his conception of the particular medicinal potion (drink) as magical; its use was forbidden either for sterility or fertility. He considered use of a contraceptive potion to be a crime of homicide. St. Martin's condemnation of contraception in the First Council of Barga was a reaction against the Priscillian movement, a form of Manicheanism. This document, universally accepted in the Spanish provinces, was later transmitted to the Western churches as the basis for future teachings and legislation.

St. Gregory the Great became Pope at the time of the moral decline of Roman civilization. To reestablish Christian morality in matters of sex, he adopted some of the extreme attitudes of the Stoics. He condemned not only contraception but also the pleasures of procreative coitus. He considered taking pleasure in legitimate intercourse to be sinful, and denied Communion to those who had not purified themselves after marital intercourse. Enhanced by Gregory's personal prestige and the increasing authority of the papacy in the Middle Ages, this doctrine assured the absolute condemnation of contraceptive practice by the entire ecclesiastical institution.

Penitentials. From the sixth to the eleventh century, the teaching on sexual morality in the Church is found especially in the Penitentials, books which assigned appropriate penances for particular sins. The rigidity of the Penitentials on sexual morality could hardly be exaggerated. Examples of the rigors of some Penitentials include: sterile couples were forbidden to have intercourse; intercourse during menstruation was to be punished by twenty to forty days of penance; dorsal intercourse was to be punished by forty days of penance. Contraception is condemned in the Penitentials, at least in the eighth century and, perhaps, even in the sixth century.

Canonists. Beginning in the eleventh century, the canonists (principally Ivo, Bishop of Chartres (1091-1116), Gratian, the Camaldolese monk, and Peter the Lombard, the Bishop of Paris) systematized the teachings of earlier authors on human sexuality, including condemnations of contraception, with singular attention to the doctrine of St. Augustine. These canonical collections, in the opinion of some interpreters, were compiled in response to the spread of Catharism, a new form of Manicheanism which opposed procreation in marriage. However, in the midst of this movement against neo-Manicheanism, "dissenting" theologians, such as Abelard and Hugh of St. Victor, asserted that marriage served values other than procreation, such as love, spiritual union and avoidance of fornication. Their teachings on this topic failed to win wide audiences among their contemporaries.

Scholastics. St. Albert the Great and his disciple, St. Thomas Aquinas, rejected the view that contraception was a sin of homicide, but both considered contraception unnatural. They considered any sexual act in which procreative insemination was impossible to be a "sin against nature," e.g., masturbation, sodomy, bestiality, *coitus interruptus* (withdrawal) and contraceptive acts in marriage. Moreover, they were of the opinion that "nature" also specified the proper position for intercourse. "The fit way," so-called, "was with woman beneath the man"; they considered any deviation from this position unnatural and seriously sinful.

Aquinas distinguished the order of human reason from the order of nature, which is considered sacred and unchangeable: Just as the ordering of right reason proceeds from man, so the order of nature is from God Himself; wherefore in sins contrary to nature, whereby the very order of nature is violated, an injury is done to God, the ordainer of nature.[18] Natural coitus as instituted by God should not be altered by man. A sin against nature is an affront to God, although "no other person is injured" (as distinguished from adultery or rape, which are against the order of reason in so far as another person is injured).

The Thomistic analysis considers the biological function of the sexual act as given by God and unalterable by man, and postulates that offspring are the natural end of copulation. Therefore, copulation for pleasure alone, or without procreative intention, is against nature. Similarly, Aquinas holds that an intention to have intercourse for the sake of health is against nature.[19] Coitus is naturally ordained for procreation and nothing else.

However, Aquinas teaches in his *Summa Against the Gentiles* that "if *per accidens* generation cannot follow from emission of the seed, this is not against nature, nor a sin, as if it happens that the woman is sterile."[20] Thus, *insemination* appears to him the essential act required by nature. When insemination is made impossible, it is against nature, with or without the possibility of procreation. However, in an earlier work Aquinas condemned the potions of sterility as against nature, even though *insemination* would not be prevented by their use.[21] He never repeated this latter analysis, nor did he ever subsequently suggest that the use of contraceptive potions was a sin against nature.

Thomas posed three types of seminal ejaculation: (1) acts in which insemination was impossible (these were unnatural); (2) acts in which insemination was possible and conception resulted (these were natural and normal); and (3) acts in which insemination was possible, but conception did not occur (these were normal, but accidentally different from the norm). Aquinas does not demonstrate (2) as the norm and (3) as accidentally different; rather, he presupposes it. This presupposition was accepted by all theologians of his time, and Aquinas was never called to demonstrate it. Aquinas did not ask whether it makes sense to postulate one type of coitus as normal and to treat every variation from it as accidental, even cases in which it was known that conception was impossible, or to hold that old age was an "accidental" exception to the ability to generate.

Early Dissent from the Thomistic Analysis. No doubt Aquinas was influenced by the Augustinian view on sexuality; he in turn influenced later theologians and the Church in the teaching against contraception. But there was also an undercurrent of dissenting opinions, including that of Duns Scotus. From 1450 to 1750, certain radical departures from tradition had taken place. Martin Le Maistre (1432-1481) held that rendering the marital debt, avoiding fornication, seeking bodily health and calming the mind were proper purposes for marital intercourse. Denis the Carthusian (1402-1471) considered love a legitimate object of coitus. The Augustinian view declined in Church circles as other values, such as education of children, love and the welfare of married partners, were considered in regard to marital intercourse. However, the prohibition against contraception was maintained.

Factors in the Emerging Controversy. Faced with a crisis of overpopulation, theologians began to consider what means of regulating birth are permissible, and what are not. Among the means discussed are: *amplexus reservatus* (uncompleted copulation), *copula dimidita* (partial penetration), certain sterilizing operations, "the pill" and other methods of contraception.

The contemporary controversy on birth control has taken place in a context marked by many new factors:

Population. The reduction of infant mortality and the prolongation of life have created the possibility of dangerous increases in population.

Status of Woman. With education and equal opportunity in modern society, woman is no longer considered a machine of procreation, but rather a person.

Education. Education today is not considered a luxury, but a necessity (including higher education). This fact adds new burdens to family finance.

Scientific Knowledge and Philosophy. Biological, psychological and sociological sciences provide new data which must be considered in the moral evaluation of human sexual behavior. Contemporary philosophy has also developed many different perspectives. The traditional notion of nature as static has been replaced with a more dynamic, more historical notion. In this integrated, dynamic and historical conception of the human person, the traditional and static analysis of human acts is no longer applicable. Contemporary theologians are developing a contextual, historical norm of human behavior.

Hierarchical Magisterium and Theologians: Contemporary State of the Questions of Contraception

Magisterial Pronouncements on Responsible Parenthood before Humanae Vitae. The need for regulating births and the moral permissibility of so doing have gradually been recognized in magisterial pronouncements of the Church. Pope Pius XII taught that serious motives—which are very numerous and broad—can exempt the married couple from the duty of procreation for a long time, even for the entire duration of their marriage.[22] Pope John XXIII referred to this as a responsibility under certain circumstances.[23] The Second Vatican Council spoke of fulfilling the task of parenthood "with human and Christian responsibility."[24] "The parents themselves should ultimately make this judgment in the sight of God."[25]

No word of doubt is expressed in the Church today concerning this basic moral duty (responsible parenthood), but the teachings of the popes continued to reiterate the absolute condemnation of artificial contraception taught by Pius XI in *Casti Connubii.* There was, however, even before *Humanae Vitae,* a division of opinion in the Catholic Church as to the binding force of this norm on contraception.

Magisterium, Theologians and Contraception: Pre-1963 Statements. The principal pre-1963 statements condemning contraception were those of Pius XI (*Casti Connubii,* 1930) and Pius XII (Address to the Midwives, 1951).

Relevant portions of the Encyclical *Casti Connubii,* which was dated December 31, 1930, include:

> But no reason, however grave, may be put forward by which anything intrinsically against nature may become comformable to nature and morally good. Since, therefore, the conjugal act is destined primarily

by nature for the begetting of children, those who in exercizing it deliberately frustrate its natural power and purpose sin against nature and commit a deed which is shameful and intrinsically vicious. (paragraph 51.)

Since, therefore, openly departing from the uninterrupted Christian tradition, some recently have judged it possible solemnly to declare another doctrine regarding this question, the Catholic Church, to whom God has entrusted the teaching and defense of the integrity and purity of morals, standing erect in the midst of the moral ruin which surrounds her, in order that she may preserve the chastity of the nuptial union from being defiled by this foul stain, raises her voice in token of her divine ambassadorship and through Our mouth proclaims anew: any use whatsoever of matrimony exercized in such a way that the act is deliberately frustrated in its natural power to generate life is an offense against the law of God and of nature, and those who indulge in such are branded with the guilt of a grave sin. (paragraph 56.)

Most theological evaluation of Pius XII's statement on the subject would refer to *Casti Connubii* as the magisterial source of Pius XII's pronouncements. Thus, critiques of *Casti Connubii* would by implication involve the Address to the Midwives. A few authors said Pius XI's condemnation in *Casti Connubii* was an *ex cathedra* definition (hence infallible); others said the teaching was infallible from the ordinary and universal magisterium; others said it was "certain" from tradition, etc.; others (the clear majority) said it was noninfallible. Influential on the American scene was John C. Ford, S.J., who argued that the "common denominator" of all the commentators on *Casti Connubii* was that the condemnation of contraception was at least definable doctrine: while prescinding from infallibility, this approach safeguards the teaching's irrevocability.[26] This attempt to create a category of "irrevocable" halfway between infallibility and noninfallibility (an evaluation which Ford is apparently repeating since *Humanae Vitae*) is highly tendentious.

The ecclesiology of the moralists in this period was strongly post-Vatican I (an infallibility-minded era); there was no open dispute (not even open discussion!) on the morality of contraception. The norm was simply accepted and not tested or contested by Catholic theologians.

Period from 1963 to Humanae Vitae. Commencing in 1963, a number of prelates, an ever-increasing number of theologians and a large segment of the faithful, in view of scientific, historical, sociological, psychological, demographic and theological considerations, began questioning the Church's ban of "the pill" and other forms of contraception when used for purposes of responsible birth control. The question asked was whether *every* contraceptive intervention—not simply that done from egoistic and hedonistic motives but even that done for very weighty and responsible reasons—is morally evil in itself. Profound scriptural, traditional and theological reasons were given for revision of the norm. The public discussion brought out for the first time a grave difference of opinion, bringing a measure of uncertainty to all those Catholics—laity, priests and bishops—who were earnestly seeking the truth. It is clear that during this period the Church was experiencing a widespread and seriously-based atmosphere of perplexity and uncertainty concerning the licit means for implementing the duty of responsible parenthood.

Any analysis of the certitude and binding force of the magisterial teaching, and of the ways in which magisterial pronouncements may or may not allow of a variety of theological interpretations within the Church, must at least take into account what those theological interpretations were between 1963 and 1968. It will become evident that, among reputable Catholic theologians, a great variety of moral theories were being proposed during this time which found their way into pastoral practice on the part of bishops, priests and laity.[27]

1) Defense of Absolute, Intrinsic Immorality of Contraception.

Some theologians, even in the years of new debate on this topic, were defending on philosophical and theological grounds the teachings of Pius XI and Pius XII that contraception (understood as positive methods of directly preventing conjugal intercourse from resulting in conception) is intrinsically and gravely immoral. Though admitting in many instances that these arguments are rarely convincing to all, particularly to those who do not share the Roman Catholic faith, they advance clarification of the papal teachings and philosophical considerations of their own to support this teaching, arguing from either the procreational purpose of the conjugal act, or from its purpose of mutual self-donation or both.[28]

One of the most thoroughly elaborated defenses of this position is that proposed by Germain Grisez.[29] He contends that the arguments customarily advanced to support the authoritative teachings of recent pontiffs—the "perverted faculty" argument and the argument from loving self-donation—are based on an inadequate theory of natural law. More recently, many philosophers and theologians have pointed to a number of grave weaknesses in Grisez's natural law argument. However, Grisez's approach at least illustrates the fact that natural law does not indicate a monolithic philosophical system.

The minority report of the pope's commission on the problem of the family, population and natality maintained this same view that contraception is always (i.e., intrinsically) seriously evil. It admitted, however, that clear and cogent arguments based on reason alone could not be given. Instead, it based its position largely on the fact that the magisterium has consistently upheld this position in the past.[30]

With an increasing awareness of the almost insufferable hardships entailed in a truly responsible parenthood, and cognizant of newer insights into the psychology of moral imputability, a number of authors were prepared to admit that, although the use of contraceptives is objectively gravely immoral, subjectively its use may rather frequently be only venially sinful, or perhaps not sinful at all. Thus they were willing to admit a more lenient pastoral approach, while still maintaining that contraception is objectively wrong.

2) Possibility of Change in the Teaching of the Hierarchical Magisterium.

The aforementioned authors were operating on the stated assumption that the magisterial statements of the popes condemning contraception were irreversible and admitted of no change. A considerable number of theologians, however, addressing themselves more recently to the question of contraception and the development of doctrine within the Church, and taking into account new knowledge which is available, concluded that the formulation of the norm as expressed by Pius XI in *Casti Connubii* admitted of development to a formulation which would morally permit the use of contraceptives, at least in some cases, without thereby betraying the core or basic value conveyed by the Church's traditional teachings on marriage. This position was proposed by Gregory Baum and others.[31]

The possibility, and perhaps desirability, of a change in the norm was also promoted both in the public mind as well as in theological reflection by the interventions of several cardinals during the Second Vatican Council in the Fall of 1964. Cardinal Leger said that fundamental principles must be reinvestigated—not simply to meet a popular demand, but rather because of a keener theological analysis of marriage and from new discoveries in biology, psychology and sociology. He said that fecundity should be described as affecting the whole state of matrimony rather than every single act. Cardinal Alfrink pointed to real doubts, in the case of a serious marital dilemma, as to whether complete or periodical continence is the only efficacious, moral and Christian solution. Patriarch Maximos IV Saigh asked whether the official positions of the Church should not be revised in the light of modern science, both theological and medical, psychological and sociological.

3) Distinction among Various Forms of Contraception—Approval of "The Pill."

Theologians generally do not hold that the magisterial pronouncements, especially *Casti Connubii,* condemning contraception apply to contraceptive sterilization with the same authoritative and juridical force.[32] However, Pius XII explicitly condemned direct (contraceptive) sterilization in an authentic, noninfallible way, and applied this teaching to the progestational steroid (the so-called "birth control pill"), condemning as immoral its use for the direct purpose of suppressing ovulation for the sake of avoiding conception.[33]

The first public questioning of the traditional teaching argued in favor of the use of "the pill," but these early probings still condemned other forms of contraception. Certain theologians—Louis Janssens, W. van der Marck and Josef M. Reuss—said that the natural process of the individual sex act should be respected, but procreation may licitly be excluded as an effect of the sex act through the anti-ovulation pills when serious reasons justify this method of responsible parenthood.[34] This opinion came to be held very widely. Ambrogio Valsecchi, who summarized virtually all the writings of the theologians during this period on every moral aspect of "the pill," established that the majority of European theologians, writing on this topic after the above-mentioned three articles, saw this view as possible, or were outright favorable towards it.[35] He found the theological situation in America the reverse: there was opposition to the new moral opinion, but not by many theologians; and those Americans who continued to oppose it failed to offer new development of thought in reference to the newer problems which had been raised.

4) Each Individual Act Need Not Be Open to Procreation: Acceptance of All Forms of Contraception as Such.

The new opinions just referred to were followed by a more basic examination into the moral question of contraception itself. After studying the implications of biology (and the merits of employing a biologically determined moral norm), anthropology (which sees marriage as a whole, having one complex aim), psychology (and the importance of a sustained and harmonious love for marriage), sociology (newer elements in the social structure of the family, overpopulation) and other newer dimensions of sex in marriage, many theologians (eventually the majority) could see no moral difference between the use of "the pill" and other methods of conscientious birth regulation. In many cases, the arguments already offered by some theologians to justify the contraceptive use of "the pill" were also found applicable to other contraceptive methods generally. Thus the opinion began to be proposed by many theologians that the meaning of marriage always includes the notion of procreation, but that every individual human sexual act in marriage need not be open to procreation.[36]

The climax of this trend was the majority theological opinion of the so-called papal birth control commission. Without making any important distinctions among the various methods, the majority view holds that the use of contraception should not always be considered intrinsically and gravely immoral. It should be noted that the use of contraception is not thought to be good in every case, nor preferable, as though its unreasonable use could not lead to selfish hedonism. Instead, these theologians concluded that, in the face of serious reasons for limiting family size, and considering the duty of maintaining family harmony and fidelity through the more or less regular use of full sexual intimacies in marriage, it cannot be held that *every* sexual act must remain "open to procreation."[37]

5) Ideal/Real Situation; "Lesser of Two Evils": A Pastoral Approach.

A final unique category of theological opinion on the morality of contraception teaches that the marital act is both unifying and creative of fruitful love, and that neither purpose should be effectively excluded from the act. But this opinion holds that the Catholic teaching is a *positive* vocation to an *ideal*. The ideal would be to attain the full beauty and truth of sexual consummation by realizing *all* the levels of its meaning in the act. This cannot be attained all at once: it calls for a morality of growth. This viewpoint suggests that it is difficult to arrive at the *prohibition* of any particular act, that there is usually a combination of values and disvalues in human acts in man's fallen state, and the overriding value is to achieve as many "goods" as possible toward implementing the moral order.[38] This perspective certainly mitigates the "objectively and intrinsically immoral" designation of every contraceptive act. It maintains that, when the marital embrace involves both values and disvalues, the moral decision should not be based on whatever may be defective in the specific shape the act takes here and now but on the best that can be done. Such a decision must not be considered sinful: in view of the total end aimed at, it may be a proof of wisdom. To know how to accept imperfect behavior as, at the moment, the "least bad" choice is to behave wisely and virtuously. This moral analysis differs only little from the opinion which held that contraception may be chosen, when necessary, as "the lesser of two evils."[39]

Responses of the Magisterium to the Mid-60's Controversy. With respect to this mounting controversy, the highest ecclesiastical authorities (Ecumenical Council and Pope) were not able to remove doubts by stating a definitive or unchangeable norm.

1) Vatican II (1965). The Council manifested an awareness of a crisis of responsible Christian parenthood in the lives of many married people. The *Constitution on the Church in the Modern World* honestly acknowledged and described this dilemma: that sometimes couples should not procreate; yet they should not forego all sexual intimacy, for otherwise family harmony would be threatened—an unfortunate outcome which would militate against the basic educational purpose of marriage.

> This Council realizes that certain modern conditions often keep couples from arranging their married lives harmoniously, and that they find themselves in circumstances where at least temporarily the size of their families should not be increased. As a result, the faithful exercise of love and the full intimacy of their lives is hard to maintain. But where the intimacy of married life is broken off, its faithfulness can sometimes be imperiled and its quality of fruitfulness ruined, for then the upbringing of the children and the courage to accept new ones are both endangered.[40]

The uncertainty concerning whether *every* prevention of conception is morally evil in itself, or whether contraceptive measures cannot be justified for serious objective reasons, was heightened by the decision of the Council not to decide this question.[41] The Council affirmed that there are "illicit practices against human generation," and admonished Catholics that, in practice, it is not permissible for them to "undertake methods of regulating procreation which are found blameworthy by the teaching authority of the

Church in its unfolding of the divine law." An explanatory footnote in the conciliar document, after referring to previous papal norms, added:

> Certain questions which need further and more careful investigations have been handed over, at the command of the Supreme Pontiff, to a commission for the study of population, family, and births, in order that, after it fulfills its function, the Supreme Pontiff may pass judgment. Since the doctrine of the magisterium is such, this holy Synod does not intend to propose immediately concrete solutions.[42]

It has been claimed that the Council's handling of this matter *condemned* contraception, excluding any practical doubt on the matter.[43] If this were so, the teaching of *Humanae Vitae* on this topic would have been quite superfluous with respect to the judgment of the certitude of the teaching. Others have sharply denied that the Council reaffirmed as certain and unchangeable the unexceptionable moral malice of contraceptive interventions.[44] The Council, in its examination of the votes *iuxta modum,* rejected any *modi* which called for incorporation of suitable formulations of the traditional norm in the conciliar text.[45] Pope Paul himself said that the Second Vatican Council was not able to resolve the question: deeper study was needed.[46] Vatican II, therefore, without explicitly and substantially *changing* the traditional teaching that every contraceptive action is evil in itself, did not confirm with conciliar authority such earlier teaching.[47]

2) Paul VI—The Commission Period. Having appointed a special commission to study the morality of contraception, Pope Paul admitted that the question was "an extremely complex and delicate problem," and that new knowledge was shedding light on the question.[48] He said the norms of Pius XII should be regarded as valid, but that such traditional authoritative teaching was not irreformable in the sense of a final definition; he declared himself prepared to announce a change if he felt bound in conscience.[49] He requested expert advice so that he could give guidance without ambiguity.[50] He said that the consciences of men should not be

left exposed to painful uncertainties;[51] that deeper study was needed because the Church's teaching authority cannot establish moral standards unless it is certain it is interpreting God's will; and that the Church was trying to reach such certitude.[52]

Pope Paul, who had reserved the birth control question to himself,[53] received the report of his birth control commission in 1966, but declared that no decisive pronouncement could be made until he studied further the doctrinal, pastoral and social implications of the change in the norm proposed by his commission.[54] The Pope stated, on the same occasion, that the Church's norm prohibiting contraception "cannot be considered not binding as if the magisterium of the Church were in a state of doubt at the present time, whereas it is in a moment of study and reflection concerning matters which have been put before it as worthy of the most attentive consideration."[55]

Theologians' Positions on the Binding Force of the Magisterial Norm before Humanae Vitae. It has already been pointed out that the majority of theologians writing on the question of contraception at this time began to favor the use of the pill as a legitimate means for regulating birth. Likewise, a growing number of theologians, even the majority in the later years, as indicated in the majority report of the birth control commission, came to the conclusion that there was no decisive theological difference between the pill and other forms of contraception, such as rhythm, and argued for a change in the teaching of the Church on contraception. It is common knowledge that a substantial number of Catholic theologians asserted that in certain circumstances Catholic couples could in good conscience use contraception in the responsible planning of their families. These theologians saw no objective or subjective evil in the use of contraception in these circumstances.

How could Catholic theologians come to this conclusion in the light of the teaching of *Casti Connubii,* the later addresses of the popes, and especially the most recent statements of Paul VI? These theologians maintained there could be a development of teaching from the time of Pius XI and that the teaching of the magisterium on this issue could change. Various propositions were articulated by these theologians in support of their dissent.

1) Probable Opinion to the Contrary. The teaching of *Casti Connubii* was no longer binding, nor were the more recent but less authoritative statements made by subsequent popes, especially by Paul VI, binding. The weight of theological opinion was now so strong that there was a probable opinion that one could use contraception in certain circumstances.[56]

2) Norms as Disciplinary. The teaching of *Casti Connubii* was no longer true in the light of a development of the teaching, and the recent statements of Paul VI were more in the nature of disciplinary norms. In his statements, the Pope admitted that he had not yet given his final view. Thus one could treat the statements of Paul VI as practical rules, or as what theology has traditionally called merely disciplinary norms. Such norms would not be binding in the face of a proportionate, *grave incommodum* (serious inconvenience) in observing them.[57]

3) Conditional Assent to Noninfallible Teaching: Possibility of "Dissent." The question of contraception naturally gave rise to the question of the magisterium in moral matters. There was dissatisfaction with some solutions which did not go to the heart of the problem. The question of whether or not Catholics could use contraception was intimately tied up with a proper understanding of the magisterium. In this light, it is interesting to read the following citation from Richard A. McCormick. (Note that McCormick has the reputation of a very modern theologian who, later than many others, saw the need for a change in the teaching on contraception.)

> Theologians would contend that the precise obliging force of papal statements on contraception is their doctrinal force. That is, authoritative Church interventions on questions of natural law are educative in the moral order. This educative aspect is the basic source of their obligatory power. In other words, the Catholic recognizes in the *magisterium* a divine commission to teach, to enlighten consciences.

Because of this divine commission and the promise of aid in its execution, authentic noninfallible Church interpretations of natural law enjoy the presumption of correctness, and it is this presumption which founds the duty in prudence to accept in a human way these teachings; for we are all bound to prudence in the formation of our consciences. The obligation is not the result of a legal directive.

Once it is shown, therefore, that there are intrinsic reasons (good and probable) why the Church may change her teaching on contraception, it would seem that the foundation for a certain obligation has ceased to exist—precisely because the obligation never derived in the first place from a legal directive, but from a teaching or doctrinal statement. If the teaching statement becomes doubtful, does not the obligation also? And if the pertinence of past norms to divine law is doubtful, is not the teaching statement doubtful?

But, it has been claimed, the address of Pope Paul VI on October 29, 1966, repudiated the existence of a doubt. Verbally, yes. But a careful reading of this address (wherein the Pope said explicitly that he was not making his decisive statement on contraception) will lead one to the conclusion that it could not have been a doctrinal or teaching statement. Noonan admits this when he asserts that the Pope was actually admitting a "doubt as to the divine immutable character of the law." Only an authentic teaching statement is capable of dissipating a genuine doctrinal doubt. And that is why I would agree with the many theologians who contend that the matter of contraception is, as of now, at least for situations of genuine conflict, just where it was before the papal address—in a state of practical doubt.[58]

Thus before *Humanae Vitae* theologians could and did responsibly teach that, on the question of contraception, there was sufficient reason to dissent from the authoritative, noninfallible, papal teaching on this point. On July 29, 1968, a Roman Catholic theologian familiar with the historical development of the question of contraception was generally aware of these two theological positions: the right and at times the obligation to dissent even in a public way from authoritative, noninfallible papal teaching, and the insufficiences of the natural law reasoning proposed in defense of the absolute condemnation of artificial contraception.

Conscience as a Framework of Dissent

The penultimate paragraph of the Statement by Theologians maintains: "Therefore, as Roman Catholic theologians, conscious of our duty and our limitations, we conclude that spouses may responsibly decide according to their conscience that artificial contraception in some circumstances is permissible and indeed necessary to preserve and foster the values and sacredness of marriage."

The Statement by Theologians is not based on an unnuanced, universal moral principle that subjective conscience can be followed without moral wrong in each and every situation. In the total context, the Statement has indicated that in the matter of artificial contraception, there are sufficient reasons to reject the absolute ban on artificial contraception proposed in *Humanae Vitae*. Whether or not sufficient reasons are present in a particular case is a judgment that must ultimately be made by the conscience of the couple themselves as they try to weigh all the values involved in the situation. Such an approach to conscience is neither new nor startling for one familiar with Catholic theology; in fact, the same approach has been followed in the matter of responsible parenthood itself. The *Pastoral Constitution on the Church in the Modern World* recognizes that couples may "find themselves in circumstances where at least temporarily the size of their families should not be increased."[59] The same Constitution affirms that "the decision concerning the number of children they will have depends on the correct judgment of the parents."[60] Thus the Council document merely summarizes what all Catholic theologians would teach about responsible parenthood—parents do not have to bring into the world all the children they can possibly procreate but should responsibly plan their families in the light of all the values present, with the ultimate judgment in this case left to the honest decision of the couple themselves.

Scholastic Terminology. Conscience is generally described in manuals of Catholic moral theology as the judgment of the practical reason about the moral goodness of a practical act.[61]

Scholastic theologians have traditionally distinguished various types of conscience, although not all have agreed on the terminology employed. The problem of conscience in the context of moral theology arises from the tensions between the subjective pole of morality and the objective pole of morality, or between freedom and truth (although some contemporary theologians are striving to overcome the total dichotomies implied in such terminology).

Conscience is true (*vera*) if it corresponds to the objective order; erroneous (*erronea*) if it does not correspond to the objective order. A sincere conscience *(conscientia recta)* is one subjectively formed in the proper way but which may be erroneous. A true and sincere conscience must always be followed. Theologians generally admit that a sincere but invincibly erroneous conscience (sometimes called the erroneous conscience in good faith) must be followed by the individual. However, a vincibly erroneous conscience cannot be followed without moral guilt. To properly appraise statements made about the rights of conscience by people speaking in the context of the scholastic idiom, it is necesary to be familiar with the above distinctions.

Concerning the decision of conscience to use artificial contraception, three possibilities exist:

1) Some theologians would hold that the decision to use contraception could come from a true and sincere conscience. The Statement by the theologians is consonant with this understanding.

2) Some statements by Catholic bishops and theologians indicate that such decision could reflect a sincere but erroneous conscience; the error on the part of such a person would be invincible, and he would not be guilty in following such a conscience although there would remain a moral obligation to overcome the error and arrive at the truth.

3) Others maintain that, after *Humanae Vitae,* such a conscience would be vincibly erroneous and, consequently, could not be followed without moral guilt.

Contemporary Catholic Moral Theology. Catholic moral theology avoids any simplistic, absolute norm based on the rights of the individual conscience. Such an unnuanced universal norm would destroy the efforts of moral theology and Christian ethics which endeavor to point out the good, fitting and right thing to do. One cannot appeal merely to such an unnuanced moral norm to justify his actions. Some confusion apparently arises from a poor understanding on the *Declaration on Religious Liberty (Vatican II),* but the declaration studiously avoids the technical term "freedom of conscience," probably because of the many simplistic understandings of this term.

Catholic moral theology has attempted to present an ethical approach based on reality rather than on mere subjectivistic whims and fancies. Conscience ultimately must conform itself to the moral order. However, Catholic theology is recognizing more and more that such a moral order cannot be spelled out beforehand in very specific terms.

The just war theory proposed by Catholic theologians maintains that the *individual* must decide in each and every case whether the war is just. The same argument is being employed in support of civil law recognition of selective conscientious objection—a position adopted in the 1968 Pastoral Letter of the American Bishops. Catholic theology stresses that the conscience must be properly formed before making its decisions. However, this obligation does not require a scholar's grasp of all the issues involved. If such were required, people could not realistically make decisions of conscience. A commensurate amount of diligence and inquiry is what is required. In addition, conscience itself does not properly operate only in a coldly rationalistic way. In fact, the rationalistic aspect of conscience has been overemphasized to the detriment of other aspects, such as intuition and connaturality.

A greater emphasis is being placed upon conscience in the contemporary milieu. More stress is placed on the dignity of the human person and the need for man to respond to the call of God in a personal manner from the very depths of his own person.[62] Such personal responsibility requires man to take a more active and creative role in bringing about the betterment of the world and society. Sociological changes have given more people an education and an opportunity to make creative contributions to society. The emphasis on historicity, growth and development has focused on the responsibility of man to direct such growth and change. The objective moral order is no longer conceived as a minute plan spelled out in unchanging patterns which will always be existing and normative for the Christian.

In moral theology today the question of conscience frequently arises in the context of the debate about "situation ethics" and absolute norms in moral theology. A responsible theologian must avoid the simplistic "either/or" approach to problems (e.g., either follow conscience or follow objective norms as taught in Catholic moral theology). Catholic moral theory has always tried to avoid subjectivism by holding that morality is based on reality. Today, newer epistemological theories are coming to grips with the problems of reality. Reality cannot be considered merely in terms of the objectivity of the object "out there." These newer epistemological approaches strive for a critical realism, which ultimately tries to overcome some of the simplistic, subjective-objective dichotomy of the past.

The brief discussion of scholastic terminology and newer trends in the understanding of conscience illustrates the complexity of the problem and the need to avoid simplistic solutions. The conclusion of the Statement by Theologians is not based on a simplistic and universal principle that subjective conscience can be followed without wrong in every situation. The entire context of the Statement and the six chapters of this volume indicate the true interpretation of the conclusion: in this particular case of artificial contraception, there are sufficient reasons for dissenting from the absolute ban enunciated in *Humanae Vitae,* but in the individual case, the final judgment must be made by the consciences of the couples after carefully weighing all the values involved.

Notes

1. C. Ryan, O.P., "The Traditional Concept of Natural Law: An Investigation," in Illtud Evans, ed., *Light on the Natural Law* (Baltimore: Helicon Press, 1965).

2. J. M. Aubert, "Le droit naturel: ses avatars historiques et son avenir," *Supplément de la Vie Spirituelle* 81 (May, 1967), pp. 282–322.
3. *Pastoral Constitution on the Church in the Modern World,* paras. 74 and 79.
4. F. Boeckle, ed., *Das Naturrecht im Disput* (Dusseldorf: Patmos, 1966).
5. B. Lonergan, *Collection* (New York: Herder, 1967), pp. 252–267; "A Transition From a Classicist Worldview to Historical Mindedness," in J. E. Biechler, ed., *Law For Liberty* (Baltimore: Helicon, 1967).
6. K. Rahner, *Spirit in the World* (New York: Herder, 1968); B. Lonergan, *Insight, A Study in Human Understanding* (New York: Philosophical Library, 1957); *Collection* (New York: Herder, 1967); E. Coreth, *Metaphysics* (New York: Herder, 1968).
7. R. Johann, *Building The Human* (New York: Herder, 1968); F. Simons, "The Catholic Church and the New Morality," *Cross Currents,* 16 (1966), pp. 429–445; W. van der Marck, *Toward a Christian Ethic* (New York: Newman Press, 1967); F. Boeckle, ed., *Das Naturrecht im Disput* (Dusseldorf: Patmos, 1966); B. Schueller, "Zur theologschen Diskussion ueber die lex naturalis," *Theologie und Philosophie,* 41 (1966), 481–503.
8. In this section the subject professors again want to express their gratitude to Herder & Herder for the permission to publish in book form materials which in substantially the same form were published in *Contraception: Authority and Dissent,* C. E. Curran, ed. (New York: Herder, 1969), especially pp. 159–175.
9. 43 *AAS* (1951), p. 838.
10. T. L. Hayes, "The Biology of the Reproductive Act," *Cross Currents,* 15 (1965), pp. 393–406.
11. S. Mudd, ed., *The Population Crisis and The Use of World Resources* (The Hague: Dr. W. Junk, 1964); M. Cepede, F. Houtart, L. Grond, *Population and Food* (New York: Sheed & Ward, 1964).
12. B. Haering, "The Inseparability of the Unitive-Procreative Functions of the Marital Act," in C. Curran, ed., *Contraception: Authority and Dissent* (New York: Herder, 1969).
13. R. O. Johann, "Responsible Parenthood: A Philosophical View," *Proceedings of the Catholic Theological Society of America,* 20 (1965), pp. 115–128; W. H. van der Marck, *op. cit.,* pp. 48–60.
14. Lonergan, *Collection* (New York: Herder, 1967), pp. 121–267.
15. D. H. Johnson, "Lonergan and the Redoing of Ethics," *Continuum,* 5 (1967), pp. 211–220.
16. This section follows very closely the highly respected historical research found in J. T. Noonan, Jr., *Contraception* (Cambridge, Mass.: Harvard University Press, 1965); full citation and references cited herein are available in Professor Noonan's book.

17. Noonan, *op. cit.*, pp. 34–35.
18. *II–II,* 154, 12, *ad obj.* 1.
19. *On the Sentences,* 4.31, 2.2.
20. *Summa Against the Gentiles,* 3.122.
21. *On the Sentences,* 4.31.
22. Address to the Midwives, October 29, 1951, in *AAS* 43 (1951), pp. 835–54, at pp. 845–46; Address to the Family Front, November 26, 1951, in 43 *AAS* (1951), pp. 855–60, at p. 59.
23. *Mater et Magistra,* May 15, 1961, in 53 *AAS* (1961), pp. 401–64, at pp. 447–48.
24. Vatican II, *Pastoral Constitution on the Church in the Modern World,* para. 50.
25. *Ibid.*
26. J. C. Ford and G. Kelly, *Marriage Questions: Contemporary Moral Theology II* (Westminster: Newman, 1963), pp. 256–78.
27. Among the better surveys of the theological literature on contraception at this time is: A. Valsecchi, "La discussione morale sui progestativi," *La Scuola Cattolica* 93 (1965), supplemento 2, 157*–216*.
28. G. Kelly, "Contraception and Natural Law," *Proceedings of the Catholic Theological Society of America,* 18 (1963), pp. 25–45, and reiterated in the book he coauthored with J. C. Ford *(op. cit., supra).* Their works appeared, however, before the traditional teaching was thoroughly challenged in Catholic theology.
29. G. Grisez, *Contraception and the Natural Law* (Milwaukee: Bruce, 1964).
30. "Report of the Commission for the Study of Population, Family and Births," *The National Catholic Reporter* (April 19, 1967), pp. 9–12.
31. G. Baum, "Can the Church Change Her Position on Birth Control?" in T. Roberts, ed., *Contraception and Catholics* (New York: Herder, 1964), pp. 311–344; Dewart, "*Casti Connubii* and the Development of Dogma," *ibid.*, pp. 202–310; F. H. Drinkwater, "Ordinary and Universal Magisterium," *The Clergy Review* 50 (1965), pp. 2–22; E. Schillebeeckx, "De Naturwet in verband met de Katholieke huwelijksopvatting," *Jaarobek der Katholieke Theologen 1961* (Hilversun, 1963), pp. 5–51; and others.
32. G. Kelly, *op. cit.*, pp. 26–27.
33. 43 *AAS* (1951), 843–44; 50 (1958), 734–35.
34. L. Janssens, "Morale conjugale et progestogenes," *Ephermerides Theologicae Lovanienses,* 39 (1963), pp. 787–826; W. van der Marck, "Vruchtbaarheidsregeling," *Tijdschrift voor Theologie,* 3 (1963), pp. 378–413; J. M. Reuss, "Eheliche Hingabe und Zeugung," *Tuebinger Theologische Quartalschrift,* 143 (1963), pp. 454–476.
35. A. Valsecchi, *op. cit.*

36. Louis Dupré, *Contraception and Catholics* (Baltimore: Helicon, 1964), W. van der Marck, *Liefde en vruchtbaarheid. Aktuele vragen over geboorteregcling* (Roermond: Romen, 1964). (This work is also available in English translation: *Love and Fertility. Contemporary Questions about Birth Regulation* [London: Sheed & Ward, 1965]; E. Schillebeeckx, "De Naturwet in verband met de katholieke huwelijksopvatting," *Jaarboek der Katholieke Theologen 1961* (Hilversum, 1963), pp. 5–51.
37. "Report of the Commission for the Study of Population, Family and Births," *The National Catholic Reporter* (April 19, 1967), pp. 8–12.
38. P. de Locht, *La morale conjugale* (Brussels: CNPF, 1964).
39. For a summary of the various approaches, see *Concilium,* Vol. 5 (1965), articles by F. Boeckle, "Birth Control, A Survey of German, French and Dutch Literature on the Question of Birth Control," pp. 97–129; E. McDonagh, "Recent English Literature on the Moral Theology of Marriage," pp. 130–154.
40. Vatican II, *Pastoral Constitution on The Church in The Modern World,* para. 51; Pope Paul VI speaking to the College of Cardinals on June 23, 1964, had already acknowledged the existence, the complexity and the delicacy of this problem: 56 *AAS* (1965), p. 588.
41. Bishop Reuss, *Verantwortete Elternschaft* (Mainz: Matthias-Gruenewald-Verlag, 1967), pp. 83–116.
42. Vatican II, *Pastoral Constitution on The Church in The Modern World,* paras. 47 and 51, Fn. 14.
43. J. C. Ford and J. J. Lynch, "Contraception: a Matter of Practical Doubt?" *Homiletic and Pastoral Review,* 68 (1968), pp. 563–574.
44. V. Heylen, "La Note 14 dans la constitution pastorale 'Gaudium et Spes,' " *Ephemerides Theologicae Lovanienses,* 42 (1966), fasc. 3.
45. Cf. *Expensio modorum partis secundae,* approved by the Council, paras. 1c, 1e, 42a, 56d, 71, 79, 93, 98a, 104f, 105a, 107h.
46. Pope Paul VI, February 12, 1966, 58 *AAS* (1966), p. 219.
47. Reuss, *op. cit.,* pp. 85–86, who also states, from the study of Heylen, that footnote 14 points to a doubt in the Church, "dubitante ecclesia."
48. June 23, 1964, 56 *AAS* (1964), p. 588.
49. *Ibid.,* pp. 588–589.
50. March 27, 1965, 57 *AAS* (1965), pp. 388–390.
51. *Ibid.*
52. February 12, 1966, *AAS,* 58 (1966), p. 219.
53. 56 *AAS* (1964), pp. 581–589; *Pastoral Constitution on The Church in The Modern World,* para. 51; 58 *AAS* (1966), pp. 1168–1170.
54. October 29, 1966, 58 *AAS* (1966), p. 1169.
55. *Id.,* pp. 1169–1170.

56. E.g., R. A. McCormick, "Notes on Moral Theology," 26 *Theological Studies,* (1965), p. 646.
57. J. T. Noonan, "The Pope's Conscience," *Commonweal* 85 (1967), 559ff; R. A. McCormick, "Notes on Moral Theology," *Theological Studies,* 28 (1967), pp. 796–800; B. Haering, "Aber wir Beichtvaeter . . . !" *Theologie der Gegenwart* 10 (1967), pp. 40–43; J. M. Reuss, *Verantwortete Elternschaft* (Mainz: Matthias-Gruenewald-Verlag, 1967), pp. 83–116.
58. R. A. McCormick, "Notes on Moral Theology," *Theological Studies,* 28 (1967), pp. 799–800.
59. Vatican II, *Pastoral Constitution on The Church in The Modern World,* para. 51.
60. *Ibid.,* para. 87.
61. The treatment on conscience in this section merely summarizes the consideration as found in the manuals of Catholic theology. These considerations are then applied to the question under discussion.
62. Vatican II, *Declaration on Religious Freedom,* para. 1.

7

The Dissent from *Humanae Vitae* Onset and Aftermath

A Contemporary Context: Actions and Declarations of Others. The preceding chapters have explained the rationale justifying the actions and declarations of the Catholic University professors who made public their dissent from the specific ethical conclusion of *Humanae Vitae* which absolutely condemned artificial contraception. There is, however, another methodological approach in judging the actions and declarations of these professors: their conduct must be seen in the total context of other responses to the Encyclical. If other respected theologians, and especially entire national hierarchies, made public interpretations of the papal letter which in some way dissent from the absolute ban on contraception, then the Catholic University professors and their American colleagues could also find justification in the actions and declarations of other prudent and respected people. But a word of caution is in order. Although the public dissent of American theologians bears many similarities with other dissent throughout the world, there are important, distinctive characteristics about the dissent in which the Catholic University professors were involved. Their dissent was unique and unprecedented in its immediacy and in its concerted expression of co-responsibility on the part of a large number of theologians. The actions and declarations of national hierarchies and other theologians, nevertheless, furnish an incontestable basis for justifying even the unique characteristics of the dissent spearheaded by the professors at Catholic University.

Dissent Within the Hierarchical Magisterium. The Statement by Catholic Theologians had upheld as a "common teaching in the Church that Catholics may dissent from authoritative, noninfallible teachings of the magisterium when sufficient reasons for so doing exist." Most of the national hierarchies throughout the world also made public their collective interpretation of the papal letter. Some of these statements of national hierarchies merely restated the papal teaching with no further interpretation. Others tended to interpret the Encyclical in a pastoral way by indicating that in practice there may not be subjective sin when a couple uses artificial contraception in a given situation. Other national hierarchies, however, did refer to the possibility of dissent in practice from the absolute ban of the Encyclical's teaching, although each approached the problem in a somewhat different way. A sampling of this latter approach follows.

a) On July 30, 1968, Cardinal Alfrink of the Netherlands publicly announced that Catholics do not have to accept the Encyclical without discussion or debate and called an emergency conference of the Dutch hierarchy. On August 2, Cardinal Alfrink and six other Roman Catholic bishops of the Netherlands issued a joint letter, with copies to the press, to the effect that the Encyclical is not infallible, and that while "the personal conscience cannot pass over an authoritative pronouncement such as a papal letter . . . there are many factors which determine one's personal conscience regarding marriage rules (for example, the mutual love, the relations in a family and the social circumstances)."[1]

b) On August 30, at their conference at Malines, the Belgian hierarchy issued a statement to the Belgian Church and the press, which included the following:

> Someone, however, who is competent in the matter under consideration and capable of forming a personal and well-founded judgment—which necessarily presupposes a sufficient amount of knowledge—may, after a serious examination before God, come to other conclusions on certain points. In such a case he has the right to follow his conviction provided that he remains sincerely disposed to continue his enquiry.[2]

c) On August 30, at Koenigstein, Federal Republic of Germany, the German hierarchy issued to the German Church and to the press a statement concerning the Encyclical, which included the following:

On the other hand, we know that many are of the opinion that they cannot accept the encyclical's statement on the methods of regulating births. They are convinced that this is the exceptional case of which we have spoken in our doctrinal letter of last year. As far as we can see the main questions voiced are: Is the teaching tradition obligatory on the decision stated in the encyclical; do not the recently prominently stressed aspects of marriage and its consummation, also mentioned in the encyclical, cast a doubt on the decisions rendered on the methods of birth control?

He who believes that he must think this way must examine himself conscientiously to determine whether or not he is free of subjective pride and arrogance so that he can account for his position before the judgment of God. In adopting this position he will have to give consideration to the laws of intra-Church dialogue and try to avoid giving any scandal. Only the person acting in such a manner can avoid conflict with the properly understood obligation due authority and the duty of obedience. Only in that way does he contribute to their Christian understanding and realization.[3]

d) On September 21, at Graz, Austria, the Austrian hierarchy issued a statement to the Austrian Church and press concerning the Encyclical, which included the following:

Since the encyclical does not contain an infallible dogma, it is conceivable that someone feels unable to accept the judgment of the teaching authority of the Church. The answer to this is: If someone has experience in this field and has reached a divergent conviction after serious examination, free of emotion[al] haste, he may for the time being follow it. He does not err, if he is willing to continue his examination and otherwise affords respect and fidelity to the Church. It remains clear, however, that in such a case he has no right to create confusion among his brothers in the faith with his opinion.[4]

e) On September 27, at Winnipeg, Canada, the Canadian hierarchy issued a statement to the Canadian Church and to the press concerning the Encyclical, which included the following:

We must appreciate the difficulty experienced by contemporary man in understanding and appropriating some of the points of this encyclical, and we must make every effort to learn from the insights of Catholic scientists and intellectuals, who are of undoubted loyalty to Christian truth, to the Church and to the authority of the Holy See. Since they are not denying any point of divine and Catholic faith nor rejecting the teaching authority of the Church, these Catholics should not be considered, or consider themselves, shut off from the body of the faithful. But they should remember that their good faith will be dependent on a sincere self-examination to determine the true motives and grounds for such suspension of assent and on continued effort to understand and deepen their knowledge of the teaching of the Church.[5]

f) On October 17, at Copenhagen, Denmark, the Scandinavian hierarchy issued a statement to the Scandinavian Church and to the press concerning the Encyclical, which included the following:

There are, however, other declarations of the Church, which do not present the mark of infallible definition. Such decisions do not, indeed, claim to be the object of supernatural faith, but that should by no means be interpreted as if such decisions lacked the assistance of the Holy Ghost. The history of the Church, it is true, can show documents which contained statements later rectified or amplified. Something similar with regard to the encyclical *Humanae Vitae* should therefore, on principle, not be excluded. for everyone agrees that it contains no infallible definition.

Thus, it is evident that no one should question the contents of the encyclical without adequately and equitably, in the presence of God, having studied the thought and final intentions of the encyclical. Should someone, however, for grave and carefully considered reasons, not feel able to subscribe to the arguments of the encyclical, he is entitled, as has been constantly acknowledged, to entertain other views than those put forward in a noninfallible declaration of the Church. No one should, therefore, on account of such diverging opinions alone, be regarded as an inferior Catholic. Whoever, after conscientious reflection, believes he is justified in not accepting the teaching and not applying it in practice, must be answerable to God for his attitude and his acts.[6]

g) On or about December 11, at Solothurn, Switzerland, the Swiss hierarchy issued to the Swiss Church and to the press a statement concerning the Encyclical, including the following:

> The faithful who cannot accept all the encyclical's instructions regarding birth control, when they are not motivated by selfishness or complacency and when honestly striving towards an ever better fulfillment of God's will, may be permitted to assume that they are not guilty before God.[7]

h) On November 8, at Lourdes, France, the French hierarchy issued to the French Church and to the press a statement concerning the Encyclical, including the following:

> Contraception can never be a good. It is always a disorder, but this disorder is not always guilty. It occurs in fact that spouses consider themselves to be confronted by a true conflict of duty.
>
> On this subject we simply recall the constant moral teaching: When one faces a choice of duties, where one cannot avoid an evil whatever be the decision taken, traditional wisdom requires that one seek before God to find which is the greater duty. The spouses will decide for themselves after reflecting together with all the care that the grandeur of their conjugal vocation requires.[8]

This statement of the French hierarchical magisterium publicly "dissents" in another way from the Encyclical: the Encyclical specifically stipulates that no one may licitly apply the concept of the "lesser of two evils" to permit the use of artificial means of contraception (*Humanae Vitae,* paragraph 14).

All the foregoing statements were widely publicized throughout the world. Many of them were reported, occasionally in full text, by the *New York Times*; they were quoted very liberally in other leading American newspapers. In many instances, these newspaper reports were carried as front-page news. Such was the manner and mode of those portions of the hierarchical magisterium that expressed public teaching negative to the absolute binding force of the Encyclical and publicly acknowledged the legitimacy of dissent.

Other Theological Dissent. The declarations and actions of other Roman Catholic theologians parallel in significant details the declarations and actions of the professors at Catholic University and the more than 600 qualified subscribers to the Statement by Theologians. Public dissent from the Encyclical by Roman Catholic theologians began in the press, on television and on radio as early as July 29, 1968. In many instances, this dissent was "organized" in the sense that groups of theologians, or faculties of particular institutions, issued joint statements. The professors at Catholic University documented instances of such dissent in fourteen pages of the prepared materials they submitted in their defense to the Inquiry Panel. Professor Reich, who was in Germany for the summer, was able to document from the German press many of the reactions to the Encyclical in that country. Professor Smolko, with many hours of volunteer help, combed the leading secular papers in this country as well as the leading religious news services to document similar examples of public dissent on the part of theologians.

The following were among the groups who issued public dissenting statements: a group of faculy members at Pope John XXIII National Seminary in Weston, Mass.; Professor Bernard Cooke, S.J., and thirteen colleagues in the theology department of Marquette University; seven members of the theology department of St. Peter's College in Jersey City; six members of the Boston College Department of Theology; fifty-five members of the faculty of St. Francis Xavier University, Antigonish, Nova Scotia. Other groups, such as the faculty of Alma College, Los Gatos, Cal., issued statements which allowed for the possibility of dissent from the Encyclical. Another very significant public dissent emerged from a meeting of twenty European theologians who had gathered in Amsterdam on September 18-19 for the express purpose of commenting on *Humanae Vitae*. The signatories to the resulting public statement include some of the most outstanding contemporary Catholic theologians in Europe: J. M. Aubert, A. Auer, T. Beemer, F. Boeckle, W. Bulst, P. Fransen, R. Gallewaerd, J.

Groot, P. Huizing, L. Janssens, R. van Kessel, W. Klijn, F. Klostermann, O. Madr, F. Malmberg, E. McDonagh, S. Pfeuertner, C. Robert, P. Schoonenberg, C. Sproken and M. de Wachter. The group included professors from the Universities of Louvain, Nijmegen, Tübingen, Bonn, Maynooth, and several other European universities. These theologians, in their organized consensus statement, publicly dissented from the teaching of *Humanae Vitae,* and stated, "If we believe that these considerations may and should be presented to the public, it is because we are convinced that we bear a part of the responsibility for the crisis through which many of our better faithful are passing and above all, because, far from wishing to create any unwarranted agitation, we desire to work for the common good and the salvation of our brethren."[9]

Conclusions concerning the Declarations and Actions of the Catholic University Professors

Declarations and actions of Roman Catholic theologians must be within the pale of the Roman Catholic faith-commitment. The testimony presented to the Inquiry Board did not, however, attempt to demonstrate that the position taken by the professors concerned was the *only* legitimate position within the pale of the Roman Catholic faith-commitment. The purpose of the preceding chapters, and of the prepared testimony they recount, is to prove that the declarations and actions of the Catholic University professors in publicly dissenting from *Humanae Vitae* were within the ambit of responsible Roman Catholic theology.

The Question of Dissent. It is within the pale of responsible Roman Catholic theological activity that Roman Catholic theologians may, and in some cases even should, dissent from authoritative, noninfallible teaching of the hierarchical magisterium when there are sufficient reasons for so doing.

This conclusion flows from the interpretive function of the theologian vis-à-vis the tradition in and for the Church; the very nature of noninfallible teaching itself; the "common teaching" among the manualists that dissent from authoritative, noninfallible teaching of the papal and hierarchical magisterium is possible; Vatican II's *Constitution on the Church,* as interpreted in the light of the *modi* to the document, and its historical development; statements of national hierarchies, including the American bishops, which acknowledge the right to dissent from authoritative noninfallible teaching of the hierarchical magisterium; unanimous expert testimony that the right to dissent from noninfallible papal teaching is a "common teaching" among Catholic theologians.

More specifically, dissent from the ethical conclusion of *Humanae Vitae,* which absolutely condemns any form of artificial contraception, is a responsible action within the pale of Roman Catholic theological options. The reasons adduced in chapter six (which amplify paragraphs 5, 6, and 7 of the Statement by Theologians) justify specific dissent from the teaching that artificial contraception "is absolutely excluded as a licit means of regulating birth." The Encyclical speaks as if there is a monolithic philosophical system called the natural law. Newer approaches acceptable in Catholic theology today are not employed in the Encyclical. The particular theory of natural law proposed in the papal Letter does seem to suffer from a "biologism" and a "physicalism" described in chapter six. The arguments traditionally advanced in favor of the teaching proposed in *Humanae Vitae* were not convincing to the majority of Roman Catholic theologians, to say nothing of other Christian theologians and philosophers, even before the issuance of *Humanae Vitae*, and the Encyclical offered no new or different reasons to support its conclusion. For some years critics had faulted the argument against contraception as a "single act" analysis; this analysis was essentially and uncritically reiterated in *Humanae Vitae.* The Statement by Theologians noted the many positive values concerning marriage expressed in the Encyclical: among these, the insistence on the twofold characteristics of marriage and sexuality—the unitive and the procreational. As the dissenters recognized, however, a growing number of people today tend to deny the inseparable union of these two necessary characteristics of human sexuality and marriage in each and every marital act. The assertion that these two aspects must be, or even can actually be, present in every single marital act is not convincing in its mere restatement.

The Theologians' Statement pointed out further deficiencies in the encyclical which were not set forth in detail in the presentations to the Inquiry Board. These faults of the Encyclical were not only evidences of uncritical assumptions leading to unconvincing scholarship; perhaps more importantly, they were evidence of insufficient sensitivity to the personal dimensions of the question of contraception. The Encyclical cited the evil consequences of artificial birth control: but no data were given to support the existence of such consequences. Thus, some persons could rightly be offended by the assertion in the Encyclical that "it is also to be feared that the man, growing used to the employment of anticonceptive practices, may finally lose respect for the woman and, no longer caring for her physical and psychological equilibrium, may come to the point of considering her as a mere instrument of selfish enjoyment, and no longer as his respected and beloved companion" (paragraph 17). The dissenting Statement of July 30 also suggested that the Encyclical showed disregard for the dignity of millions of human beings brought into the world without the slightest possibility of being fed and educated decently. The Encyclical does not show the concern for demographic problems which was evident in the earlier encyclical of Paul VI on the *Development of Peoples.* Not even a footnote reference to that earlier Encyclical was included in *Humanae Vitae,* although the teaching on responsible parenthood proposed by the hierarchical magisterium in recent decades affirms the need to limit family size on some occasions because of demographic problems. If *Humanae Vitae* had made more explicit mention of responsible parenthood in the context of the demographic problem (there is an implicit reference in paragraph 10), there would have been less reason to criticize it on this particular score.

In addition to the intrinsic weight of the scholarly case that the Encyclical was not convincing, expert testimony of distinguished

Catholic theologians was presented before the Inquiry Board to confirm the Roman Catholic viability of the scholarly criticism. Professor Bernard Lonergan, S.J., of the Gregorian University in Rome and Regis College in Toronto, who is a member of the International Commission of Theologians recently appointed by the Pope, and Professor Walter Burghardt, one of the two American theologians on this commission, affirmed that the dissent from the Encyclical was a permissible Catholic option: Professor Burghardt appeared in person to present his views to the Inquiry Board; Professor Lonergan sent a written statement from Canada agreeing that the Theologians' Statement was defensible "on principles acceptable in Catholic Theology," and that the materials on which this presentation is based set forth such a defense. Another expert witness, Professor Austin Vaughn, contended that dissent in this case was outside the pale of responsible Roman Catholic theological activity; his position, of course, represents one of a variety of theological options on the matter. In any event, without judging the ultimate validity or invalidity of the theological views offered, the testimony given to the Inquiry Board by these witnesses and by the Catholic University dissenters makes clear that there is a manifest diversity of theological judgments on the issue *within the pale of responsible Roman Catholic theological activity.* In the light of the reasons adduced, the expert testimony received, the statements of some national hierarchies and of some individual bishops in this country and throughout the world, and the declarations and actions of overwhelmingly large numbers of distinguished American and European theologians, therefore, dissent from a particular ethical conclusion of *Humanae Vitae* is definitely a responsible Roman Catholic theological activity.

The Question of Public Dissent. It is within the pale of responsible Roman Catholic theological activity that Roman Catholic theologians may dissent *publicly* from the authoritative, noninfallible teaching of the hierarchical and papal magisterium and, in particular, from the absolute condemnation of artificial contraception enunciated in *Humanae Vitae.*

Although theological manuals of the nineteenth century had

either limited dissent to private expression, or not explicitly acknowledged the right to public dissent, the foregoing material shows that the rationale set forth in such manuals provides the basis for development toward the right and, in certain circumstances, the duty of public dissent. Expert historical testimony given by Professor John Noonan indicated that in other historical cases of theological dissent, the dissent was made public and communicated to the faithful who were affected by the teaching dissented from, i.e., to those who had a right to knowledge of the dissent. Professor Noonan also suggested that historical factors peculiar to the times may have contributed to the insistence on private, to the exclusion of public, dissent in the manualists. The contemporary theologian has a responsibility to many different constituencies who have a right to be informed of his theological judgments and interpretations: the Church as a whole, the hierarchical magisterium itself, the people directly concerned with the matter in question, priests, non-Catholics, fellow academicians. In the present ecclesiological context, with its stress on co-responsibility, it is within the pale of responsible Roman Catholic theology to say that the theologian has an obligation to communicate his dissent to all who have a right to know it. In the last few years, the hierarchical magisterium and the theologians have emphasized the right to know in the Church and the need for a true public opinion in the Church. The Catholic Church in the twentieth century, like all contemporary mankind, is more acutely aware and conscious of the mass media of communication existing in the world today. The methods employed by both the pope and hierarchies throughout the world made extensive use of press conferences and the mass media of communication. The 1968 Pastoral Letter of the American Bishops acknowledges the legitimacy of public theological dissent, while cautioning against scandal. Even the one expert witness, Professor Vaughn, who disagreed with the basic theological position taken by the subject professors, agreed that in this day and age the theologian has an obligation to use the mass media in some circumstances, even in the case of dissent. Such use of the mass media is acceptable academic procedure for theologians. Public silence on the part of professors who "privately" dissent from authoritative, noninfallible teaching could be looked upon as irresponsible by many people in theological and academic circles, both Catholic and non-Catholic. (This possibility was suggested by a number of expert witnesses: Professor Burghardt, Reverend Hotchkin, President Bennett, Mr. Woodward.)

The Encyclical itself, and the rumors preceding its release, were prominently mentioned and discussed on radio, television and in newspapers and magazines. The news media were actively seeking the opinions of theologians. Many people were directly affected by the teaching of the Encyclical and needed theological interpretation. Priests needed guidance in their role as counsellors and confessors. Non-Catholics, both theologians and other interested persons, were wondering what the Catholic reaction would be concerning the Encyclical. In this context, it was hardly irresponsible for theologians to state their views candidly and publicly.

The expert testimony of Roman Catholic theologians (Professors Lonergan and Burghardt, Dean Thirlkel) recognized the need for public dissent in this case. Other expert testimony from Catholic academicians (Presidents Yanitelli and Hesburgh) and Christian ecumenists (Reverend Hotchkin, President Bennett), as well as a religion editor for a national news magazine (Mr. Woodward), testified to the responsibility of public dissent in this case. In addition, more than 700 American Catholic theologians, in various statements and announcements, publicly dissented in this case, and many of the most highly respected European theologians similarly publicly dissented in a joint declaration. One could likewise characterize as "public dissent" some of the statements made by national bodies of bishops.

The Immediacy of the Dissent. The Statement by Catholic Theologians was released to the press about thirty hours after the Encyclical was officially released. Such a quick response was responsible; indeed, it could have been irresponsible not to respond accurately as soon as possible.

The draftsmen of the Statement had read and studied the Encyclical before they formulated their response; almost all who have commented on the Encyclical admit there is little or no development over the reasons proposed in *Casti Connubii* of Pius XI, issued in 1930 and repeated in the conventional arguments in the manuals of theology. Anyone conversant with the debate of the last few years was in a position to evaluate the Encyclical without the need for additional study.

The original Statement by Theologians has stood the test of time remarkably well. Some subsequent comments on the Encyclical have lacked the moderation and precision of the statement of July 30. One commentator, not a subscriber, referred to it as a moderate document. The lengthy theological analysis presented to the Board of Inquiry and contained in this volume shows that the Statement is theologically sound and accurate.

Some who had criticized the immediacy of the response seem to imply there is an inherent good in delay—a false assumption. There is no wisdom in delay if one is able to speak accurately and competently without delay, especially when the question was urgent; when many persons required a theological interpretation as quickly as possible, and when there was grave danger of distortion and false dilemmas if competent theologians did not speak out. By expressing themselves quickly, the theologians were able to modulate the situation and perhaps prevent disastrous consequences.

Norms Governing the Public Expression of Dissent from Authoritative Noninfallible Teachings of the Hierarchical Magisterium

The public expression of theological dissent should, of course, be subject to the responsibilities of the theologian in and for the Church. The American bishops, in their 1968 Pastoral Letter, enumerated certain specific norms for expressing dissent publicly which appears to state guidelines which all parties concerned can substantially accept. The norms enunciated by the American bishops (presupposing well-founded reasons for dissent) can be reduced to the following:

> They (i.e., "Norms of licit theological dissent") require of him careful respect for the consciences of those who lack his special competence or opportunity for judicious investigation. These norms also require setting forth his dissent with propriety and with regard for the gravity of the matter and the deference due the authority which pronounced on it.
>
> The reverence due all sacred matters, particularly questions which touch on salvation, will not necessarily require the responsible scholar to relinquish his opinion but certainly to propose it with prudence born of intellectual grace and a Christian confidence that the truth is great and will prevail.
>
> The expression of theological dissent . . . must be such as not to give scandal.[10]

The declarations and actions of the subject professors with respect to *Humanae Vitae* were in full accord with the foregoing "norms of licit theological dissent."

"Respect for Other Consciences." In this context it has been alleged that the dissenting professors showed a disregard for the pastoral implications of their dissent, especially in terms of the confusion among faithful Catholics regarding their obligations and rights on the subjects of contraception and dissent. In expressing their opinions with respect to the Encyclical, however, the professors did not attempt to create, and did not create, any false impression that they were acting as anything but dissenters. They expressly and publicly acknowledged that their dissent from the teaching of the papal magisterium, and large portions of the hierarchical magisterium with respect to the binding force of the Encyclical, was a conclusion of "Roman Catholic theologians conscious of their duties and limitations." They emphasized that their action was not to be considered a rebellion or a revolution. Their conduct was not an effort to establish a second or alternative magisterium in competition with the hierarchical magisterium; nor were they trying to usurp the bishops' teaching prerogatives and merely cause confusion

among conscientious laymen. The context of their dissent, however, as recalled in chapter one, was a situation in which many sincere laymen were not informed of their right to dissent conscientiously from such papal teaching as the Encyclical and still remain in the Church. The Statement by Theologians, far from being insensitive to the consciences of others, was in fact particularly sensitive to this problem of conscience and showed the highest respect for those who lacked the special theological competence but yet had the right to know the common teaching on dissent.

"Propriety and Due Deference for the Teaching Authority." The facts indicate that the subject professors used the public communications media with propriety. The purpose of the theologians was not to gain publicity or notoriety for themselves; many of them turned down numerous requests to appear on radio and television programs after they were assured that their Statement had already reached its intended audience. The professors' actions were dictated by an understanding of the responsibilities of Roman Catholic theologians which is shared by many competent theologians.

The major thrust of the position taken by the dissenting professors was that one could be a loyal Catholic with true Catholic respect for the pope and still dissent from the absolute ban on artificial contraception contained in the Encyclical. The Statement of July 30 begins: "As Roman Catholic theologians we respectfully acknowledge a distinct role of hierarchical *magisterium* (teaching office) in the Church of Christ." The press thus frequently cited the professors as saying their declarations and actions were neither a rebellion nor an uprising. It was suggested by the Catholic University Trustees that many were puzzled at the professors' public dissent "because their actions seemed to some to be done without a proper regard for the person of the Holy Father. . . ."[11] But there are no grounds for such puzzlement. The record of the Inquiry into the dissent shows no support for even the suggestion that the professors, by their declarations or actions, failed to show proper regard for the person of the Holy Father (expert witnesses who were questioned on this had difficulty even appreciating the question). At least in the academic world, scholarly criticisms, and even sharp disagreements, are never conceived as "personal." It is clear from the testimony that each of the subject professors acted out of respect and concern for the pope and the papal office and was not trying to cause confusion, or to mislead, but simply to communicate views which people have a right to know about. Professor Vaughn, while disagreeing with the professional conclusions of the subject professors, made it clear that he did not consider the tenor of their criticism of the Encyclical to have exceeded the customary limits of academic criticism; two college Presidents, Victor Yanitelli of St. Peter's, and Robert Cross of Hunter College, and now at Swarthmore, found the Theologians' Statement a model for such criticism.

The allegation that the subject professors apparently undertook to *organize* public opposition to the Encyclical must also be considered. The word "organize" has many different connotations. The Inquiry Board specifically inquired as to whether any undue force or pressure was used to induce other theologians to subscribe to the statement of July 30 and did not discover even the hint of such pressure. The subject professors could not be said to have "organized opposition to the teaching of the pope," as those terms are generally understood. Roman Catholic theology has always attributed theological importance and significance to the number of theologians who maintain a certain position. In moral theology, the number of theologians maintaining a particular judgment furnishes sufficient weight for a person to safely follow that judgment in his actions. As an academician, the theologian is conscious of the need to consult with his peers about his own opinions. As a Roman Catholic theologian, he is aware that the number of theologians holding a particular judgment has importance both in the theological and the practical order. As a prudent person, the Roman Catholic theologian also realizes the added weight given to a judgment because of the stature and number of qualified people who adhere to that position.

Expert theological witnesses, including Professor Vaughn, who could not accept the substance of the position proposed by the subject professors, saw no impropriety in the manner, style and method of the actions of the professors. Similar manners, styles and methods were employed by other groups of American and foreign Roman Catholic theologians, both in the instance of the response to *Humanae Vitae* and in other cases. The expert testimony of Professor Burghardt, as editor of *Theological Studies,* and of Mr. Woodward, as religion editor of *Newsweek,* made clear that the professors could not have restricted their views to publication in technical theological journals. The mass media subscribe to the theological publications and in fact are often sent advance copies of articles dealing with subjects of public concern. In any event, the press would have undoubtedly immediately sought the comments of leading theologians concerning the Encyclical, and the joint public Statement gave the dissenters time to compose a concise response which reflected the considered judgment of a large number of scholars. From the viewpoint of Roman Catholic theology, in short, there was no impropriety in the manner, style and method in which the subject professors expressed their dissent publicly.

"Prudence and Scandal." Scandal, strictly so-called, is a technical, theological term classically defined as a word or deed, evil, or at least with the appearance of evil, which furnishes to another an occasion of sin. Thus scandal in the strict sense exists only when the act or word itself is evil, or has the appearance of evil, and is an occasion for leading others into sin. The declarations and actions of the subject professors cannot constitute scandal in the strict sense of the term.

In a looser and nontechnical use of the term, scandal is understood as the wonder of questioning which arises in respect of an unaccustomed action, such wonderment not resulting in sin on the part of the questioning party (although it may constitute for some persons an obstacle, at least temporarily, to the smooth development of their Christian lives). However, the fact that such questioning might arise in a particular case is not of itself a convincing reason for not acting. The ultimate decision must take account of many factors under the norm of prudence.

Prudence is practical wisdom in weighing all the pertinent factors involved before arriving at a conclusion. In complex human questions there will always be some negative effects resulting from one's actions. It is inhuman and contrary to reality to suggest that one cannot act if there *may be* some negative results. Public dissent, of course, would not be prudent in every situation. All the pertinent elements must be taken into consideration, weighed and balanced. While the declarations and actions of the dissenting professors did occasion some wonderment and questioning among some Catholic people, much greater harm could have resulted if the theologians had not made their dissent public. According to expert testimony, many other people—concerned spouses, many priests, non-Catholics and even the Roman Catholic Church itself—would have suffered harm if the dissent were not made public. In view of all the factors involved, one can legitimately conclude that the public dissent of the subject professors followed one of the possible responsible prudential options open to Catholic theologians in the circumstances; in fact, they could have been irresponsible if they had not expressed their dissent in the way they did.

Theological Dissent and the Ongoing Life of the Church

This volume has been a defense of the theological dissent from the Encyclical *Humanae Vitae,* but such dissent is not merely limited to the realm of *speculative* theology. The Statement by Theologians intended to express a theological opinion which could be followed *in practice* by loyal Roman Catholics. But there seems to be a definite tendency on the part of some to draw too sharp a dichotomy between speculative theological dissent and pastoral practice. The Pastoral Letter of the American Bishops, *Human Life in Our*

Day, furnishes a prime example of such a false dichotomy between speculative theology and pastoral practice.

The American bishops explicitly recognize the possibility of theological dissent: "There exist in the Church a lawful freedom of inquiry and of thought and also general norms of licit dissent. This is particularly true in the area of legitimate theological speculation and research."[12] While implicitly recognizing the possibility of practical dissent through a citation from Cardinal Newman, however, the American bishops nonetheless make many absolute statements about the ban of contraception as being of divine law: "The Encyclical does not undertake to judge the consciences of individuals but to set forth the authentic teaching of the Church which Catholics believe interprets the divine law to which consciences should be conformed. . . . We feel bound to remind Catholic married couples, when they are subject to the pressures which prompted the Holy Father's concern, that however circumstances may reduce moral guilt, no one following the teaching of the Church can deny the objective evil of artificial contraception itself."[13] Speaking of some negative reactions to the Encyclical, the bishops further declare: "Some reactions were regrettable, however, in the light of the explicit teaching of Vatican Council II concerning the obligation of Catholics to assent to papal teaching even when it is not presented with the seal of infallibility." After citing paragraph 25 of Vatican II's *Dogmatic Constitution on the Church,* the bishops continue: "Pope Paul has recalled this obligation several times with respect to his Encyclical on the regulation of birth, beginning when he exhorted priests to be the first to give, 'in the exercise of your ministry, the example of loving internal and external obedience to the teaching authority of the Church' " (*Lumen Gentium,* 25).

The letter of December 23, 1968, over the signature of Acting Rector Scheel in the name of a subcommittee of the Board of Trustees to the Inquiry panel, speaks of "speculative theology" and "free speculative inquiry." These phrases seem to be indications of a dichotomy between speculative theology and practical decisions of everyday life; but theological dissent in this case does not merely constitute a theoretical exercise which has no bearing on practice.

Theological dissent in this case has very practical repercussions. It is not theologically possible to admit the possibility of dissent in the theoretical order and to deny it in the practical order. Such a dichotomy attacks a very basic assumption of Catholic theology, that is, that *truth* is *one*. The ultimate basis for the possibility of theological dissent from the authoritative, noninfallible magisterium must be understood. The manualists properly made an important distinction between the assent of faith and religious assent. Religious assent is conditional and not absolutely certain precisely because the teaching is not proposed as being absolutely certain, i.e., infallible. The reality or truth itself is not absolutely certain; thus the religious assent can admit of error; one cannot give a greater assent than that warranted by the reality itself. This epistemological realism has been a commendable part of the Roman Catholic theological tradition. Thus dissent is not merely a speculative prerogative of philosophers and academicians; rather dissent, both in practice and in theory, is rooted in the fact that the teaching proposed is not absolutely certain. It is both unrealistic and erroneous to assert that a teaching is or should be treated as absolutely certain when in reality the teaching is not that certain. Dissent from authoritative, noninfallible hierarchical teaching is possible for a Roman Catholic precisely because such a teaching makes no pretension of being absolutely certain. If sufficient evidence exists, one may dissent both in theory and in practice. The contention of this volume remains that sufficient reasons do exist in this case for one to dissent both in theory and in practice from the absolute ban of artificial contraception proposed in *Humanae Vitae*. Dissent in theory and in practice always remains at least a possibility for the Catholic in respect of authoritative, noninfallible teaching of the hierarchical magisterium. The manualists rightly speak of a presumption in favor of the authoritative teaching, but this presumption always is provisional and cedes to the truth.

But when the right to dissent itself has been challenged, and as dissent has become manifest in many forms and shapes in our contemporary culture and society, disturbing many established institutions, there has been a great temptation to brand all dissent as disloyal and destructive. There have been many Catholics who have sought to discredit the dissenting theologians precisely on such grounds. Undoubtedly there are instances in our culture and society in which dissent has exceeded the bounds of propriety and of truth, but loyal dissent remains absolutely vital for any human society, including the Church, which claims to be the presence in time and space of the saving activity of the Risen Lord.

Dissent does not ipso facto connote rebellion or disloyalty but rather can be one of the truest forms of service to and loyalty for the Church. The foregoing chapters emphasize how the model of the Church has changed from the static notion of a perfect society, structured pyramidically from the top down, to the more dynamic notion of the pilgrim people of God who, precisely as pilgrims, are always on the march toward the new heaven and the new earth and always in need of reform. Without loyal critics and critical loyalty, the Church cannot be faithful to its Founder. The proper understanding of the pilgrim Church demonstrates the continual need for criticism and dissent without, however, canonizing every possible form of dissent and criticism. Obviously there are limits to dissent; but the thrust of these pages has been to show that dissent from the absolute condemnation of artificial birth control as taught in *Humanae Vitae* is both possible and appropriate. Those who engage in such dissent are neither traitors nor reprobates.

The dissenters do not claim for themselves any type of infallibility. The dissenters can and should present arguments to show that their particular dissent is responsible and within the pale of responsible Roman Catholic options. The tendency, in some circles, to automatically brand dissenters as disloyal traitors should not force dissenters to assume a defensive position. Dissent is not to be assumed to be treacherous until it proves its loyalty. The outcome of the Inquiry at Catholic University shows that it is time for a fresh understanding of the function of dissent and for a new appreciation of the purposes of those who dissent. An older, triumphalistic concept of the Church as a perfect society independent of the conditions of culture, history and time tends to minimize change and development and avoid the tensions which accompany all growth. From a theological viewpoint, however, the Church, existing in the times between the two comings, of Christ, will always experience the tension of trying to do the truth in love. Tension and loyal dissent are thus absolutely necessary for the Church and its mission. Merely to reject all dissent as disloyalty without studying the reasons for it is just as erroneous as an approach which uncritically accepts all dissent.

The concerted dissent to the absolute ban on artificial contraception will certainly affect the Catholic Church not only in theory but also in practice. In theory, the conditional nature of authoritative, noninfallible teaching is now understood by all in the Church. Further, the teaching office in the Church can no longer be considered as simply coincident with the hierarchical teaching office. But the practical consequences of this dissent in the life of the Church will be even greater. Even those who are reacting most negatively to theological dissent realize the enormous changes that it portends. An editorial in the *Catholic Standard and Times,* the official paper of the Archdiocese of Philadelphia, on the occasion of the publication of the Report of the Catholic University Board of Inquiry, begins in this fashion:

> Who directs the Church and who speaks for Christ—individual theologians or the Pope?
>
> While it may seem an oversimplification, this is the basic question which must be answered in the light of clearance given by a Catholic University of America board of inquiry to 20 professors who dissented from the conclusions of Pope Paul's encyclical letter, *Humanae Vitae*. This action, it seems to us, brings to a boiling point the crisis in moral doctrine and, even more fundamentally, the crisis in Church teaching authority which has been actively simmering since the issuance of Pope Paul's encyclical last July.[14]

One can both accept the Petrine office and hierarchical office in the Church, however, and realize that the entire teaching function of the Church is not identified with these two offices. Such an understanding of the teaching function of the Church is definitely within the pale of the Roman Catholic faith-commitment. Nor does such a view of the teaching function of the Church mean that the Church's teaching is reduced to a majority consensus. The primary teacher in the Church always remains the Holy Spirit; but no one person or office in the Church—pope or bishop, theologian or dissenter—has a monopoly on the Holy Spirit.

The time of renewal and tension within the Church is not finished. The dissent discussed in this volume demands a reevaluation and better understanding, on the theological level, of a number of important aspects of the Catholic Church: the proper place of the *whole* Church in the magisterial function; the proper weight and place of the Christian Churches and Ecclesial Communities in the determination of authentic Christian teaching; the role and function of the papal and hierarchical teaching officers in the light of the teaching function of the whole Church; the manner in which the Church exercises its teaching function in the modern world; the role of the theologian in the Church; the relationship between the individual conscience and the entire Church. It will be even more difficult to put into practice a life style in the Church which follows from the theoretical admission of such dissent. The Church today desperately needs new and different structures and organizations in order to fulfill its mission. These are the challenges which the Church faces in the immediate future. It is hoped that the loyal theological dissent explained in this volume will help the Roman Catholic Church to meet these challenges.

Notes

1. *New York Times,* August 3, 1968, p. 1.
2. N.C. News Service (Foreign), September 4, 1968.
3. N.C. News Service (Foreign), September 11, 1968.
4. N.C. News Service (Foreign), October 4, 1968.
5. N.C. News Service (Foreign), September 30, 1968.
6. N.C. News Service (Foreign), October 24, 1968.
7. N.C. News Service (Foreign), December 12, 1968.
8. N.C. News Service (Foreign), November 9, 1968.

9. N.C. News Service (Foreign), September 23, 1968, and *London Tablet,* September 28, p. 973.
10. National Conference of Catholic Bishops, 1968 Pastoral Letter, *On Human Life in Our Day* (November, 1968).
11. Letter dated December 23, 1968, from Acting Rector Nivard Scheel, C.F.X., on behalf of the committee of Trustees of Catholic University, to Dean Donald E. Marlowe as Chairman of the Board of Inquiry.
12. *On Human Life in Our Day* (November, 1968).
13. *Ibid.*
14. *The Catholic Standard and Times,* April 18, 1969, p. 6, cols. 1–2.

8

Epilogue
Conclusions of the Catholic University Faculty Board of Inquiry

"The 30 July statement of the subject professors represents a responsible theological dissent from the teaching of the Encyclical *Humanae Vitae,* and this dissent is reasonably supported as a tenable scholarly position.

"The right of a theological scholar to dissent from noninfallible teachings of the magisterium is well documented, most recently in the 15 November 1968 pastoral letter of the American Bishops.

"From the perspective of the Church, there well may be novel elements in the use of the public media which must be resolved in the future, but the release of this statement cannot be regarded as contrary to the accepted norms of academic procedure. Neither the timing, the content, nor the means of securing circulation and concurrence of colleagues are to be regarded as extraordinary or improper in the light of current academic practices. The alternatives of either repressing the statement or of adopting a policy of concerted silence would have been more truly improper. Given the realities of the public media, the extensive theological dissent on this issue and the possibility of such dissent were certain to quickly become matters of widespread public knowledge. All allegations of surprise, confusion, scandal and related concerns must be judged in the light of this certain, public knowledge. The subject professors were compelled to some kind of honest response, and we conclude that the statement thus may have averted at least as much harm as it is alleged by some to have caused.

"The statement does not conflict with the Profession of Faith taken by subject professors. The statement of the professors constitutes a measure of dissent from a noninfallible statement of the authentic papal magisterium. Whether this dissent can better be described as reinterpretation or an attempt at development is not at issue; it is beyond the Board's competence to delineate the doctrine concerning contraception, or to resolve other questions raised by the Encyclical itself, or the substantive content of the Theologians' Statement. The question whether such dissent violates any special commitments of the subject professors as teachers of theology or other sacred sciences may be answered as follows:

A. "With regard to the primary role of the theologian as a scholar, the following needs to be said:

1) "The theologian is properly limited to the data of his science, which include, among other elements, the pronouncements of the official papal and episcopal magisterium, which the theologian evaluates and interprets.

2) "Like any other scholar, the theologian is bound to communicate his findings to others, a responsibility which may be defined more extensively in view of his position in the Church (below).

3) "The theologian is ultimately constrained only by truth itself. Since it is Catholic doctrine that any conflict between the faith and truth, as variously investigated and discerned, is only apparent and not real, the Roman Catholic theologian operates properly without any fear of the developments of his science. At the same time he recognizes the limitations of his own fallibility and his need to engage in a theological endeavor that is shared by other scholars.

4) "Inevitably, the theologian has been influenced by the ecclesiological dimensions associated with the Second Vatican Council. In particular, he is aware that his theological reflection must develop in dialogue with the entire Church and with others (cf., *Pastoral Constitution on the Church in the Modern World, Gaudium et Spes;* Paul VI's Encyclical Letter *Ecclesiam Suam*).

B. "Since theologians are rightly conscious of other responsibilities which flow from their scholarship, the role of the theologian as a member of the Church requires consideration:

1) It is clear that the theologian has a true teaching function in the Church, which is part of the prophetic role common to all the baptized, although enhanced by the theologian's professional competence and reflection. This office is nonofficial and nonauthentic in comparison with the hierarchical magisterium, but the latter is itself dependent upon the formulation of theologians. (Cf., Paul VI, Address to the International Congress on the Theology of the Second Vatican Council, 1966.)

2) "In the resolution of apparent conflicts between the findings of theological science and the expression of the hierarchical magisterium, both the hierarchy and the theologians are bound to enter into dialogue. This need has been explicitly recognized by the National Conference of Catholic Bishops, especially in the light of contemporary means of communication (cf., pastoral statement, *Human Life in Our Day,* November, 1968). This dialogue may be unstructured or structured (cf., proposal of the School of Sacred Theology, stipulation of facts).

C. "With regard to the right of theologians to dissent from noninfallible teachings of the hierarchical magisterium:

1) "From the classical instances of major, discernible change in the teaching of the hierarchical magisterium, such as the teachings on interest taking, religious freedom, and biblical science, it is clear that noninfallible pronouncements are reversible. It is not pertinent whether the change takes place because of theological reflection and publication, the words or actions of the members of the Church who are not theologians, or intrinsic factors in human society: the fact of such change means that the door to theological inquiry is not closed.

2) "There has been an explicit and formal recognition of the right to dissent from noninfallible teaching, although couched in limited terms, even in the common teaching of theologians prior to the Second Vatican Council, that is, during the post-Tridentine

period when the likelihood of such dissent was considered remote. (Cf., the theological manuals enumerated and cited in the prepared testimony.)

3) "The position of the Second Vatican Council, in speaking of the 'religious assent' required by noninfallible pronouncements of the hierarchical magisterium (*Lumen Gentium,* n. 25), must be understood in the light of the development of the text itself. The Council, by accepting the proposals of its Doctrinal Commission, deliberately omitted the text in the original scheme, which stated that a matter decided by the ordinary magisterium 'can no longer be regarded as a matter for free debate among theologians' (Pius XII, Encyclical Letter *Humani Generis*). The Council likewise accepted the statements of the Doctrinal Commission: (a) that when an educated person is unable, for solid grounds, to give internal assent (to noninfallible teaching), approved theological explanation should be consulted (i.e., the common teaching of 'approved theologian' referred to above); and (b) that an observation seeking a conciliar statement of freedom for further investigation (i.e., of noninfallible teaching) and doctrinal progress 'is true, but does not need to be brought in at this point.'

4) "The right to dissent in such cases has been most recently acknowledged by the National Conference of Catholic Bishops in the pastoral statement already mentioned.

5) "Finally, attention should be given to the arguments advanced concerning the usefulness of dissent by theologians within the Church community: it is a means of informing the sense of the faithful and of hastening the legitimate development of doctrine; it is a means of correcting a noninfallible statement and thus strengthening and supporting the continuity of the hierarchical magisterium; in Catholic doctrine it may be regarded as a working of the Spirit in the Church.

D. "With regard to the public character of dissent by theologians, in particular, by means of the popular communications media:

1) "The historical cases of doctrinal development through the dissent of theologians cannot be expected to provide parallels for

the present time. Ecclesiological dimensions were not as fully developed or understood, nor were our contemporary means of communication available. Similarly, the theoretical position taken by theologians prior to the Second Vatican Council, largely restricting theological dissent to private expression, has to be reevaluated.

2) "With regard to the distinction between public and private dissent, the restriction seems to have been objectively invalid and a disservice to truth, which the theologian should express freely and without reservation, even though aware of his own fallibility and careful to respect the rights of others, especially the role of the hierarchical magisterium.

3) "In any event, a clear development has taken place in the official recognition of the 'right to know,' as formulated in the documents of the Second Vatican Council, and by Pope John XXIII's (encyclical letters *Mater et Magistra, Pacem in Terris*; Second Vatican Council, *Inter Mirifica,* December 4, 1963). (U.S. Bishops' Committee for Social Communications, May 4, 1967; Exhibit 50). In effect, this recognition demands that those who have knowledge should communicate it to those who have a need and a right to it. It means, moreover, that the new means of communication should be put at the service of the Gospel and, in the application to the legitimate teaching of theologians, that these means may be appropriate to cases of dissent by interpretation.

4) "The judgment whether a particular dissent should be communicated in one way or another must almost always be a matter of opinion, as the decision so to act must be dictated by practical wisdom. Attention must be paid to the arguments presented in the prepared testimony, in particular to the immediate need to correct a false notion of the Encyclical's precise authority and to forestall a diffuse presentation of less-informed theological opinion by the media.

E. "With regard to the present case, the following may be added to the above more general principles:

1) "It is evident that theologians other than the professors have publicly dissented, in greater or less degree, in accord with the above concept of the theologian's office, from the papal

teaching in the Encyclical *Humanae Vitae*. In particular, there were the other signatories of the Statement, principally members of the Catholic Theological Society of America and the College Theology Society, as well as individual theologians and groups of theologians in various countries. The several statements of the episcopal magisterium in other countries, which included interpretations differing in some measure from the Encyclical and which were based upon theological data, may also be mentioned.

2) "The Pastoral Statement of the National Conference of Catholic Bishops, *Human Life in Our Day* (November, 1968), issued after the Encyclical *Humanae Vitae,* recognizes the right of theologians to dissent from noninfallible teaching and takes into account the contemporary circumstances which may affect the public expression of that dissent.

3) "The Board feels that specific reference should be made to the several publics to which the professors felt responsible as theologians, according to their own statement: (a) to the whole Church; (b) to the pope and the other bishops; (c) to their fellow theologians; (d) to the individuals touched by the contraception issue; (e) to the priests of the United States, including former students; (f) to the University community; (g) to the public communications media; (h) to non-Catholics, especially those already engaged in dialogue; (i) to men of good will, to whom *Humanae Vitae* was addressed.

"It is clear that a Roman Catholic theologian may fail in his responsibility by excess or defect. In most instances the measures of excess or defect would be difficult to determine and would in fact be largely a matter of opinion.

"Only in the clearest instance of grave failure would a theologian be subject to the censure of his peers, and then his competence as a teacher should be judged by the same criteria as that of a scholar in any other discipline.

"In the present case the Board does not judge the correctness of the teaching of the professors nor does it feel that their course of action was necessarily the only one available. The Board has received substantial evidence of the seriousness of the theological endeavor in which the professors engaged and of the professors' consciousness of their pastoral obligation as theologians.

"Acknowledging the legitimacy of theological dissent by way of evaluation and interpretation of noninfallible teachings of the hierarchical magisterium, and in the light of the above considerations, the Board recognizes the right of the professors to act as they did, in their capacity of Roman Catholic theologians, and it accepts their conviction that they had a duty so to act. It therefore finds that the professors acted responsibly as theologians.

"The statement was released within a very short time after the publication of the Encyclical. The question of the propriety of this suddenness has been raised. There are circumstances, however, to be considered. As already mentioned, the controversy was by no means new. Moreover, it was an important issue, and even those who are not moral theologians in the strict sense had had full opportunity and incentive to inform themselves and to take some position on the issue. The Encyclical's teaching on artificial contraception purported to be and was in fact essentially the same teaching with which the theologians were familiar before the appearance of the Encyclical. The theologians were careful to read the document before framing their statement. It should also be noted that, had the theologians withheld or delayed their announcement, reporters would have sought their interpretations, as happened elsewhere. It is at least possible that any statements would have been issued with less opportunity for careful preparation and with much less control over the conditions of their release.

"With respect to the timing of the release, therefore, it is the opinion of the Board of Inquiry that the subject professors acted responsibly and in accord with American university practice.

"It is common academic practice to use all effective and rational means of publication and discussion. The dissemination of information and opinion in various ways is the most general service which the university performs for the public. The practice is encouraged by leaders outside the universities, including churchmen. Responsible dissemination to an appropriate audience is meant to improve the quality of information and understanding concerning religious issues.

"Moreover, as already mentioned, the dissemination of the theologians' views through the public media was unavoidable. The press and television in America do not wait for news to come to them, but instead go to experts when this is appropriate. In the present instance the press and television took the initiative in trying to elicit statements from the theologians. The latter, for their part, showed professional restraint by refusing to make a statement until they had read the document and talked over their own response to it.

"Furthermore, it is unrealistic to suppose that all theological discussion of the issue could have been withheld from the public media, even if this were desirable. No one seems to argue for this position. On the other hand, any attempt to present only "approved" theological interpretations would have been contrived and even ominous, and would have strained the credibility of those who had already followed the controversy through the same public media. When controversy has been open, dissent inevitably becomes public.

"The public promulgation of the Statement has raised the question of 'scandal' in the minds of some. However, a suspicion that an opinion affecting the lives of millions had been self-suppressed through fear or silenced by authority would have strongly and adversely affected the credibility of the theologians and the hierarchical magisterium, and this might have led to other allegations of 'scandal.'

"The Board of Inquiry does not find in the theologians' use of public media any departure from accepted standards of responsible academic procedure as practiced in American universities.

"A further question has been raised concerning the profession of faith taken by professors of theology, among others, in virtue of canon 1406 of the Code of Canon Law and the Statutes of the University (art. 50).

"This profession of faith has taken different forms. Until 1967 the formulas of Pius IV, as enlarged after Vatican Council I by Pius IX, were employed; since May 31, 1967, the Nicene-Constantinopolitan Creed has been used, with the following abbreviated addition: 'I also embrace and retain each and every thing regarding the doctrine of faith and morals, whether defined by solemn judgment or asserted and declared by the ordinary magisterium, as they are proposed by the Church, especially those things which concern the mystery of the holy Church of Christ, its Sacraments, the Sacrifice of the Mass, and the Primacy of the Roman Pontiff.'

1) "It is evident that the profession of faith made by professors of theology differs in no way from the profession made by other believing Roman Catholics.

2) "In the formula for the profession of faith, a distinction is made between the Nicene-Constantinopolitan Creed, which is explicitly made the object of divine faith, and the additional text which is introduced: 'I also embrace and retain. . . .' In this added text the expression, 'as proposed by the Church,' illustrates the precise issue already discussed, namely, the potential area for permitted dissent, for cause, from noninfallible teachings.

3) "There is no incompatibility between the formula of assent to Catholic teachings and the declaration of the Second Vatican Council (*Constitution on the Church,* n. 25) concerning religious assent, in that 'each and every thing' commands varying degrees of consideration, as this has been explained above in the light of the conciliar development of its own text.

"The Board therefore finds that the professors in no way violated the profession of faith."

Subject Index

Academic Freedom and due process, 23
Ad Extirpanda, 76
American Association of University Professors, 19-21
American Civil Liberties Union, 19
Aristotle, condemnations of, 71-72
Assent, absolute, 5,42;
  conditional, 43,48,186;
  internal, religious, 42,111;
  and magisterium, 125f.;
  and manualist tradition, 43-51;
  and Vatican I, 114
Authority of Papal Encyclicals, 84-86,118f.
Authoritative teachings, altered, 73-80

Baltimore Sun, 15-16
Birth Control Commission, 4,184f.
Bishops' Pastoral Office in the Church, Decree on, 60

Canon Law, Code of, 114,228;
  and definitions, 63;
  and faith, 109;
  and *Humanae Vitae,* 124;
  and obligation to assent, 114;
  and rights of accused, 76
Casti Connubii, 3,26,114,176,177, 180,185,186,209
Catholic Standard and Times, 218
Catholic Theologians, Statement of, 6,7,12,13,16,188,197;
  text of, 24-26

Catholic University of America, 5, 10;
  Academic Senate, 18,19,23;
  Board of Inquiry, 14,20-23,212, 215,218; Report of, 221f.;
  Board of Trustees, 9,11,12,15-23, 215;
  Chancellor, 9-16;
  Professors, 4,5,24;
  Statutes of, 18,108,228
Church. *See* Ecclesiology
Church and Public Opinion, 138
Church in Our Day, 7,66,138
Church in the Modern World, Pastoral Constitution on, 26,120, 222;
  and diverse moral solutions, 64;
  on faithfulness and sexual morality, 164-66;
  and freedom of inquiry, 120;
  on marriage and procreation, 183-84;
  and natural law, 157;
  and responsible parenthood, 188
Coelibatus Sacerdotalis, 74
Collegiality, 102
Communications media, duty to inform, 37;
  moral responsibility, 136;
  natural law, 135;
  need to be informed, 143;
  pastoral function, 37;
  and testimony of witnesses, 149f.
Conscience, framework of dissent, 188f.;

right of, 26;
and situation ethics, 190;
and war, 190
Constitution on the Church, 12,100, 101,120,204,215,229;
and assent and dissent, 12;
authentic teaching authority, 55;
ecclesiology of, 124;
freedom and responsibility, 120;
history of, par. #25, 112-116;
modi on dissent, 115-16;
right to dissent, 112-14
Contraception, absolutely immoral, 3,4,178-79;
history of morality of, 169-174;
and natural law, 155f.;
new factors, 175f.;
and papal commission, 184;
and the Pill, 180-81
Cum Onus, 75

Declaration on Religious Liberty, 26,76,77,79;
and freedom of conscience, 190
Decree on Ecumenism, 79
Decree on Media of Social Communications, 135f.
Decree on the Oriental Catholic Church, 77
Demography and *Humanae Vitae,* 165,205
Detestabilis Avaritiae, 75
Development, doctrinal, 32-35
Development of Peoples, 205
Dissent, theological and American Bishops, 215;
authentic, fallible teaching, 7,14, 20,26,40,43,186-87;
balance of values, 146f.;
Church in Our Day, 7,20,40-48
as dialogic, 118;
examples in history, 66-72;
and Faith, 8, 222
within Hierarchical Magisterium, 197f.;
Human Life in Our Day, 20,47;
as irresponsible activity, 206; (cf. Report, 221)
as interpretation, 121-123;
interpretive value, 40;
in Manual tradition, 116f.,134, 206-07;
mode and manner, 13,17,76,91, 206-08;
need for reinterpretation, 47-51;
norms for, 77,209;
not rebellion, 6,201,217f.;
as responsible activity, 203f.;
and University Statutes, 17
Dissenting groups and theologians, 202-203

Ecclesiam Suam, 83,84,222;
and Ecclesiology, 99
Ecclesiology, "Counter-Reformation concept," 92-93;
Development of, 91f.;
of *Humanae Vitae,* 123-27;
of Vatican II, 92,116f.
Encyclicals, genre, 82-87;
history, 83;
recent debate, 181
Ethical theory, newer approaches, 160f.

Faith and the theologian, 108-112

Gaudium et Spes. See Church in the Modern World
Guidelines for Baltimore and Washington, 4,5

Human Life in Our Day, 20,47,207, 209,214,215,226
Humanae Vitae, 3,8,9,13,16,17,50,84, 86,91,107-08,111,124,133,141

defective concepts, 25-26;
ecclesiology, 123f.;
inadequate concept of moral law, 155f.;
as "Law of God," 15;
Natural Law methodology, 155f.;
as noninfallible, 86;
Statements, hierarchical, American, 8-9; others, 198-201
Humani Generis, 80,85,114-15,224

In Eam, 75
Infallibility and specific morality, 63; and Vatican II, 120
Interest taking, condemnation of, 75-76
Interpretation, dynamic, 101;
need to communicate, 36;
problem of, 33f.
International Congress on the Theology of Vatican II, 106

Jews in Public Life, teaching changed, 78

Lateran Council II, 75
Lateran Council III, 75
Lateran Council IV, 78
Lumen Gentium. See Constitution on the Church

Magisterium, 24,55-87,105,186
authentic, fallible magisterium, 42f.,224;
communal aspect, 56;
extraordinary, 55-56;
hierarchical, 56,104;
and theological community, 103-27;
and possibility of change, 179-180;
object of, 62-65;
ordinary, 42f.,56;
norms pre-*Humanae Vitae,* 185f.;
responses of, 183-87;
subject exercising, 56-62;
Theologians and Contraception, 176-78
Mater et Magistra, 119,134-35,225
Mirari Vos, 77-81
Mystici Corporis, 80,95

Natural Law, as monolithic, 204;
pluralist, 155f.
National Catholic News Service, 16
National Catholic Reporter, 4
National Review, 119
National Conference of Catholic Bishops, 8,9,223
News media. *See* Communications media
Newsweek, 150-51, 213

Oriental rites, changed attitude, 77

Pacem in Terris, 84,135,225
Peace and War, altered teaching, 73
Personalism, 166
Physicalism, 157,162
Probabilism, 39f.
Profession of Faith, 108,222;
New Formula, 110-111
Prudence, 213-14;
as Practical Wisdom, 146f.
Public Opinion in the Church, 137f.

Quanta Cura, 76,78,79

Relationality, 166-67
Right to Dissent, 116f.
Right to know, 78; to be informed, 134-39
Rights of Accused, changed teaching, 76

Sapientiae Christianae, 114
Scandal, 213

Scholasticism, 33;
and contraception, 173-74
Sexual ethics, altered, 73-75
Situation ethics, 195
Sobernost, theology of, 60
Statutes, University, 18

Theology, nature and function, 29f.;
and documents of Vatican II, 100-101
Theologians, obligations, 36f.,139-45,222;
and Profession of Faith, 17;
as scientists, 33f.
Theological dissent. *See* "Dissent"
Time magazine, 5
Transcendental Method, 167-68

Ubi Primum, 83-84
Unam Sanctam, 78
United States Catholic Conference, 5

Vatican Congregation for the Teaching of the Faith, 110
Vatican I, on faith and theology, 30f.;
and magisterium, 58-59
Vatican II, ecclesiology, 97f.;
and infallibility, 120
Vienne, Council of, 75

War and Peace, teaching altered, 73
Washington Lay Association, 6
Washington Post, 15
Washington Priests' Association, 4,5
Washington Star, 4,15

Proper Name Index

Abelard, 173
Adam, K., 94
Aegidius, Romanus, 78
Albert the Great, St., 72,173
Alexander III, Pope (Roland Bandinelli), 70,71,75
Alfrink, B. Card., 180,198
Amaury of Bene, 71
Ambrose, St., 171
Aquinas, St. Thomas, 33,34,36,39,60, 64,72,121,124,156,158,164,173,174
Aristotle, 64,71,72,156
Athanasius, 67
Aubert, J. M., 202
Auer, A., 202
Augustine of Canterbury, St., 74
Augustine of Hippo, St., 34,170,171, 173

Bacon, R., 72
Bandinelli, R., *See* Alexander III, Pope, 70
Bassett, W., xvi,6
Baum, G., 104,180
Beemer, T., 202
Bencini, F. D., 83
Benedict XIV, Pope (Prospero Lambertini), 77,83
Benedict XV, Pope, 84
Bennett, J. C., 23,105,151,208
Bernardin, J. L., 9,10
Billuart, L., 58
Blondel, M., 35
Boeckle, F., 160,202
Boniface VIII, Pope, 78,80,81
Brown, R. E., 104
Bulst, W., 202
Burch, T. K., 8
Burghardt, W. J., 10,23,149,150,206, 208,213

Caesarius of Arles, 172
Cajetan, 62
Cavanagh, J., xvi
Celestine III, Pope, 44
Celsus, 73
Ceroke, C., xvi,6,14
Choupin, L., 85
Chrysostom, St. John, 171
Clement VIII, Pope, 77
Clement of Alexandria, St., 171
Congar, Y., 34,35,58,105,121
Connelly, T. R., xvi,19
Constans II, 69
Constantine, 73
Constantius II, Emp., 67,68
Cooke, B., 202
Coreth, E., 160,167
Corrigan, J. E., 5
Cravath, Swaine & Moore, 19
Cronin, J. F., 7
Cross, R., 22,212
Curran, C. E., ix,xvi,4,5,7-10,13-17
Cushing, R. Card., 138
Cyril of Alexandria, St., 171

D'Avanzo, 58
David of Dinant, 71
Dearden, J. F., 8
Denis the Carthusian, 175

Denzinger, H., 33
Dejaifve, G., 104
Dieckmann, H., 12,41,44,45
Donlon, S. E., 117,133
Duns Scotus, 175

Eugene III, Pope, 75

Facundus of Hermiane, 68
Falteisek, E. F., 7
Farley, L., 16
Foley, L. A., xvi
Ford, J. C., 177
Fransen, P., 104,202
Franzelin, J. B., 58
Friedman, C., 23

Galileo, 44
Gallewaerd, R., 202
Gallati, F., 117
Gasser, V., 46,58,59
George, D., xvi
Granfield, P., 76
Gratian, 73,74,156,173
Gregory the Great, St., Pope, 73,74, 80,171,172
Gregory VII, St., Pope, 73,74
Gregory IX, Pope, 72,75
Gregory XVI, Pope, 76-78,80-81,83
Grisez, G., 14,179
Groot, J., 203

Haering, B., 10,166
Hannan, P., 10
Hellegers, A., 8
Heraclius, 69
Herberg, W., 119
Herve, J. M., 12,41,93
Hesburgh, T., 23,208
Hochwalt, C., ix,16,17
Honorius, Pope, 44,66,69,70
Hotchkin, J.H., 23,151,208
Hugh of St. Victor, 173
Huguccio, 74
Huizing, P., 203
Hunt, J. F., xvi,19
Hunt, R. E., xvi,5-7,10,14-16,19

Ibas of Edessa, 68
Ignatius of Antioch, St., 57
Innocent III, Pope, 74,78,80
Innocent IV, Pope, 72,76,84
Irenaeus, St., 59
Ivo of Chartres, 173

Janssens, L., 181,203
Jerome, St., 171
Johann, R., 160,167
John XXIII, Pope, 36,84,99,119,134-136,141,176,225
Johnson, D., 168
Jones, D. L., 5
Journet, C., 94
Joyce, T., xvi
Justinian, 68

Kaesemann, E., 104
Kanoti, G., xvi,6
Karrer, O., 12
van Kessel, R., 203
Kearney, P., xvi,6
Klitjn, W., 203
Klostermann, F., 203

Lagrange, J. M., 121
Lambertini, P., *See* Benedict XIV, Pope, 83
Lambruschini, 86,144
Leger, E. Card., 180
Leo II, Pope, 70
Leo XII, Pope, 77
Leo XIII, Pope, 84,114
Lercher, L., 12,41,43,45,46
Liberius, Pope, 44,66,67
Lonergan, B., 23,34-35,160,167,168, 206,208
deLubac, H., 94,121

Madr, O., 203
Maguire, D. C., xvi,5,6,8,10
Malmberg, F., 203
Malone, G. K., 86
vanderMarck, W., 160,167,181
Marechal, J., 167
Marlowe, D. E., 19
Marthaler, B., xvi,6
Martin of Braga, St., 172
Martin le Maistre, 175
McBride, A. E., xvi, 5
McCormick, R. A., 63, 186
McDonagh, E., 203
McGinn, B., xvi, 6
McIntyre, F. Card., 17
McKeever, P., 10
McNamara, K., 98
Medina, B., 39
Medina, J., 75
Megivern, J., 10
Mersch, E., 94
Moehler, J. A., 35,94
Murray, J. C., 35
Murray, R., 103
Murphy, F. X., 5
Murphy, R. E., xvi

Nau, P., 85
Neill, J. K., 19
Newman, J. H. Card., 34-35,46,48, 121,215
Nicholas I, Pope, 76
Noonan, J. T., Jr., 8,23,49,75,81,82, 104,207

O'Boyle, P. Card., ix,9,11-12,14-16
Onan, 170
Origen, 34

Palmieri, D., 12,41,43,44,48
St. Paul, 171
Paul VI, Pope, vii,3,4,24,25,36,74, 82-84,86,91,99,106,112-113,123-124,141,150,184-187,215,223
Perriot, 85
Pesch, C., 12,41,43,45,48,93
Peter, C., 10
Peter the Lombard, 70,71,173
Peter of Poitiers, 71
Pfeuertner, S., 203
Pius IV, Pope, 229
Pius V, St., Pope, 82
Pius IX, Pope, 76,77,79,80,83,229
Pius X, St. Pope, 80,84
Pius XI, Pope, 3,26,84,114,170,176, 177,178,180,209
Pius XII, Pope, 80,84,85,86,95,114, 137,141,143,162,176,177,178,180, 224

Quade, Q., 104

Rahner, K., 34,35,57,118,133,160, 167
Reich, W., xvi,202
Reuss, J. M., 181
Rhodes, J., 104
Robert of Courcon, 72
Robert, C., 203
Ruffino, R. G., xvi,5,6,14

Saigh, Patriarch Maximos IV, 180
Salaverri, J., 41,43,44
Scheeben, M. J., 94
Scheel, N., 215
Schillebeeckx, E., 34
Schmaus, M., 94
Schmitz, W. J., 14
Schoonenberg, P., 203
Schreitmueller, H. J., 5
Schueller, B., 117,133,160
Sergius, 69
Shannon, J. P., 22,136
Simons, F., 160
Sloyan, G., 23
Smolko, J. F., xvi,202
Soto, D., 75

Springer, R., 5,8,9
Sproken, C., 203
Straub, 12,43
Suarez, F., 58
Sullivan, F. A., 41,43,44

Tanquerey, A., 93
Teilhard de Chardin, P., 121
Tertullian, 59,171
Theodoret of Cyrene, 68
Theodore of Mopsuestia, 68
Thirlkel, J. H., 23, 208
Tong, P. K. K., xvi
Tracy, D. W., xvi,6,7

Ulpian, 156,158
Urban II, Pope, 73,80
Urban III, Pope, 75
Urban IV, Pope, 72
Urban V, Pope, 72

Valsecchi, A., 181
Van Noort, 12
Vaughn, 10,206,212,213
Vigilius, Pope, 44,66,68,69

deWachter, M., 203
Webb, R. K., xvi,19
Weiler, 58
Whalen, J. P., 9,10,11,14,18,19
Wills, G., 119
Woodward, K., 23,150,208,213
Wright, J. Card., 10,11

Yanitelli, V., 23,208,212

Zaleski, A., 10,11